JOY GIRL

JOY GIRL

A NOVEL OF OLIVE BORDEN

LAINI GILES

To Allan Giles
1968-2020
My graphic designer, photographer, accountant, banner model, tea bringer, flatterer, sounding board, salesman, pack mule, lover, muse, and best friend.

I miss you, baby.

A ROUNDUP LULLABY

CHAPTER ONE

LAGRANDE STATION, LOS ANGELES, CALIFORNIA,
September 20, 1925

"Excuse me, sir," Momma asked the desk agent in her slow Old Dominion drawl. "Which platform for the 10:15 to Victorville?"

"Number two, ma'am."

"Thank you kindly," she said, pouring on the syrupy charm. She snapped her fingers at a porter to take care of our trunks. At forty-one, hard work and widowhood had aged Momma, but she was still a handsome woman with red hair and fair skin. She hadn't drifted toward fat as other matrons had. But her overprotectiveness wore on me. I tried to steer her into seeing attractive older gentlemen, but Momma insisted that I was her life and always would be.

We were headed to a giant staging area outside Victorville where we'd be shooting my latest film, *3 Bad Men*. I searched the faces in the station for the cast and crew and at last saw George O'Brien's muscled arm waving near the door out to the platforms. George was playing Dan O'Malley, my love interest.

"Olive! Mrs. Borden! Over here!" he called.

Next to George were Tom Santschi, J. Farrell MacDonald, and Frank Campeau, the character actors who would be playing Bull, Spade, and Mike, the three bad men of the title. Tom was a tall, chiseled Missourian with dark shaggy hair and an easy way about him. When I'd asked him about his last name, he smiled broadly, his pale blue eyes twinkling, and said he was Swiss, "like the cheese."

Mr. MacDonald was balding and graying, with a gray beard and beetle brows. He'd been with Universal when it was originally IMP. He'd done work with Harold Lloyd, and like me, with Hal Roach. Tom teased him about his "Kinnect-i-cut" accent, and nobody knew him by anything other than "Mac."

Frank was a Michigander with a rugged face, and he teased me in his nasal Michigan inflection, calling me Ollie and "little lady." He'd decided to get into character early and had worn his stovepipe hat to the depot for fun.

Lou Tellegen was a tall, handsome Dutchman who'd once worked with Sarah Bernhardt. His long legs were like stilts, and he was nothing like Sherriff Layne Hunter, the villainous rustler he portrayed. He was charming, debonair, and he flirted with me good-naturedly, causing Momma to insert herself between us. Also clustered on the platform were pretty blonde Phyllis Haver, who played Lily, one of the good-time girls at the saloon in Custer; Priscilla Bonner, who played Millie, Tom's onscreen sister; and Alec Francis, an Englishman, who played Reverend Benson.

George smiled as he helped me up into the train. What could I say about George, other than that my heart beat a little faster when he was around? He looked like he should be on a plinth in a museum holding a discus. I tried not to be obvious, but it was hard not to let my eyes follow him, especially when Momma was around. The trades said he had been a boxer, and it was obvious from his physique, with bulging biceps and a barrel chest, along with dark slicked back hair and gorgeous eyes.

The first time I'd met George, on the Fox lot, he'd offered to carry my makeup case and Momma's mothering bag. It was a woven Mexican tote she'd filled with everything from extra handkerchiefs to Kotex feminine products. It also held a tub of Pacquin's hand cream, a bottle of camphor liniment, a sweater, a towel, a velvet ring box for storing my pansy ring when I was shooting, and a flask for helping to keep warm when it was chilly.

Even though I was nineteen years old, Momma still treated me like a schoolgirl, and I was determined to shrug off the yoke. Later that afternoon, as we played pinochle in the lounge car, I caught George glancing at me once or twice, and I did the same. Momma always brought me back to the game.

"That's a meld for me," Momma said. She paused, watching us. "Olive, are you listening?"

"Yes, Momma," I said.

"Victorville, next stop! Next stop Victorville!" the conductor said, as he strode through the lounge car.

Momma tallied the scores and gathered up the cards, placing them in the card box. "Thank you for a pleasant game, George. See you in the station."

I looked at George longingly as Momma and I exited the car, and he gazed back. Momma quickly filed down the corridor, and I followed docilely so we could collect our things. On the platform, we ran into George again. He gallantly took my piece of hand luggage and swung it as if it were made of air. "Hey, look, there's our ride," he said. He pointed to Lefty Hough, the property man, waving near the door into the depot.

Lefty guided us through the station and out to a series of cars and trucks parked in front of the station. Lou and George sat down next to me in back, and Momma reluctantly took the passenger seat in front. When everyone's trunks were collected and we were all accounted for, Lefty put our car in gear, and we bounced off down the road and into the desert.

"How did *you* get started in this crazy business?" George asked.

"When I was sixteen, I told Momma I didn't want to go to school anymore. It bored me." I lapsed into Momma's drawl: "'I don't believe in idling, young lady. If you won't go to school, you will get a job. Work is the most vital thing in life, so you must love what you do. If you tell me what you want to do, I'll try to help you do it.'"

Momma looked crossways over the front seat at me.

"What did you tell her?" George asked me.

"That she wanted to be an actress, of course," Momma said with a brittle laugh.

George listened raptly as I told him how we chose Hollywood over New York, and then how we sold every stick of furniture to finance the trip. I was only a baby when Daddy died, and Momma had worked her fingers to the bone as a hotel cleaning lady for years to make ends meet. It got no easier in Los Angeles. We opened a candy store for a while, but even with the popularity of Granny Shields' meringue bites and divinity fudge, we couldn't keep it afloat.

"Candy's not the healthiest thing to eat," George said.

"It was something in my stomach though. Things were

getting desperate for a while. I finally got a job at Christie Studios, but only for three days," I said. "The director said I was awful and I should go home."

"She cried the entire night," Momma called over the front seat. "I nearly went and gave that man a piece of my mind, I can tell you, but she begged me not to."

"I did work for them again, and for a few other studios, but only bit parts."

"Then came Sennett," Momma said. "Olive was a Bathing Beauty."

"You worked for Sennett?" George asked. "Would I have seen anything you were in?"

"A couple of Jack White shorts," I said, brushing them off as the minor roles they were. "Nothing big."

"What happened to turn things around?" he asked.

"WAMPAS happened," I said.

Every year, the Western Association of Motion Picture Advertisers picked several new actresses whom they thought were up-and-comers, and in 1925, they had chosen me, along with my cousin Natalie.

"From that, Paul Bern selected me for *The Dressmaker from Paris*. He's a director at Paramount, and such a darling. When I didn't think I could afford a frock, he bought me one with his own money. Then he put me in *Grounds for Divorce* too. I desperately needed acting experience, and he gave it to me. He took me to the Trocadero and the Cocoanut Grove, he introduced me to people I would never have met otherwise. I met Tom Mix when I was out with Paul. *The Yankee Señor* changed my life."

"Mix is a swell guy," George said.

"How about you? I asked. "How did you start out?"

"I used to wrangle horses for my pop up in San Francisco. He's the chief of police there. They have a mounted patrol, and I love horses. I call my dad Cap, short for Captain. Well, one day, Cap took me to a rodeo, and Mix was there. He told me if I ever got to Hollywood to look him up and he'd give me a job as a cameraman."

"And you did?"

"It took a while. I enlisted during the war. Saw lots of action as a stretcher bearer, and I was on a sub chaser for a while. After the war, I was at Santa Clara College, thinking about going to medical school, but I liked playing football and boxing more than studying."

"I can believe that," I said, eyeing his muscles. "You don't strike me as the egghead type."

"Then I got tackled in a pile-on when we played Stanford. Broke a couple bones, and bruised my ego pretty bad. I decided life was too short. Told Cap I was gonna go look up Tom Mix and ask about that job. He couldn't believe it."

"How'd it go?" I asked.

"About as well as you, it sounds like," he said with a laugh. "Trying to make it in Los Angeles for fifteen dollars a week. Living at the YMCA with my buddy, Dan Clark, who's an assistant cameraman. We had two cots and a rug. That was it."

I laughed.

"I paid close attention to what was going on, and eventually, they gave me more responsibility and bigger parts. The nice thing about westerns are the chuck wagons. I learned to load up at meals when I could."

He slapped his knee, and I laughed along.

"So many fellas helped me then they didn't have to—Art Acord, Richard Dix, Hobart Bosworth, and Tom. I almost gave up a couple times. George Walsh did his dog-gonedest to get me into *Ben Hur*, but when I lost that, it was almost the last straw."

"What happened?" I asked. "That changed things?"

He got quiet for a minute. "Wally Reid died."

I'm sure my mouth made a little O of surprise.

"Everyone was looking for 'handsome and friendly' to fill the big hole that Wally left. Suddenly, people started paying attention to me. Ford helped me get *The Iron Horse* and that's all she wrote. Holy moley, look! So that's Fordville."

The company's series of tents stretched for acres across the patch of Mojave that Fox had staked out. They'd built a giant corral, with separate pens for the multitude of horses, cows, mules, and oxen. Parked in a separate area were the hundreds of Conestoga wagons, buckboards, and prairie schooners. We were due to be here for four months, shooting the massive land rush scenes. There were going to be around 2400 people here, mostly extras and stuntmen.

It had been sixty miles, give or take, from the train station to the filming site, and we were coated in sand by the time we arrived. We found our tents and unpacked, ready to begin the big adventure. *3 Bad Men* had been adapted from Herman Whittaker's novel *Over the Border* and told the story of a great Dakota land rush in 1877. Tom, Mac, and Frank began the film as cattle rustlers, but turned over a new leaf when they ended up the inadvertent caretakers for Lee Carleton, played by me. Lee had seen her father murdered by another band of rustlers, led by Lou, who was out to get her inheritance. However, the three bad men became Lee's protectors and ended up turning over a new leaf. To that end, they also decided to find her a husband, and settled on happy-go-lucky cowboy, Dan O'Malley, played by George.

The commissary and meal tents full of tables could deal with over six-hundred fifty of us at a time. The cooks were real chuckwagon types, turning out true cowboy cooking for the cast and crew. Every day, we could choose breakfasts like bacon, sausages, flapjacks, and sourdough biscuits, along with gallons and gallons of strong coffee. Lunch and dinner were variations on cowboy beans and hamhocks, chuckwagon or sonofabitch stew, frybread, and baking powder biscuits, with vinegar pie, rice pudding with raisins, cobbler, or mock apple pie for dessert.

With his longish hair and cassock, Alec added a gentlemanly touch to our primitive existence. He'd brought several tins of tea along for the shoot, along with a proper teapot and cups, ginger biscuits, and currant scones so he could enjoy a proper teatime around three in the afternoon. I had to laugh when I found our three bad men seated in a circle around Alec, and he was showing Mac how to raise his pinkie while drinking his brew.

The night after our first day of shooting, we stars enjoyed a campfire that Tom and Mac built to truly get into the spirit of the picture. Mac whittled and Tom rolled his own cigarettes, while Frank played his harmonica, and Lou strummed his guitar. Coyotes howled in the distance as we sang traditional songs like "Home on the Range" and "Little Red Wing." Then we traded stories of shooting other pictures.

"So we're shooting in Nevada for *The Iron Horse*," John Ford began, piling tobacco into the well of his pipe. He lit a match and began to puff before continuing. "George, what was the name of that hellhole again?"

"Dodge," George said.

"Dodge. That's it. I rented a train from the Barnes Circus, and we lived in it, on a siding next to where we were shooting."

"The one that came infested with fleas?" Mac said with a laugh. "*That* train? I risked my life outside in a tent instead."

"Then it started snowing," George added.

"I was getting to that. What a cockup," Ford said, shaking his head. "Far too early in the season. The sets were covered. And I mean *covered*. Lord was it cold! My fingers were blue for most of the shoot. And the outhouses were too far from the train. You needed showshoes just to take a piss."

"I remember it all," Mac said. "I also remember keeping Jack here from killing his own brother."

"They don't wanna hear about that, Mac," Ford said.

Phyllis and I looked back and forth at each other.

"*I* wanna hear about it," said Phyllis, leaning forward.

"*Everybody* was fighting," Mac continued. "They had to take the ketchup bottles off the tables. Afraid they'd kill each other. Ford there was using live ammo and his brother Eddie told him it was dangerous—"

"Shut *up*, Mac," Ford said.

Mac continued, undeterred. "So they start throwing punches, and George tries to break it up, but you've never seen two more murderous Irish bastards go at it in your life, and..."

Ford made a noise of disgust, stood, and brushed the dirt off his denim dungarees. Then he marched off muttering all the way. Not surprising, I'd discovered. Jack Ford could turn on the charm one minute and the next, berate Lefty,

George Schneiderman, the cameraman; or anyone else who incurred his wrath.

"Was it something I said?" quipped Mac.

"So then what happened?" asked Priscilla Bonner, passing her cigarette to Tom so he could light another.

"One of 'em—I didn't even see who—threw an alarm clock that happened to be in that train compartment, and it hit the window. *Smash*! The glass flew everywhere. Got me right here above the eyebrow and drew blood. I've still got the scar," Mac said.

"Where?" Phyllis said, leaning over to examine the area of his forehead he was indicating.

"Right here," he insisted.

"I don't see it."

"Well, it's there. George saw it all too."

"Mac's right. It was crazy. Worst shoot I've been on," George said.

"Don't forget the buffalo stampede," Mac said.

"How could I forget!" George said.

"Buffalo stampede?!" echoed Phyllis, Priscilla, and me in unison.

"Yup," said Mac. "Reggie Lund, one of the camera jockeys, was down in a pit, aiming up at the stampede—you know, for low-angle shots. One of the damned beasts tripped on the plank above him, and it went down. I mean *down*." He smacked one hand on top of the other so hard we all jumped. "The poor thing died and almost took Reggie with him."

"Oh dear..." said Priscilla.

"One guy actually *did* die." George said.

"Oh yeah," Mac said. "Circus guy. What was his name,

George? Do you remember?"

"Kelly," George said. "Nice guy. I talked to him a couple times."

"Died?!" I said. "From the stampede?"

"No, pneumonia," Mac said. "Poor bastard. They sent him to the hospital in Reno, but he didn't make it."

We shook our heads and tippled out of the flask that Frank passed around. The temperature had dropped since nightfall, but nothing like the disastrous conditions for *The Iron Horse*. George and I sat close, propped against the wheels of a wagon, and as the long day shooting took its toll, my head dropped to his shoulder. I could barely keep my eyes open.

"She shore is cute," Mac said.

"I think so too," George replied. He helped Momma get me up and back to our tent, where I promptly passed out. Each day went something along those same lines, but the night before we filmed the big land rush scene, I was too keyed up to sleep. I strolled over to the corrals, where I climbed up on one of the fences the company had erected. An Appaloosa and a bay mare both ambled over for attention, and I laughed as they quarreled over my hand. I'd stroke the gentle head of the bay and the Appaloosa would move in, wanting affection too. A deep rumble of a laugh came from behind me.

"He acts so tough when anyone's on him, but Ole Devil really is a big softie. Aren't ya, fella?" George sidled up to the fence and joined me, placing a boot on the bottom cross beam of the fence and petting the Appaloosa's muzzle. "Can't sleep?"

"No. I'm too excited," I said. "I'm enjoying the quiet. It's so peaceful out here."

"Where's your mother?" he asked, looking around cautiously.

I laughed. "Asleep, if you can believe that."

"I didn't think she slept. She seems to always have at least one eye on you."

"I know, but she worries. I was only a year old when Daddy died, and I had a baby brother die too. I'm all she has left."

"That's gotta be hard."

"Yeah," I said, fondling the bay's silken ear. "I mean, I understand. She's done a lot for me. Private schools back in Virginia and moving us out here when I told her I wanted to act. She used to be so wonderful when I was little, but now I feel like she's strangling me."

"Does she let you date, even? How old are you?"

"I'm nineteen. Old enough. But if you ask her, Momma will insist I'm eighteen, so you didn't hear it from me."

"My lips are sealed," he said. He moved a little closer along the fence and touched my pansy ring. "I notice you never take this off. There's gotta be a story there, right?"

"It used to be a tie tack. Daddy had it made because Momma had pansies in her wedding bouquet. I had it made into a ring so I could keep him with me." I splayed my fingers so he could get a good look. "It's my good luck ring."

"Olive?" he said softly.

"Yes?"

"What would your mother say if she knew how badly I wanted to kiss you right now?"

I turned toward him, flipped a leg over the top plank, and hopped down off the fence.

"She'd be scandalized. Especially when she saw me kissing you back."

When he leaned down to kiss me, I closed my eyes and the earth seemed to shift beneath me. I'd gotten a stolen kiss from Harold Linebecker when I was thirteen, but Momma had kept all other boys away since then. On movie shoots, she was always a few feet away, with crocheting in her lap and her mothering bag at the ready, but Momma wasn't here now, and this kiss was sweet and perfect. When I opened my eyes, George smiled.

"I've been wanting to do that ever since the first time I saw you," he said.

"When was that?"

"A couple months ago on the Fox lot. You must have been working on *The Yankee Señor* because you were wearing a lace dress and a fringed shawl. I saw you stop outside the administration building and fix the buckle on your shoe. You looked up with those huge dark eyes and I was smitten. When they told me you were going to be in *3 Bad Men*, I couldn't believe my luck."

"I remember that day. I looked up and there you were. My heart did a little flip-flop."

"Mine too." He gazed down at me. "I'd love to take you out on my boat sometime. I sail up the coast to Oregon or down to Mexico to fish and relax. There's something about the ocean that gets me right here." He gave his chest a thump near the area of his heart.

"I'd love to go out on your boat."

"Ever sailed?"

"No, but I'd love you to teach me."

He kissed me again. "Then it's a date. When we get back, we'll ditch your mother and sail over to Catalina or down to San Diego. Your pick."

"I'd sail around the world if you asked me to."

"Could you be ready to go in twenty minutes?" he asked with a laugh, smoothing my hair back from my face.

"Fifteen," I said.

I gazed up at him, unable to stop smiling, and I must have looked like a complete fool.

"It's late. Must be after midnight," George said, as the singing around the campfire reached louder, drunker levels and the coyotes harmonized in the distance

"I don't want tonight to end," I said, snuggling against his chest, clad in its plaid shirt. The aroma of flannel and male musk was intoxicating.

"This is To Be Continued," he said, kissing me again. "But we should hit the hay. We've got a big day tomorrow."

"You're right." I hesitated, not wanting the kiss to end, but finally coming up for air. I reluctantly turned to go back to my tent. "Good night, George."

"Goodnight, Olive. Sweet dreams."

Sweet dreams? How was a girl supposed to sleep after a kiss like that?!

3 BAD MEN SET, OUTSIDE VICTORVILLE, CALIFORNIA:
September 1925

"Schneidy, give me a sweeping shot across those wagons. Panoramic, straight across," John Ford said, pointing with his pipe. "I want tension. I want to capture the restlessness. Got it?"

"Got it," Schneidy said. George Schneiderman was Ford's regular cameraman. He had a sloped forehead and Brylcreemed hair, and his voice was a mutter out of the side of his mouth. He chain smoked everywhere except next to the film. That was too dangerous.

As Ford scanned the crowd, Schneidy rotated the camera in a wide arc, capturing all the wagons, horses, and extras who'd been brought out for the shoot. Added to that were a number of motorized vehicles outfitted with special platforms for the cameramen to shoot from front, back, and side vantage points. On the raised filming scaffold that stood over the plain, Ford stood ready with a giant megaphone to yell commands. Before George and I saddled up, we'd decided to get a good look at everything from above.

Suddenly Ford got a strange look on his face. "Tension," he muttered over the pipe in his mouth.

"What?" Schneidy said beside him.

"Tension," Ford repeated, removing the pipe. "Hey, Lefty, where's the other baby?"

Lefty swallowed hard, and every bit of color drained from his face. "Shit," he said. This scene had two babies in it, and somehow, we only had one.

"I'll find one someplace," Lefty said, dashing toward the ladder. "It might be a while. Babies don't exactly grow on trees around here."

Ford shook his head in frustration. We had children among the extras, but no babies.

"I'll be back!" Lefty called up to us. He sprinted off toward an Oldsmobile that wasn't being used for filming. With a quick roar of the engine, he disappeared in a cloud of dust.

"Take a break!" Ford yelled. "One hour!" There was no way Lefty could make anything happen in an hour, but he'd already impressed plenty of folks with his resourcefulness. I was curious to see how far it stretched.

The stuntmen and extras looked around in confusion, but soon shrugged and whipped out pemmican and decks of cards. Those riding solo guided their mounts back toward camp. But no more than forty-five minutes later, the Oldsmobile advanced across the desert flats toward us, trailing dust. A buckboard struggled along behind it.

Eventually, they all pulled to a stop near the scaffold, Ford climbed down, and we followed him. Using his hand to block the mid-morning glare, he looked up at the driver's bench of the wagon. There sat a man, a woman, and a baby in arms. Lefty rushed over from the car.

"Jack, this is Elmer Stanley, his wife Loretta, and their boy, Franklin." Lefty looked inordinately pleased with himself.

"How d'ya do?" Ford said. "Did Mr. Hough tell you what we need?"

The dazed couple nodded, and Ford further explained the film and the scenes in which Franklin would appear, stressing multiple times how safe he would be.

"We'll take real good care of him," Lefty said. "He'll be in no danger. Like he's lying in his crib."

I wanted to laugh, but held it in. In addition to his other talents, Lefty was a hell of a liar.

Ford nodded to try to convince the Stanleys. "Why, he'll be famous!" he offered. "You can tell your friends he's in a flicker."

"And don't forget the token of our appreciation," Lefty added, nudging Ford. "The fifty bucks for five days of work.

A couple for the stampede and one for the fire? We should be able to get it done in five days, right Jack?"

"Of course," Jack said, obviously trying not to choke on the price tag. How many more babies would he find in the back of beyond? He'd have to make some sacrifices to the budget.

When everything was agreed upon, Ford, Lefty, and Schneidy briefed the Stanleys on the basics of the land rush, and Franklin's role in it. The couple reluctantly handed Franklin to the two stunt people playing his parents, then stood back on the platform to watch the production. After finding our mounts and saddling back up, George and I joined the others at the base line and waited. The pre-arranged signal was a pistol shot, and with a gesture from Ford, Lefty fired the gun.

From the giant megaphone, Ford yelled at the top of his lungs. "Action!"

CHAPTER TWO

3 BAD MEN SET, OUTSIDE VICTORVILLE, CALIFORNIA,
September 1925

In a moment, the true majesty of the land rush came alive. The wagons surged forward in a cloud of dust, the ground shook, and all around us echoed a symphony of horses' and mules' hooves that sounded like rolling waves of thunder.

From cameras mounted on platforms at the rear of a pair of Chevrolets, two cameramen captured the stampede from ahead. Two Buicks with similar retrofitting traveled on either side of the mass of wagons as they galloped across the barren plain. The last few cameras had been sunk in pits along the route, the better to film the galloping horses and wagons from below.

A fellow on a penny farthing towed by a horse provided a quirky touch, along with Margery and Mary Agnes, sisters on a tandem bicycle that had been built especially for them. One wagon hit a bump and turned over. The driver plunged down a hill. Another stunt woman's horse stumbled, so she trick fell and was snatched up by another rider.

An even more daredevil horseman drove his buckboard

onto uneven ground, and like a choreographed ballet, he dived forward as it tumbled over itself.

Otis Harlan, playing Zach Little, the editor of *The Pathfinder* newspaper, bumped along in his wagon, with his printing press alongside him.

"Cut to mom and pop!" Ford yelled through his colossal megaphone.

The stunt people carrying Franklin on their wagon pretended to lose a wagon wheel and the others frantically navigated around them. The man worked quickly to repair the wheel. The woman set Franklin on the ground to help the man fix it. At last, they finished with their fake wheel repair and ran back to the seat of their wagon. But they'd "inadvertently" left Franklin behind on the ground. George leaned down in the saddle and grabbed the kid, who proceeded to yowl piteously. Franklin was handed off to Otis for safekeeping.

When most of the crucial action had been filmed from various angles by multiple cameras, Ford watched carefully and stepped back to the giant megaphone.

"Cut!!" he hollered. "One more time!"

The scene was shot again and again over four days, amassing hundreds of yards of footage, each take focusing on a different area of interest: George and me, the three bad men, and the others. Every night, the horses, wagons and vehicles pulled to a halt and traversed the sandy soil back to camp, then, at Fordville, empty film cans were filled with new reels and labeled. The latest rushes would be transported to the studio for producers to critique. Wires would be sent back to Victorville via Western Union with the latest comments, and we'd reshoot as necessary.

The heat, even in the shade, was stifling, at over 100 degrees. It was impossible to stay fresh under the glaring sun, and the constant onslaught of dust kicked up by the livestock and wagons was like the world's smelliest incense cloud. The makeup people had their work cut out for them, plastering layers of powder on top of layers of dirt. I went through bottles of witch hazel trying to keep my face clean. At night, the desert heat became bone-chilling cold. It was hard, sweaty work. But with George and I growing closer every day, I wouldn't have changed any of it for the world.

3 BAD MEN SET NEAR VICTORVILLE, CALIFORNIA,
September 29, 1925

"Olive, honey, it's time to wake up. Everyone's already in the meal tent," Momma said, bustling around our trunks. Thunder rumbled in the distance, and raindrops began to pelt the tent canvas. "You look pale. Are you all right?" She placed the flat of her hand against my forehead. "Good gravy, you're burning up."

"Momma, I feel dreadful." I rolled over and clutched my belly, wincing.

"I'm going to get Doc Powell, Baby. Don't move."

"I don't think I can," I said with a moan.

She hurried out of the tent, and I stared at my trunk a foot away. A few minutes later, she was back, soaking wet, with Doc in tow.

"…and she's running a fever too," Momma was saying, using her hand to push damp hairs out of her face.

Doc leaned down next to my pallet, the moist earthy smell of his rawhide jacket filling my nostrils. "Miss Borden, how are you feeling?" he asked.

"Awful, Doc. My stomach hurts, and my head is splitting." By now, the rain was beginning to find its way between the seams in the canvas.

"Roll over on your back, if you would."

I did with a groan.

"Mrs. Borden, excuse me for a moment, please, but I'm going to unbutton your daughter's shirt."

He undid my top two buttons, placed his stethoscope on my chest, then examined my skin.

He shook his head as he took my pulse.

"Please tell me it's not what I think it is," Momma said in a panicked voice.

"Priscilla and Grace are sick too. Same symptoms. Headache, gut ache, fever, rose-colored spots on her chest… I saw it this past winter in New York from oysters. It's typhoid."

"Noooooo," Momma moaned. "Not again. My sweet Harry died of it when Olive was a baby, and then my little Frankie. How did it happen?"

"Out here? Could be almost anything. Bad water, dust, improper hygiene…"

"Hygiene?"

"Well…to be blunt…someone hasn't washed their hands after using the privy…either before eating or before making the food."

I moaned.

"We'll have to get you to a hospital, Miss Borden. I'll also need to have some fresh water brought in, in case ours is polluted."

"But what can we do in the meantime?" Momma said.

"Try to rest. I'll talk to Mr. Ford about getting that water." He hurried out of the tent. In a little while, he was back.

"All right. Lefty is going to contact the hospital in Victorville, and let them know to expect you. In the meantime, George is going to ride to the hot springs nearby and get some fresh water and fruit to keep you eating, since we need to monitor what you're taking in. We're not sure what's contaminated."

"But it's pouring," Momma said. "The poor boy will catch pneumonia."

"He insists," Doc said. "Try stopping him."

That afternoon, Tom and Mac devised a sling out of long poles and canvas and got me to the infirmary tent, while Momma ran alongside, holding a jacket above me to block the rain.

Unfortunately, the situation there was no better than in the tent that Momma and I shared. The rain shower had turned into a gullywasher—the kind the desert experienced so rarely. Two of the extras were put to work holding a thick army blanket over me to fend off the rain. The floor became a muddy lake.

I drifted in and out of consciousness that day and night, and Momma sat and held my hand. When things seemed darkest, morning finally dawned, and like some kind of angel in buckskin, George stepped through the entry into the tent. He was completely drenched, and water dripped from the brim of his hat. He pulled it off and grinned, then sat down on the camp stool between Momma and me.

"Hello, pretty ladies," he said. He set his knapsack down and undid the buckles holding it closed. Out of it, he pulled five canteens. He handed one to me. The others he gave to Doc to give to Priscilla, Grace, and Alec, who was also fighting the sickness now. Momma had also begun feeling poorly, so she got one too.

"I have a few more if anyone else starts showing signs," he said.

Doc nodded.

"And... here you go," George said as I looked on weakly.

Out of the sack he pulled a handful of oranges. "I filched these from a grove I passed on my way back from the spring." He used his thumbnail to break open the skin, pulled some of the white pith loose, and held it out for me. I took it.

"I can't believe you did all this," I whispered. "It's so sweet, George. Did you ride through the night?"

He shrugged, like it was nothing, really, and at that moment, I realized I was besotted with him.

Several hands drove Priscilla, Grace, Momma, Alec, and I to the hospital in Victorville, and by the fifth, we were all stable enough to be transported back to Los Angeles to St. Vincent's. After that, it was home to convalesce. Although it took several weeks, I finally began to regain my color and my health.

NEAR VICTORVILLE, CALIFORNIA, *Late October 1925*

There is no more majestic animal than the horse, and there was no sweeter horse than Rawhide, the bay they'd assigned to me at the beginning of the shoot. Before I'd worked with Tom Mix, I'd never been near a horse before in my life, so they'd had to find me a gentle one. I had to look convincing as a horse-woman, and I still wasn't sure if I passed muster, even though George spent some time showing me how to work with them.

Rawhide and I developed a terrific working relationship. I didn't goose him in the ribs too hard, and he did what I told him. But about a week after I got back from my sick leave, I got too cocky. It seemed harmless, but I stood tall in the saddle like I'd seen George, Mac, and the others do. I think a fly must have buzzed too close to the old boy's ear and made him nervous. Whatever it was, that horse lost its ever-loving mind. He took off across the sandflat, whinnying and squealing hysterically, trying to knock me off his back.

"Whoa!" I screamed. "Whoa!" I grabbed the horn of the saddle and held on for dear life. A couple of the cowboys took off after me.

"Hold on, Miss Borden!" one yelled as they saddled up and gave chase.

"The thought occurred to me!" I yelled back.

Rawhide writhed and twisted beneath me, and I tried tugging my foot out of the stirrup, but with the bulky western boots I was wearing, that was impossible. It was jammed in tight. If he bucked me off, I'd be dragged to my death. All I could do was clutch the saddle horn and pray.

At a dry creek bed, Rawhide broke his stride to leap

across. When he landed, my boot finally shifted, and I was able to work it free of its leather prison. I let out a sigh of relief, but then felt myself go airborne, and the earth tilted crazily beneath me. After that, everything went black.

I don't know how long it was. It could have been five minutes, it could have been five hours. The first thing I saw when I opened my eyes was Momma's frightened face directly above me. As I came to, I glanced around. George, Ford, Lefty, Mac and Phyllis clustered behind Momma, and they all wore her worried look.

"Wait!" said Doc Powell, catching up to the others. "Don't move her! Let me examine her first!"

He checked my head and neck, then my spine and my hips. He slipped off my boots and asked if I could feel my feet and my arms, then poked them with a pin. He had me raise my arms, wiggle my toes and fingers, and checked my vision.

"Can you move?" said Lefty.

I moved my shoulders to and fro, then my neck and waist to make sure everything worked.

"Do you think you can sit up?" Doc asked.

"I'm not sure," I said. I offered my arms and the fellows gently pulled me to a sitting position. After a minute or two, I awkwardly got to my feet and brushed off my denim trousers. My hip and back protested.

"Oh, Baby!" Momma said. "That beast nearly killed you!"

"Momma, Rawhide's the gentlest boy there is. Something must have frightened him."

The others looked to be holding their collective breath. I flexed first one foot, then another, stretched my legs, then my arms, but my lower back and hips would not cooperate.

How could I get back on that horse? I didn't want all these rough, tough cowboys to think I couldn't hack it. If John Ford didn't poke me to get back in the saddle, one of the Fox honchos would.

"It hurts a little when I bend this way," I said, leaning to the right. "But I can keep shooting."

"Are you sure?" George said.

"Mr. Hough, we should take a break so Olive can rest. I'll put some liniment on her back. I have some in my mothering bag," Momma said.

"Momma, I'm fine," I insisted.

"I think we should let Margie take over for you for now," Doc said. Margie Hatfield was my stunt double, and she was fearless, but I didn't want her to be hurt, so I always insisted on doing my own stunts. So far, this had made my co-stars laugh.

"Darling Baby, you're *injured*!" Momma said.

George tenderly touched my shoulder. "Olive, maybe sit for a little while. You were almost trampled. Don't force it if you're not ready. Believe me, I know. Boxing taught me to pay attention to what my body told me."

"All right," I said, and watched resentment creep over Momma's face at me listening to George and not to her.

They brought over one of the horse-drawn wagons and carted me back to camp. I felt every rock and pebble and shift in the ground. When we pulled up, George helped me out and into a folding canvas chair, then he brought me some water and rubbed my shoulders. The cooks boiled some water in a kettle, somebody found a hot water bottle, and I placed it against my back. Momma fluttered around me, trying to move closer than George.

"You need to lie down and take a nap, Baby."

"No, Momma. I'm going to be fine. Let me set a spell." People might disparage my acting, but I wasn't going to let them call me lightweight or unprofessional. I'd already been off too long from the typhoid, and I wasn't going to let this put me out of commission.

When I felt a little more rested and able to move, I approached Rawhide and he nuzzled me.

"What was that, Rawhide? I thought we liked each other, huh?" I ran my hand over his broad, shiny neck and his muzzle. "Am I forgiven?"

"Uh-uh," Lefty told me. "Olive, you're not getting back on that horse."

"Of course I am. He didn't mean to go crazy, did you, boy?"

"He tried trampling you to death," Lefty said.

"He got spooked, that's all," I said, scratching Rawhide's ears. He nickered and turned his neck for more stroking.

"He started to step on you, and was halfway up in the air on his way down. For some reason, he didn't land on you. You got *very* lucky."

But nobody could tell me different. Half an hour later, we shot the scene where Lee and her father lost their wagon wheel and she met Dan for the first time.

FOX STUDIO, 1401 WESTERN AVENUE, HOLLYWOOD, CALIFORNIA,
November 17, 1925

The Fox lot sat at the intersection of Sunset and Western. Western divided it in half, with the larger stages to the east, and the administration building, stars' bungalows, Munchers, the Fox employee commissary; and other buildings to the west.

The interiors would be the easiest part to shoot because they could be done at the studio. I'd finally bounced back from the typhoid and the bucking (after plenty of medical care), so we moved ahead on the scenes inside the saloon and the tent. After interiors were done, we had to wait for spring thaw before we could head north to Wyoming for the mountain scenes.

In the story, Bull, Mike, and Spade wanted to keep their new ward clean so she'd stay pretty and marriageable. They offered Lee their tent for some privacy to bathe in a barrel, bringing her kettles and kettles of hot water, placing a cover over their bird's cage so he couldn't watch, then retreating, red-faced, so she could wash.

A drape was hung in front of me so I could disrobe. I did, dropping lower in the barrel so the waterline covered everything important. Momma watched from the corner, as protective as a lioness. No one would have dared to sneak a peek with her there.

It wasn't long after Ford yelled the final "Cut!" for the scene that I got the notification from the studio heads at Fox that I was being offered a contract. I'd never been so thrilled.

CHAPTER THREE

REGENT HOTEL APARTMENTS, 6166 HOLLYWOOD BLVD,
LOS ANGELES, CALIFORNIA, *December 1925*

"It's like Mr. Ford hates me," I told Momma over breakfast one morning. "He wasn't like this in the desert. I don't know what happened."

Recently, I'd noticed a change in John Ford as we shot the interiors. It was subtle at first, but then his attitude became more and more overtly nasty. I wasn't sure what to do.

"He's under a lot of pressure, Baby. He's probably taking it out on you right now, that's all," she said, pouring the coffee.

"I don't know about that. He's spitting commands at me. Real harsh-like. George says he thinks it was after the scene in the tent," I said, buttering my toast.

"George has noticed it too, then?"

"George and Jack are good friends, but George said he wanted to punch his lights out for how he was talking to me."

Momma frowned as she bit into a biscuit. "Does George know why?"

"He says he has no idea."

"Well, botheration. There is no way we are going to Wyoming

to film with him treating you like *that*. I'll have a talk with him."

"Momma, no. I don't want you fighting my battles for me. Please leave it alone."

She sighed. "All I can say is that he'd better not do it in front of me. Finish your eggs, pardner. We're headed downtown to meet with someone."

"Who is it?" I said, taking a sip of my coffee.

"His name is Ben Rothwell. "He's a show business agent, pardner. I want you to have some guidance for dealing with the studios. Lord knows I'm not much help. These problems you're having with Mr. Ford? We can nip that in the bud, like a stipulation in the contract that you will no longer work with him."

"Momma, he's one of the best directors at Fox. That would cut my choice of parts."

"I am not going to watch you be mistreated by that man— even if he does wield that megaphone like he's a king. He will at least speak to you like a gentleman. I'm looking out for your interests, my girl. That's all there is to it."

We finished breakfast, then took Western to 3rd downtown. On Hill Street, I pulled my used Nash Super Six to a stop at the curb in front of the Wright-Callender building, and I got out first. Momma gathered up her purse and mothering bag before stepping daintily out of the passenger side. We entered the building through the ornamented doors out front, then stepped into the elevator.

"Fourth floor," Momma told the elevator operator. When the cage opened, she marched off down the corridor and I brought up the rear.

"This way, baby," she said, pausing outside the door to the

Willis and Inglis Talent Agency. She held it open, and I followed quietly.

The secretary looked up from her Underwood and smiled.

"My daughter and I are here to see Mr. Rothwell," Momma said.

"I'll let him know you've arrived, Mrs..."

"Cecilia Borden."

"I won't be a moment." The woman hurried into one of the offices and returned a moment later. "This way, please."

Momma and I stepped into the office she indicated. Ben Rothwell was a tall man with closely cropped, rusty-auburn hair that coordinated well with his brown tweed suit and brown-striped tie. His eyes were a snapping blue.

"Mrs. Borden," he said. "And Miss Borden. It's a distinct pleasure. I'm so happy to meet you both."

"Everyone calls me Sibbie," Momma said.

"Sibbie it is. And you call me Ben."

I smiled and Momma forged ahead. "As I mentioned over the phone, Mr. Rothwell, I believe my daughter needs the services of an agent like yourself to look out for her interests, personally and financially. She has recently been offered a contract by Fox studio."

"Congratulations! Excellent news," he said. "Miss Borden, why don't you tell me about your work up to this point? The more I know about your previous credits, the better."

I looked to Momma for guidance.

"Go ahead, pardner," she said.

For someone who wanted to be so independent, I was too nervous to speak. "You do it, Momma," I mumbled.

"Of course," Momma said, pulling her cheaters out of the

glasses case in her handbag. She was too vain to wear them all the time, but for negotiations this important, they were definitely necessary. Consulting her notes, she outlined my early work for Christie and Sennett, described the shorts I'd made for Hal Roach, and expounded on our deep appreciation for Mr. Mix and the wonderful opportunities he'd given me, including *The Yankee Señor*. Finally, she explained my WAMPAS title, my newfound popularity, the Fox contract, and the fact that she would *under no circumstances* allow me to be spoken to or treated as John Ford had recently done.

"Miss Borden...or do you mind if I call you Olive?" Mr. Rothwell asked.

"Olive's fine," I said.

"Good. And you can call me Ben. I've heard a lot from your mother. Now I'd like to hear directly from you. Do you have anything to add?"

"She covered it pretty well," I said. "But...is it true, Ben, that you can ask for more money and better working conditions for me?"

"Yes, that's true."

"Then that's what I'd really like," I said. "To make more than I'm making. I got typhoid on *3 Bad Men*, and so did Momma. The campfires were nice, but I never want to be that sick again. It was too hot, then too cold. I fell off a horse. I don't like desert shoots."

Ben took notes as I talked. "We can try to negotiate that into a contract," he said. "And if you dislike the train compartments in which you're traveling, we can get you nicer ones. A more luxurious dressing room, perhaps, or a wardrobe allowance, so you're always perfectly turned out for premieres."

"I want enough to buy a nice house. A big house with servants," I continued. "I've been working my patoot off in films for three years. I deserve a house."

"*We* deserve a house," Momma corrected me. "Remember who helped you get this far."

Ben laughed. "I daresay most people in Hollywood want that if they don't have it already. I'll do my best to get you what you need."

A week later, Ben pulled his chocolate-colored Cadillac to a stop in front of the Fox administration building and escorted Momma and me inside.

"Benjamin Rothwell, Olive Borden and Mrs. Borden to see Mr. Wurtzel and Mr. Sheehan," he told the secretary. "We have an appointment."

"Certainly, sir. I'll let them know you're here." She rounded the desk and gave a quick knock at the double doors. At the curt, "Come in," she slipped inside. She was back in a moment and ushered us in.

Sol Wurtzel was slim and dark-haired, with featherings of gray above his more-than-prominent ears. His office was decorated in shades of gold and maroon.

Winfield Sheehan was in his early forties. He wasn't thin, but he wasn't portly either. He was solidly built, and was beginning to develop jowls. His hair was fair, but graying, and he wore a loud red bowtie. It was hard to concentrate on what he was saying because my gaze kept returning to it.

"Miss Borden, Mrs. Borden, Mr. Rothwell, it's good to see you. Welcome." Mr. Wurtzel escorted us to a polished dining-sized table at the rear of the room. "Can I have Edith bring you a coffee? Or maybe a Coca-Cola?"

"Nothing for me," Ben said.

"Nothing, thank you," Momma said.

"A Coca-Cola would be the berries," I said.

Mr. Wurtzel had the secretary bring me a Coca-Cola, then stationed himself across from us. Ben held out chairs for Momma and then for me. I made myself comfortable and he took the chair beside me. Mr. Sheehan joined us at the table, carrying a sheaf of papers, then he took the chair at the head of the table.

"Shall we continue with the pleasantries or get down to brass tacks?" Sheehan asked.

"Tacks, most definitely," I said with my most winning smile.

We went through the contract line by line, with Mr. Sheehan, Mr. Wurtzel, and Ben doing a lot of back and forth about compensation and hours worked. Momma interjected with thoughts on creature comforts and the extra benefits I would receive.

"One more thing," Momma said. "Olive has gotten better on a horse, but there was that unpleasantness in Victorville. She could have been killed. That will *never* happen again. Horseback riding is out."

"Mrs. Borden, we still have scenes to finish at Yellowstone, and despite your demands, some of that shoot will require Olive to ride a horse. We'll use a double when we can, and we'll be as careful as possible, but it cannot be avoided, I'm sorry."

Momma pursed her lips and handed the contract back to Ben to continue. Once Ben's demands were approved, Wurtzel made some further dictates of his own.

"Now then, in grooming you for this star role, Olive, we

want to develop a persona for you. Part Gloria Swanson, part Nazimova, with a dash of the Duchess of York thrown in. You will be elegant, cool, and aloof. Reporters will be *surprised* that you aren't a snob when they meet you. To *them*, you are warm and welcoming. To everyone else, you arc unreachable."

Elegant? The kid who'd once traipsed Chesapeake docks and chicken-necked for crabs? Is he kidding?

"Mr. Sheehan sees you as a replacement for Madge Bellamy. She's become testy, cranky with directors, and difficult to work with. We want you to adapt to her role. You act like an empress, and you do not deign to speak to *anyone* who does not matter. Your maid will spray perfume where you walk. It's an extra affectation, but it will be very effective at keeping up the persona."

"Effective at what? I'm no Vanderbilt," I said. "I was a tomboy growing up, and—"

"You can *choose* your favorite perfume," Mr. Wurtzel said, as if that was my main complaint.

"Olive would love to replace Miss Bellamy," Momma said, patting my hand. "She looks wonderful in frocks, and her clothes horse potential would be guaranteed, like Miss Swanson."

Momma and Mr. Wurtzel nodded at each other with big smiles. No one even asked me what *I* wanted. Gloria Swanson was more hoity-toity than I could ever *think* of being.

I tried to interrupt, but Mr. Sheehan, Mr. Wurtzel, Ben, and Momma kept up their steady discussion. It was like I wasn't even in the room.

When we'd made it through all four pages and I signed with the fountain pen Mr. Sheehan handed me, he beamed, offered me his hand and said, "Call me Winnie. Everyone does. If you need anything you let me know. Sol or me. Now, let me officially welcome you to Fox Studio."

I was given a choice bungalow (near George at my request), a close-up parking spot, a bungalow housekeeper, and more money than I'd ever seen in my life. They also gave me spending money for the train when I had to travel for shooting. I was given a stipend per month for frocks and accessories so I could always look my best. The cost of redecorating my bungalow was also covered.

From Mr. Wurtzel's office, Momma, Ben, and I went straight to my assigned bungalow, a charming white clapboard with a scarlet runner bean vine curled around the latticed porch outside. I felt bad for Gladys Brockwell, the previous occupant. Her name had not yet been taken down and replaced with mine. She'd recently been killed when the car she was riding in had plunged down an embankment near Calabasas. I unlocked the door, then flicked on the light and gasped.

"Good God," I said. "How could anyone love frills so much?"

"It's lovely. Very feminine," Momma said of the eyelet dressing table skirt I ripped off. In addition, there were more flounces on the daybed and hideous sprigged, flocked wallpaper. I opened the casements to air out the place.

Jacqueline Logan, my new next door neighbor, came over to introduce herself. She and George had co-starred in *Thank You*, and we got along famously. Over the next few weeks, George would stop by when he could, and we'd share lunch when he worked on the lot. When I could distract Momma by having her run errands, we'd also share cuddles and kisses.

Unfortunately, George had to travel to Santa Cruz to shoot *The Johnstown Flood* around Christmas, and I missed him terribly. To distract myself, I jumped into decorating my bungalow, replacing the lace and frills with taffeta and tailored lines, and then I decided the time had come to look for an off-set home too.

627 HILLCREST ROAD, BEVERLY HILLS, CALIFORNIA,
Early January 1926

"Here we are," said Mr. Danziger, the real estate agent.

He pulled his maroon Lincoln to a stop in the curved driveway, then turned off the engine.

After a lifetime of cheap, dingy flats, I'd dreamed of a gorgeous house, and I wanted one that would make Hollywood sit up and notice. When Momma and I had been living on boiled peanuts, cabbage soup, and scrapple back in Norfolk, with barely a dime to our names, I'd fantasized about it.

George had run into Hobart Bosworth recently at the Cocoanut Grove, they'd chatted, and Hobe mentioned he was selling this place. Knowing I was in the market, George told me about it.

"Oh, Momma, look!" I cried.

So far, this house fit the bill perfectly. It was a stucco beauty with Tudor detailing, and the roofline was a swooping, curved A-frame over one half of the façade. Off to one side was a port-cochère that led back to a large garage in the same style.

Two palms grew near the street, and lush landscaping welcomed us up to the arched front door. Mr. Danziger unlocked it and ushered us into the living room.

"Mr. Bosworth has been very happy here," he said.

"Why is Hobe moving?" I asked.

"He's found a home on Sunset. He remarried a few years ago, and his new wife would like to have a home of their own instead of living in this one that reminded them both of his ex-wife. That's good for you, because he's reduced the price!" he concluded brightly.

The main story featured shiny oak floors. To the right of the entry was a formal dining room with a built-in china cabinet. Straight ahead was the staircase to the second floor, and to the left, down two steps was the living room. A fireplace on the front wall was flanked by large vertical windows, and on the far side of the living room was an office nook enclosed with French doors. Toward the back was an enormous kitchen and sitting room, with banks of windows and a group of French doors out to the spacious terrace and garden.

I stepped onto the rear patio, where pots of vivid coral vincas and pastel impatiens clustered around an urn containing a dwarf orange tree. Bougainvillea climbed over the back walls.

"Gorgeous," Momma said. "Like the Garden of Eden."

"It's so big, I could host polo matches back here," I said. We crossed the garden, skirting the swimming pool to the entrance of the servants' quarters. It looked comfortable and large enough to bring on a whole slew of help, which I'd need to maintain the place. With a house like this, I'd be able to hold my head high among the Hollywood elite.

We retreated back inside, then I strolled back to the front

vestibule, admiring the wainscoting and the woodwork.

"Let's see the second floor," I said, taking the stairs two at a time. Momma and Mr. Danziger followed.

"Goodness!" Momma said, her eyes lighting up as she gazed around the master in satisfaction. "You could fit our room at the Regent in here seven times over!"

She was right. The plush wall-to-wall carpeting, sitting room overlooking the pool, fireplace, giant walk-in closet with shelving, and en suite bathroom with clawfoot tub, marble tile, and gold fixtures surpassed any room I'd ever seen.

"How many bathrooms are there?" I asked Mr. Danziger.

"Four," he said, consulting his clipboard.

"Four bathrooms..." Momma breathed. "Can you *imagine*?"

"All right, Mr. Danziger. We've seen enough. I want it. What do we have to do?"

"We can go back to my office and draw up an offer for the property. If Mr. Bosworth accepts the offer, we'll be on our way. If he counter-offers, you can consider that and negotiations begin."

He drove us back to his office on Wilshire Boulevard, we filled out a standard contract with my offer, and we settled in for a wait. Momma and I celebrated finding the perfect house with lunch at the Montmartre, hoping for good news.

Mr. Bosworth accepted, and it didn't take long to move us in, since we didn't have much to begin with. Furnishing it would have to wait until I returned from my next location shoot in Catalina. I daydreamed of antiques, luxury, and throwing the best parties in Hollywood.

CHAPTER FOUR

HOTEL ST. CATHERINE, CATALINA ISLAND, CALIFORNIA,
February 5, 1926

Since we were forced to wait until spring thaw to travel to Jackson Hole to finish *3 Bad Men*, Fox squeezed me into something called *Yellow Fingers* during the break.

The part seemed perfectly crafted for my dark hair and dark eyes. I played Saina, a girl who'd been brought up in a Malay village by Peter Shane, a white master who'd raised her to believe she was white. But in truth, her mother had been a native girl. Ralph Ince was tall and distinguished, and played Shane to a T, with arrogant brow lifting and a snobby demeanor.

Then, Nona Deering, a white woman played by Claire Adams, escaped from a white slaver, Kwong-Li of the yellow fingers, an art dealer in Bangkok. She crawled aboard Shane's ship, and he took her back to his island home. This did not sit well with Saina, who'd planned on marrying Shane. When Saina overheard a conversation between Shane and Nona in which he said Saina was actually a half-caste, she went mad. They smeared me with extra suntan stain to make me look darker complected, so I'd be more believable as a half Malay.

Most of the filming happened at the Fox lot, but for most of January, the studio carpenters had been busy building a complete native village from wood and bamboo on Catalina. It was finished the last week of January, but unfortunately, winter storms swept the coast as we were ready to sail over.

The waves were too rough for us to berth safely, and the harbormaster shut down the ship docks, so the cast and crew had to debark onto a tender that dropped us at the hotel's pier in Descanso Bay. The rain was coming down in sheets, so we got drenched dashing to the cars that dropped us at the hotel. Our director, Emmett Flynn was the one who'd chosen me to work with Mr. Mix in *The Yankee Señor*, so we were already old chums.

The St. Catherine was more popular for film stars than the Island Villa cabanas nearer to the harbor, due to its opulent interiors and plunge pool. It was nestled in the hills near Sugarloaf, and provided luxury and privacy, away from the gawkers and autograph hounds.

The day after we arrived, the skies cleared for an hour or so, and the show had to go on. We wanted to squeeze in as many exterior shots on Descanso Beach as we could, but it appeared that more storms were headed directly for us.

"Hot points!" called our take boy, Seth Martindale, as he carried the tripod through the crowd of extras before planting the legs in the sand and getting the camera set up. The musicians launched into "Aloha Oe" for our music, but complained about getting sand in their instruments, so Emmett sent them back inside.

Emmett conferred with several of the other members of the crew, then used his blue glass to visualize the scene. In this scene, Saina had discovered her Eurasian blood and was attempting to wash off her skin color in the ocean. I kneeled at the waterline near some rocks where the waves broke, and the gusting winds provided the perfect dramatic effect.

"*Yellow Fingers*, scene twenty-four, take one!" Seth yelled over the wind, clacking the halves of the slate board together.

"And...action!" Emmett called. "Olive, you're stricken! Scrub it off! You hate your native blood! Scrub off that yellow! Good! Good!"

The wind whipped the sand into a fury, sending it into our noses and mouths. I did my best to look traumatized, but I had to shut my eyes. My long hair blew wildly about, nearly strangling me.

"Olive!" called Emmett. "Get down a little more into the water!"

I tried, but the rocks were slick and treacherous. "Em, it's slippery! I'm afraid I could fall—"

At the moment I said it, a monster wave emerged from between two giant boulders and inundated the area where I was crouching. It knocked me into the ocean, and I fought the undertow that dragged me down and pulled me out a hundred yards or so. I was a good swimmer, but the salt water choked me as I tried to find my footing. At last I did, broke the surface, and began trudging to shore.

Momma was struggling a few yards away. She'd evidently forgotten that she couldn't swim and bounded into the ocean after me. Peter Anderson, one of the extras, had dashed into the water to retrieve her, and Seth Martindale had jumped in too. Pete grabbed Momma in a swimmer's carry, and Seth approached me through the waves.

"You okay, Miss Borden?" he yelled.

"I think so!" I choked out as we reached the beach. "I'm lucky I wasn't dashed on the rocks!"

Peter escorted Momma in with his arm supporting her, and she rushed to my side.

"Oh, my Baby!" she cried, coughing as she grabbed me in a dramatic embrace. As we neared her mothering bag, she ran to it and fussed over me, toweling me off, wiping my face, and finger combing my hair.

"Momma, let me be!" I said, pushing her hands away. "I'm fine. I got the wind knocked out of me. That's all."

She looked hurt, abruptly turned and packed up the bag, then stomped across the shifting sands back to the hotel without another word.

"Momma!" I shouted. "Come back!"

Determined, she kept stumbling away.

"Emmett, can we *please* call it a day? I'm freezing, I'm hungry, and I'm half-drowned. I know the audience is supposed to empathize with me, but this is too much!" I yelled over the wind.

He sighed. "Yeah, all right! God knows how much sand these cameras have ingested. Go check on your mother. That's a wrap for today, everyone!"

I plodded back to the hotel room I shared with Momma and gave a little knock before entering. There was no answer. She sat on one of the beds with her back to me, shaking with her held-in sobs.

"Momma, I'm sorry. All right?" I said, finger combing my sopping hair. Then I tugged off my sodden sarong-style skirt and bandeau top and pulled on a fluffy robe. I couldn't stop shivering, and my chattering teeth sounded like castanets.

"You may *not* speak to me that way again, young lady, especially in front of an entire crew. I am your mother. *Never* forget that."

"I said I'm sorry, Momma. You embarrass me when you do that while I'm shooting. I'm nineteen now. I'm a grown woman."

"You're hardly *grown*," she sniffed. "You're still very immature for your age."

At that moment, I'd had enough. "Do you know what would help with that? My mother not doing *every little thing* for me! I want to make decisions for myself for a change! I can't keep living my *entire* life with a chaperone!"

"Olive, I wish you would realize that I'm not perfect."

"You used to be, Momma. You used to do everything and I appreciated it. Now, you can *stop*. I can take it from here!"

"Did George put you up to this?"

"No! But since you mentioned it, I'd like to see my sweetheart once in a while without answering to you about how late I was out or what I was doing!"

"I do not want to be reading about your goings-on in the newspaper. I should be privy to everything so I can help to control what the magazine journalists say about you. This is Hollywood. You know how things are here."

"I have Ben for that. I wish you could just be my mother. Be happy for me when I'm successful and be sad for me when I fail."

"You won't even let me do *that* lately."

"Let me grow up, Momma!" I yelled.

Her face hardened, and she left the room, slamming the door behind herself. I sighed and lay down for a nap, my thoughts racing. When it came time for dinner, I took a bath in the bathroom down the hall. She was back when I returned to the room, and watched as I dressed in my black flat crêpe dress, panné velvet overcoat, and panné velvet tam.

"I'm going to dinner. Are you coming?" I asked as I slipped on stockings and shoes.

"No," she said. "You don't want me there."

"You're right, I don't," I said. "Goodnight." I turned on my heel and stalked to the elevator, feeling a combination of elation and nausea. How did she always manage to turn my desire for independence into the feeling that I was hurting someone? It didn't have to be like this. Other mothers let their children go. Didn't they?

She moped the rest of the trip. I had to ask her to go furniture shopping with me when we got back to town so she would speak to me again. I studied catalogs of antiques and attended high-priced auctions, and I was constantly on the prowl for the perfect sofas, the most comfortable occasional chairs, and the most elegant bed I could find.

I ran ads in the *Herald* for household staff, and although it took a while to find the perfect person, I did eventually find a cook, Mandy; and a personal maid, Lila.

Mandy was a light-skinned colored girl from South Central with a love of penny candy and a beautiful singing voice. She'd serenade us while doing her chores. Lila was tall and thin, with blue eyes behind round spectacles and a real way of reading my mind. It didn't matter if I needed a hot bath or a facial. Along with them, I brought on four housemaids, who were assigned to different areas of the house. I needed one maid simply to keep the bathrooms clean.

One passion I was finally able to indulge was my love of beautiful dolls. When I was little, Momma and I would go into downtown Norfolk for errands and we'd pass the W.G. Schwartz store, and sometimes they'd have a display in the window. I'd loved their delicate porcelain faces, real blinking eyes, and tiny teeth, with velvet dresses and patent shoes. We could never afford them. I got cheap baby dolls from Auntie Bessie or Granny and Grampa Shields, but now I delighted in going to the Tiny Tot Toy Store and buying as many as I wanted. I even had an entire room to display them in cases.

Wanting a car to match the house, I accompanied George to the next Los Angeles Motor Car Dealers' Association Car Show downtown at Hill and Washington Streets. We strolled through the giant tents that had been erected for the event, past streamers and bunting and embossed signs for exotic makes from every foreign and domestic car company. There were so many gorgeous models to choose from, but nothing looked quite right until we got to the Delage booth. There she sat, like a queen surrounded by lowly peasants, at least in my eyes. She was an elegant elongated touring car—deep midnight blue with rims of the same color, whitewall tires, and a landau top. There was no other car at the exhibition that came close to touching her.

"What is it?" I asked the salesman, nodding to it.

"Un Delage DM Limousin," he said in French-accented English. "An excellent choice. Mademoiselle is interested?"

"Mademoiselle is *very* interested," I said. George crossed his arms and watched, amused, as the attendant unhooked the velvet ropes surrounding the booth and allowed me to sit in the driver's seat of the vehicle.

I crawled in, and settled into the deep leather, examining all the controls on the wood-grained dashboard. Then, I got out and sat in the backseat, since that would be my usual spot. It was huge. There was room for me, for Momma, for Lila, and even for a social secretary to keep track of my appointments. Between the two seats was a glass panel that opened and closed, separating the driver from the passengers—the more to maintain a dignified distance. There were even pull-down shades on the backseat windows. It didn't get classier than that, and I imagined what it would look like pulling up in front of glamorous premieres. I wrote the salesman a check, and the Delage was delivered the same week. Even before it showed up, I ran another ad in the *Herald*:

WANTED- Chauffeur for local celebrity. On-call status desired. French a plus. Livery uniform required.

"French a plus?" George said, reading the ad and laughing.

"You can't have a French limousine without a French chauffeur," I said.

When Lila answered the door three days later, there stood a tall sandy-haired drink of water.

"*Mademoiselle* advertised for *un chauffeur*?" he asked. The minute he opened his mouth, he sounded snobby and arrogant. Winnie would be pleased.

"Yes, I did. What's your name?"

"Maurice LeBlanc."

"Have any speeding tickets? Accidents?" I asked him.

"Non, mademoiselle." He shook his head, so I named a price and he agreed.

"I have space above the garage for you to live so you can be on-call," I said.

"Bon," he said, so I had Mandy show him around the quarters and he made himself comfortable.

Not long after that, I also placed an ad for a social secretary to take care of all my fan mail and correspondence. Inez Perkins was pale and mousy, but she could type, and her shorthand was lightning fast. I hired her on the spot.

When I was shooting locally, Maurice drove Momma, Lila, Inez and me down Sunset to the studio every day. It was a routine I quite liked.

In the spring, with the announcement of a big Fox party to be held up in San Francisco, George decided we could travel together and make a quick vacation out of it before we headed to Jackson Hole to finish *3 Bad Men*.

"You can meet my parents!" he said enthusiastically.

"Your parents?" I squeaked. I'd never met a sweetheart's parents before. Heck, I'd never had a sweetheart's parents to meet before. I hoped that I'd pass muster.

"Yeah, and my brother Dan. And Beulah. She's been with the family for years."

"What are they like?" I asked, trying not to let my nerves show.

"My father will be the toughest nut to crack, but he's really a big softie. You're Irish Catholic, so you'll be fine."

"And your mother?"

"My mother is a saint. She was my biggest influence growing up because Cap was still out walking a beat. Trust me," he said reassuringly. "They'll love you."

Momma invited herself along for the event, but she would not be joining us at the O'Briens. On the train north from Los Angeles, George and I found a game of rummy to join in the salon car, and George ordered us two ginger ales. Momma followed us and pulled her knitting out of her mothering bag, taking a seat with a perfect view of the both of us.

After taking me in five sets, George laughed. "Let's take a break," he said.

I glanced to where Momma had been sitting, and she was gone. When I checked my wristwatch, it was after eleven. We'd actually outlasted her! We moved outside to the back platform of the observation car to enjoy being alone at last.

"I've had such a wonderful time with you," he said.

"Me too." I shivered when I said it.

"Are you cold?" He began to remove his coat.

"Nervous," I said. He caressed my arm as we moved closer.

"Don't be scared," George said. "I'm right here. I'm not going anywhere."

I closed my eyes and lifted my face. George spidered his hands through my hair before tenderly pressing his lips to mine.

"I know you probably think we sailors are all alike, girl-in-every-port, 'love em and leave 'em types, but that's not me. I love you, Olive."

"I love you too," I whispered.

He leaned down and kissed me again. Where the last kiss had been tender and tentative, this one was more insistent, more breathtaking, and I lost myself in it. We stood like that for a good hour or more, kissing, cuddling, and making plans for what we would do upon our return to Los Angeles. But for now, it was us, the welcoming darkness, the faint pounding of the ocean surf, and the starry skies. I thought I saw fireworks off in the distance, but it was only the pounding of my heart and the bright lights in my soul.

2951 HARRISON STREET, SAN FRANCISCO, CALIFORNIA,
April 19, 1926

"Mom! Cap! We're here!" George called after giving a quick knock. The door was unlocked.

The O'Brien home was a cream-colored stucco townhouse with squared bays and sculpted embellishments near the roof and over the windows. Crimson begonias in flowerboxes brightened up the front, and a police department insignia hung proudly over the doorbell.

"George!" said a stylish woman of uncertain age. Her hair was graying, but her face was unlined. It was obvious where George had gotten his good looks. She enveloped him in a hug, and I caught a whiff of peony blossom as she moved closer.

"Olive, this is my mother, Margaret. Mother, this is my sweetheart, Olive Borden."

"Why, you're as lovely in person as you are on screen, dear," Margaret O'Brien said with a smile, then bussed my cheek.

"Thank you. It's a pleasure to meet you, Mrs. O'Brien," I said.

"Please, call me Maggie."

She seemed so warm and welcoming, as I'd always imagined *other* mothers to be.

"Please, make yourself comfortable," Maggie said with a smile. She gestured to an overstuffed horsehair sofa the color of putty. Several antique tables and two Tiffany lamps also helped to fill the parlor. The drapes were deep brown velvet, with putty fringe tiebacks, and a calligraphed family tree hung on the wall near the fireplace. It traced O'Briens and Donahues going back for three generations.

"Happy birthday, darling," she said.

"It's your birthday?" I asked. "Why didn't you tell me, George?"

He laughed. "Sorry, with all the trip planning, I forgot."

"My beautiful boy is twenty-seven today," she said, taking his chin in her hand and planting a loud kiss on his cheek.

"Catholics," George said with a chuckle. "Mom and Cap named me for St. George of Antioch. Today is his feast day."

"Are you Catholic, dear?" Maggie asked.

"Oh, yes ma'am," I said. "Black Irish. My mother's mother was a McKenna, and her father was a Shields. I went to Catholic schools in Baltimore."

"That's marvelous," she said, sitting down with a swish of her skirt.

I started to say something else, but then loud footfalls sounded on the stairs. George stood to greet his father.

"I heard my opponent enter the ring!" a deep male voice called. Captain O'Brien joined us in the parlor and pretended to shadowbox with George. "Good to see you, my boy."

George took the manly clap on the back from his father and returned it. "Cap, this is my sweetheart, Olive Borden.

Olive, my father, Daniel O'Brien."

"Charmed, sir," I said.

He nodded at me and said hello, but immediately turned to George. There would be none of the same familiarity with him.

"How was the trip?" Captain O'Brien asked.

"Fine. Little chilly," George said.

As they caught up, I looked at the photographs on the wall. There were lots of photographs of George and his brother Dan in various poses— George in his military uniform, in school, in boxing garb, and in costume for *The Iron Horse*.

"How long have you and Olive been seeing each other, dear?" Maggie asked.

"Since last fall," George offered. "We met when we were making *3 Bad Men*."

"George was my handsome prince," I said. "He rode to the rescue for fruit and clean water when a couple of us got sick. Typhoid, they said."

"Oh how dreadful." She frowned with concern.

"But I'm better now, thanks to your son."

He waved away my compliment. "It was nothing. We weren't near a hospital, and somebody had to do something."

"That's my boy," Maggie said, smiling.

"Dinner is served," said a slim girl in black uniform with a white apron and hair net who stood at the entry to the parlor.

"Teriff!" said George, standing and rubbing his hands together. "I'm starved. I sure hope Beulah made her apple cobbler for me."

"She did. No worries there," Maggie said. "*And* a chocolate cake for your birthday. Shall we?"

Captain O'Brien gestured expansively toward the dining room, where the Jacobean table and chairs was set for four.

"I was hoping Dan could join us too," George said, looking disappointed.

"He and Madge have their hands full. He sent his regrets," Maggie said. Then to me, "They have a two-year old."

I smiled and nodded in understanding, and an older woman with gray hair and ruddy apple cheeks entered the dining room carrying a soup tureen.

"Beulah, you're a sight for sore eyes," George said. "Here, let me help you with that." He scrambled to take it from her and set it down with great care in the center of the table. Then he gave her a big bear hug and shook her gently.

She laughed and placed her hands on George's cheeks. "Don't make me have to box your ears, my lad."

"Same old Beulah," he said, beaming.

Beulah retreated to the kitchen again. She'd made a roast, and she brought the fragrant platter to the table, where Captain O'Brien proceeded to slice it. Plates were passed, and he added potatoes, carrots, and rutabagas to each one.

"Where are your people from, young lady?" Captain O'Brien asked. "You sound southern."

"Well sir, my father was from Massachusetts, but my mother is from Virginia. I grew up in Richmond and Norfolk. I went to school in Baltimore."

"Parochial schools, Dan," Maggie reassured him.

"And what does your father do?" he pressed, serving his soup first, then passing the tureen to George.

"Daddy died when I was a baby," I said. "Before he passed, he was a cook."

We ate politely for a while, and then Captain O'Brien threw me for a loop.

"How serious is all this between you two?"

George sat up straighter. "I'm thinking of asking Olive to marry me," he said. I gulped in surprise.

"You haven't even known each other a year," Maggie said, suddenly not as approving.

"Times are changing." George said. "Things aren't as old-fashioned as they used to be. Shooting on location was the best thing that could have happened to us." He smiled at me across the table.

The captain looked more concerned. "How well do you really know each other though?" he asked. "Are you suited?"

"We sure are. We feel the same about so many things. We like dancing and being out-of-doors, and...Olive says she could be ready to go in fifteen minutes if I wanted to cruise around the world."

"You're a world traveler too?" Captain O'Brien asked me.

It's the only way I could get rid of my mother, I thought, but I was cagier in my reply. "Oh, no. I've hardly been anywhere, but I can't wait to see other countries. England, France, Italy..."

"George wants to head in the other direction. Don't you, my boy?" Captain O'Brien said.

"Hawaii's on my list too," I replied. "And Australia. I want to see a real live kangaroo."

"Then it's settled. I'll have a wonderful first mate," George said, giving me a supportive glance.

Captain O'Brien chewed thoughtfully. "No need to rush into anything though, is there? I'm advising caution, that's all."

"I appreciate that, Cap. We're not in a hurry. And we have

our shooting schedules to think about."

Maggie tried another tack. "There's a lot to think about. The church, the flowers, the cake, the invitations, the priest. That's a lot to do when you're so busy. You should wait until you have more time to plan it well." From her, it sounded sensible instead of judgemental.

George and I gazed at each other and grinned.

"Of course, mother," George said, not taking his eyes off me.

Later, we left for the St. Francis, where rooms had been booked for us by the studio. The Fox party was a two-day long affair. Winnie and Sol had taken The Lark up the coast, along with some of their staff, like James Grainger, the general sales manager. George's dad was in charge of the police platoon who escorted the group around town, then he hosted a birthday luncheon for George at Tait's at the Beach, with another cake and candles.

The second day, we were treated to a tour of Chinatown, where the Chinatown police squad took over, and walked us through the area in groups of ten. We saw fireworks, a puppet show, a group playing traditional Chinese instruments, and a full Chinese dragon dance winding its way down Stockton Street.

We wound up the night at The Mandarin gobbling up chow mein, chop suey, shark fin soup, pork ribs, and fried rice. George contorted his fingers trying to work the red lacquered chopsticks, and we laughed as we read our fortune cookies. George's said, "You will travel the world," which was more than accurate.

Mine said, "You will never be happier than you are right now." I wasn't sure how to feel about that.

CHAPTER FIVE

LOS ANGELES AND SALT LAKE TRAIN, OUTSIDE OF CALIENTE, NEVADA, *Late May 1926*

"Ladies," George said, entering the lounge car from the observation car and doffing his hat. He and John Ford had spent much of their time sitting outside on the rear platform, where Ford aimed at jackrabbits with his old six-shooter.

"Good afternoon, George," Momma said, pausing in her knitting.

"Hi, George," I said, looking up from my *Photoplay.* We exchanged an affectionate look.

"It's getting close to dinnertime," George said. "May I escort you to the dining car?"

"Why y—" I began.

Momma cut me off. "We're going to go freshen up first, but thank you for your kind offer."

"Then I hope I'll see you there," he said. He nodded at us, then retreated through the connecting door to the next car.

"Momma!"

"You're getting too close to him. You're only nineteen," she said.

"You're my mother, not my jailer," I said.

I glared at her but still followed her to our compartment, where I brushed my hair and pinched my cheeks to make them rosier. The entire trip from Los Angeles had been like this, with George and I trying to find a place to be alone, and Momma bound and determined to be my shadow.

When we reached the dining car, I scanned the menu and made my dinner choice, then gazed out the window so I could keep from looking at her. My resentment roiled in my gut like bad indigestion.

"Good evening," the waiter said. "Have you decided?"

"Yes," I said. The chicken croquettes with mashed potatoes, and a slice of green apple pie."

Momma pursed her lips, then calmly put her menu down. "Actually, she'll have the tomato and cucumber salad and a glass of vegetable juice. I'll have the stuffed pork cutlet."

When I rolled my eyes, she simply smiled at me. "We don't want those riding trousers getting too tight, do we, Baby?"

I closed my eyes to quell the anger building in me, then stood before the waiter could retreat. Clutching his sleeve, I whispered in his ear: "Do me a favor. Deliver my food over there." I pointed several tables over, where George sat with Mac and Tom. There was one spot left at their table. "And bring me what I originally ordered, please."

The waiter nodded. I stood and turned my back on Momma and approached the group. When she asked where I was going, I ignored her. The fellas all stood for me.

"May I join you?" I asked.

They looked over at Momma, who sat there fuming, but they nodded enthusiastically, especially George.

"Look, here comes Jack," Mac said.

Ford sidled down the aisle, his ever-present pipe clenched between his teeth. He nodded to all of us, looked down at the number of seats at the table and began to move away.

"C'mon, Jack, we can scooch," I said. I smiled and pulled out one of the adjoining seats at the table.

Ford looked at me, then at George, then retreated to another table, alone.

I glanced at George, feeling the sting of Ford's resentment once again.

"What the hell was that?" Tom said.

"Olive and I have been trying to figure it out ever since the desert," George said. "He can be one ornery son-of-a-gun, but I've never seen him act like this."

"He hates me all of a sudden," I said.

"Maybe Schneidy or Lefty might know. They're around him more often," Tom offered.

"That's a good idea," Mac said.

"Hey look. Here comes Schneidy now," said Tom.

We all looked up at the new figure entering the dining car. He looked disappointed at the full table until he noticed the extra chair I had pulled up.

"Hey, Schneidy," George said. "Make yourself homely."

"That ain't hard," Schneidy said with a laugh. He greeted everyone, sat down, and picked up one of the menus. The dining steward came and took orders and we chatted a little before hitting Schneidy up for dirt.

"Schneidy, we need to ask you something," George said, lowering his voice, since Jack sat right down the aisle. "We've noticed a difference in Jack toward Olive since Fordville. Any idea what's going on?"

"Different how?" Schneidy asked cautiously.

"Rude, abrupt, like he hates me," I said.

Schneidy nodded sagely. "I was afraid to say anything."

"What is it? What have I done? He's angry at me, and I don't know how to fix it," I said.

"It's not you, not really," he admitted.

"Then what is it?" George said. "There's no need for him to be so awful to her."

"The studio is pressuring him," Schneidy said. "The minute Sol and Winnie saw the rushes of Olive bathing in that barrel, they had Ford change the focus of the movie." He turned to me. "Olive, word is, Winnie is bonkers about you in that barrel. 'Sex sells,' he says. Ford's been told they want more of you, and that's all there is to it. He's seeing his vision for the picture being destroyed, and he doesn't like it at all."

I chewed my lip. "So, it's *my* fault, even though it's *not* my fault," I said. "That's not fair. I can't help how I look."

"Think of it his way. He told Priscilla this would be a juicy role for her. Now, Millie barely has anything to do. I think he feels like a heel for promising something he can't deliver."

"So what should I do?"

"Honestly, I'd keep your head down and do whatever he tells you."

"I'm already doing that," I said.

"Do it harder."

VICTOR, IDAHO, *Late May 1926*

After miles of desert, the Great Salt Lake finally loomed off to our left, and in Salt Lake City, we changed trains onto the Oregon Short Line. When we reached the depot in Victor, Lefty herded us off the train.

"Step right this way, everyone!" he said. He directed the cast and crew to a line of cars parked outside the station.

Momma and I followed Lou Tellegen and he gallantly held the door of a Buick open for us. It was still hard for me to believe this big-hearted pussycat could transform into such a villain for the camera.

"How far is it to Yellowstone?" Momma drawled as our driver put the car in gear.

"About twenty-five miles," he answered. "But it's not the miles, it's the mileage," he said with a laugh.

"What do you mean?" I said.

"You'll see."

He pulled away from the station, and one by one, the rest of our caravan followed suit. The further we got out of Victor, the worse the condition of the road became. I peeked over the front seat at the speedometer, and never saw it go over seven or eight miles an hour. It was a miracle we didn't blow an axle. The car hit ruts that knocked it around, and several times we nearly careened off the edge of a cliff.

The road conditions were bad, but the scenery completely made up for it. The forest was full of evergreens of all types—fir, spruce and piñon pine. The trip took us past strangely-shaped boulders and crags, and the melting snowpack had filled the mountain streams, which threaded through the meadow vales. Wildflowers made colored specks in the bright green, now revealing itself after the long winter.

Along the route, Jim, our local guide, pointed out wild turkeys, antelopes, and pronghorn sheep climbing the lower foothills. Above us, hawks circled. The car continued to ascend, up up up, skirting the sides of peaks. There was no longer any ground visible on my side of the car.

I couldn't bear to look, and the altitude was making me queasy. "Tell me when it's over," I moaned.

Jim chuckled. "We've still got a ways to go, girlie."

"Ow," I said, slipping a finger into my right ear and wiggling it as we climbed even further into the Teton Pass. My head felt like a walnut inside a nutcracker, and my ears crackled until I yawned and the pressure lessened. The mountaintops seemed a mile in the air.

"Jim," Momma asked. "What are those pretty bright blue flowers?"

"Alpine forget-me-nots. Some folks call 'em cushion plant."

"They're lovely."

Jim described more of the scenery, including the bright yellow balsam root and pink longleaf phlox that dotted the mountainsides.

"Olive, look," Lou said. "That last crevasse was a nasty one, but I think you'll want to see this."

"Noooooo...." I moaned again, slumping in the backseat and trying to keep my head down.

"Don't look down. Look *up*."

So I did. Then I couldn't *stop* looking.

"It's so beautiful..." I said, gasping. "I've never seen anything like it."

The surrounding gray-violet peaks soared up into the heavens, laced with clouds, crowned in snow, their deep valleys pocked with rocks, stones, and evergreens. A lone eagle flapped its wings directly above us, on its way to a distant aerie.

"Purple mountains' majesty, indeed," said Momma.

Eventually, in late afternoon, we reached the camp and breathed a sigh of relief. The Wyoming campsite wasn't as large as the one in California, but we still had a full complement of horses, oxen, and Conestoga wagons for the scenes of the settlers passing mountains to reach the town of Custer. The scenes in Custer had taken a week on location in Nevada.

After an abbreviated dinner around the campfire, we hit the hay for some shuteye. Tomorrow would be a long day of shooting.

FIG LEAF RAG

CHAPTER SIX

3 BAD MEN SET, YELLOWSTONE NATIONAL PARK, WYOMING,
Late May 1926

"Lord have mercy. Ladies, are you seeing what I'm seeing?" Phyllis said.

In the shade from a small stand of aspen, Phyllis, Priscilla, and I sat in canvas camp chairs with our other female co-star, Grace Gordon, who played Priscilla's pal in the film.

"If you're seeing Mr. O'Brien over there without his shirt on, then I am definitely seeing that," Grace said.

George stood near one of the water barrels, fully tanned, splashing some of the water on his face and his muscled chest and arms. After drying off with a cloth, he grabbed a fresh checked shirt, pulled it on and buttoned it. Phyllis and Priscilla both wailed comically.

He looked in the direction of the noise, grinned, and waved amiably. "Ladies!" he said, and bowed.

Phyllis gave him a little wave. "Dreamy does not *begin* to describe that man," she said, sotto voce to us. Then louder to him, "George, why don't you come join us?" She patted the chair next to her.

"Sorry, Jack wanted to go over the fistfight scene, but I'll be back. Never fear!"

"We'll hold you to that!" Priscilla called.

George let out a deep laugh, paused and gave me a big smile and a wink before he strolled toward Ford's tent. He truly did not seem to be aware of his extraordinary good looks.

"You are one lucky girl," Phyllis said, looking over at me.

"What do you mean?" I casually tossed back.

"Personally delivering fresh fruit and spring water to his lady fair? Are you kidding? On *horseback*, even. In the *rain*. He's got it bad, my friend."

I giggled. "All right. All right."

"What's he like in private?" Priscilla asked.

I thought a moment. "Sweet, gallant, a complete gentleman."

She sighed.

"He introduced me to his parents too. He's mentioned marriage."

"I'm so jealous," Grace said.

"Me too," Phyllis said. "If you ever get bored, send him my way."

"George is the real thing. I'm already thinking about what to name our kids," I said.

"Yeah? What have you come up with?" Grace said.

"We want three boys. We'll name them Spade, Mike and Bull." I winked.

That sent them into peals of laughter.

Since I wasn't needed for scenes that afternoon, I decided to go cool off near the river. Momma had lain down for a nap, so I was able to slip away easily. The Snake wasn't far from our filming site, and I'd grown fond of taking off my boots and dipping my feet in the current. It was icy cold and felt delicious rushing over my toes. Plus, I could escape from Momma for a while, since she liked staying close to camp.

To my surprise, George was already at my favorite spot with his rods and supplies.

"Are they biting?" I asked as I approached.

George grinned. "The small ones are."

"Buy a girl a drink?"

He let out a hearty laugh, splashed back to shore, and offered me his canteen. "Better be careful. This stuff's got a real kick," he joked.

I took a sip, then handed it back and turned my attention to the equipment he'd spread out on the bank. "Need any help?" I asked.

"Sure! Thought I might be able to rustle up some dinner. I'm Irish, but even *I* can get sick of stew after a while. You fish?"

"You don't grow up around the Chesapeake and the Patapsco and not know how to fish. Or crab."

"I'm impressed!" he said with a chuckle.

I shrugged. "I was a tomboy growing up. Alex Jarrett, Clem Hooper, and I used to get into all kinds of mischief. That's part of the reason Momma sent me to an all-girls convent school." I laughed.

"Ever fly fished?"

"No, *that* part is new."

"C'mon, I'll teach you."

He demonstrated how to tie an arbor knot, secure the fly, and cast my line.

"See that spot right there? The seam where the two currents touch is a really good spot to throw a fly. Trout like to stay close to the bottom near the big stones, then they pop out and grab food as it swishes by. That's why we use weighted flies, so they'll go nice and deep."

He held out the fly so I could feel its heft, compared to the others in his collection.

"How long have you been fishing?" I asked.

"My whole life. When we were little, Cap used to take Dan and me to fish in San Francisco Bay for halibut, bass, and sturgeon. I even caught a baby shark once."

I watched him as he talked and inadvertently let my line droop.

"Oh, here," he said, pushing my rod up slightly. "You want to be careful about how you stand and how you walk. The fish spook easily, because they can feel when the water moves. Be careful because the rocks and pebbles in the river can get mossy and slippery. Make sure your foot is planted firmly, then take a second or two to move the other one. See those rings where the trout is coming up to get an insect on the surface?"

I nodded and my gaze followed the direction he was pointing.

"A lot of times, they'll drift downstream before they grab it, so it might be hard to figure out where to cast. Send the line upstream, but try to make sure the fly slips right past him. He's more likely to go for it."

We stood companionably for a time, casting and listening to the rushing of the river over the stones and watching the buzzing dragonflies glide low over the surface on their way to the swaying masses of fleecy white yarrow on the opposite bank.

"Most girls wouldn't even consider doing this. Too concerned with new frocks and shoes," George said quietly, the better not to disturb the fish.

"I love pretty clothes," I said. "But I love the out-of-doors too. I did my share of climbing trees and catching bugs when I was a kid."

"Still like sleeping rough, even after being so sick in the desert?"

I wrinkled my nose. "That, I'd prefer not to repeat."

A few casts and plenty of blown chances later, I finally felt a tug on my line.

"George! I got one!" I squealed.

He moved closer with the net, and as my catch struggled, I hoisted it out of the current with a grunt.

"Two-footer! Not bad!" he said, placing the net under it. We moved to the bank, and he knocked it senseless, then pulled the hook out of its mouth, laying it next to the others he'd already caught.

He wiped his hands on a bandana, then shoved it into his back pocket. Since shooting had begun, his hair had gotten shaggy, and I noticed again the dark lock of hair that fell over his eye. I brushed it away from his forehead. He looked at me, I looked at him, and it was understood. He took my hand and gently caressed it with his thumb.

"I've fallen hard for you, Olive. So hard. You're beautiful, but you're outdoorsy too. Perfect for me."

"I'm crazy about you too," I said. I gazed up at him, raising my face, and he leaned down and gave me a gentle kiss. It started soft, but I demanded more, opening my mouth for his tongue to creep in further. He took me in his arms, pressing me against him. Both of us were lost in the moment until a shrill whistle echoed through the canyon.

"That's Lefty," George said, reluctantly pulling away. "They need us back. Help me grab all this stuff?"

"Of course."

I helped him carry the rods and creels, and he took the net and the fish. We strolled back to camp with smiles glued to our faces.

"George! You brought dinner!" Ford said. He inspected the line full of cutthroat, ranging from pitifully small to a five-pounder that was almost three-feet long. I was especially proud of my addition.

"Thought I'd have Cookie grill these up with some butter. I was getting awfully tired of stew," George said.

"Lefty drove into Wilson today," Ford said. "He said there was a telegram for you and Olive." Then he walked away, barely acknowledging me, again. When we found Lefty, he handed George the telegram. I read over George's shoulder.

WESTERN UNION

GEORGE STOP SETUP ON FIG LEAVES ALMOST READY STOP TELL OLIVE SHOOT'S A GO EARLY JUNE STOP TELL FORD NO MORE DELAYS ON BAD MEN STOP SHEEHAN

Since Winnie had told me I'd get to play a clothes horse in *Fig Leaves*, I was eager to get back to Hollywood and see what he had in mind.

COSTUME DEPARTMENT, FOX LOT, 1401 WESTERN AVENUE, HOLLYWOOD, CALIFORNIA, *June 2, 1926*

"...a little pinning here...a few more tucks there... yes. That will be lovely. What do you think, Ollie?" Adrian said.

I gazed at myself thoughtfully in the three-way mirror. "Can you take it in a little more around my shoulders?"

"Of course, dear. Anything for you." He pulled a few straight pins out of the pincushion around his wrist, then secured them where I was nodding. "There, that's got it. Now let's do that batwing number with the metallic sleeve banding."

Fig Leaves was a lightweight frothy comedy contrasting a modern-day couple named Adam and Eve Smith with their prehistoric counterparts. Instead of cabs and buses, they took dinosaurs for transportation. Instead of an alarm clock, a coconut fell on Adam's head at the correct time, thanks to a convoluted contraption. Instead of the serpent, we were once again joined by Phyllis, playing a comely neighbor with designs on Adam. The studio had built mechanical creatures that actually moved, and the producers had brought in an archaeologist to help them with historical accuracy, such as it was.

When modern-day Eve was accidentally hit by a car driven by Monsieur André, she ended up at the House of André couturier on Rue de Fifth Avenue, so the studio had spent more than a hundred-thousand dollars on the frocks for me and for the other characters who worked at the fashion house. Needless to say, I was in heaven.

Adrian and I had already been through a black suit with white piping and metal accents, a Valencia blue organdie with ruffles and flower petal trimmings; an aubergine velvet with ostrich feather trim, and the showstopper, a scarlet spangled frock with bands stretching over the tops of my arms with a series of crimson streamers fluttering from them.

Near us, rolling racks stood filled with more costumes for the customers of the fashion house and the women running the House of André—satin gowns, silk lounging pajamas, and sheer chiffon gowns trimmed with fur and marabou. On more racks behind those were a series of hats and dozens of pairs of shoes—slippers, oxfords, and high heels.

I slipped off the dress and reached for the sheer white concoction he indicated. He helped me pull it over my head and I stood on the carpeted dais awaiting his verdict. He circled me, tucking and nodding.

"How was it filming *3 Bad Men*? Phyllis told me you got sick," he said.

"Oh, it was awful." I told him about the typhoid and Rawhide throwing me. "But it wasn't *all* bad. I met George."

"You two are quite the item now, aren't you?" He winked as he made another gather.

I giggled. I wasn't sure what it was about Adrian, but chatting with him was like spending time with a best girlfriend.

"We are. We're talking about sailing his boat up to Santa Barbara. He even took me to meet his parents."

"Santa Barbara? How *will* you get away from Sibbie?" he asked, his voice muffled from the one or two pins in his mouth.

"I'm trying to figure that part out," I said.

Adrian grabbed the hem of the gown and fluttered it so the skirt hung correctly.

"I don't think there's anything that could look bad on a body like yours," he said as he adjusted the gossamer fabric. "You'd be my perfect model if only you were a few inches taller!"

"I know," I lamented as he pinned the hem. "I even had problems pulling down my bunk on the train on the way up to Yellowstone."

"Oh, yes. How *was* Yellowstone" I've heard it's beautiful there."

"Stunning. You must go if you get a chance. I imagined what God must have felt when he created it."

"Ready to pack up and live in a cabin are you?" he said as I admired the shimmery fabric.

"Are you kidding?" I did a little turn and gazed at myself in the three-way. "If I did, I'd never have anywhere to wear this!"

FIG LEAVES SET, FOX LOT, HOLLYWOOD, CALIFORNIA,
June 1926

"Cut!" called Howard Hawks. "Break for lunch! Everybody be back here in an hour! Sol, I need to run something by you." The men took their discussion to a corner of the set as George and I paused.

"God, I'm starved," I said, stretching and letting out a yawn. "I hope Munchers has the Salisbury steak special today."

"Come on, Ollie. Last one there is a rotten egg," Phyllis joked. "Sibbie, are you coming?"

"Yes, one moment," Momma said, collecting her knitting.

I was still in my orchid negligee and felt vulnerable wearing it. I tried not to let it bother me, but this was now the third film where I appeared in skimpy lingerie or in something approaching my birthday suit, and the critics were beginning to pay more attention to my underwear than my acting.

"I'm going to call Maurice to take me across the street," I said. "I won't be a minute. Y'all go on ahead."

Eulalie Jensen, who played Lela, Monsieur Andre's assistant, turned and laughed. "You're taking a limousine? From the east half of the lot to the west? You're either the laziest woman in Hollywood or the snobbiest. Must be nice to be Olive Borden." She smacked her gum to make her point.

Momma glared at her, and was ready to pounce, but this time I saw red. Enough to defend myself.

"Are you *blind*?" I snapped. "I know you've already decided I'm high hat, Eulalie, but let me direct your attention to my attire. *I'm wearing a negligee.* I'm not going to parade across Western Avenue in it. Why don't you mind your own beeswax?"

She shrank away, Momma looked on, gloating, and I pulled on a robe, then had a set boy walk a message out to Maurice. He pulled into the lot outside Stage 2, picked Momma and me up, and deposited us outside the Administration Building, which was close to my bungalow.

I thanked him, then hurried inside and threw on a long robe. Momma followed me. When we joined George and Phyllis at Munchers, they were only a few bites in. George and I had the Salisbury steak special, and Momma and Phyllis had the crab Louis.

"The nerve of that woman!" I exploded at last. "Do you believe her? Calling me out in front of everyone like that? It looks like Winnie and Sol's campaign to make me look snobby is working *too* well." I blew on a spoonful of mashed potatoes.

"She's jealous, honey," Phyllis said, as Momma nodded. "She'd give her eye teeth to have a chauffeur and a limousine. It must chap her backside that she'll never be as big as you."

"Thanks, Phyl. I mean, how could she not see what I was wearing?"

"She's an idiot," Momma said. "Forget about her."

I speared a carrot with more force than was necessary. "I don't understand Hollywood. When I try to stay friendly with everyone—even the lighting whizzes and the prop boys, Sol and Winnie get mad and say I need to be snobbier. Then, for something like this that's practical, I get accused of *being* high-hat when I'm not. I'm damned if I do and damned if I don't."

"Keep being you. Sweet, lovable you," George said. "You can't do anything about everybody else."

I smiled at him and we all chatted more about the shoot. Dobbin the Dinosaur had malfunctioned and nearly knocked Phyllis off her feet with his tail.

"Hey, I almost forgot," George said. "You'll never guess what happened."

"What?" I said.

"That German director, Murnau, that they brought over? He wants *me* for his new picture. *Me*! Can you believe it?"

"You want to work with a Kraut?" Phyl asked.

Momma's eyebrows lifted and her mouth flattened into a thin line of disapproval.

"Murnau's a *brilliant* director. He's so interesting to talk to about lighting and atmosphere. I can't wait to work with him," George replied.

"What about *Seventh Heaven*?" I asked.

"I told Winnie and Sol that Charlie Farrell would be better in that than me. I really want to do this picture."

"Are there any female parts?" I asked. If George was getting this excited, maybe there was something to it. An opportunity for real acting with real clothes, no lingerie. Phyl leaned forward too.

"Two, as it happens. I'll talk to him and see if he bites." He smiled at us.

"You can still do *Pajamas* though, right?" I asked.

"Of course," he said. "Winnie wants to keep pairing us up, I know that much. It's a solid sell."

A week later, we got the update. George and I would be in the Murnau flicker together. When Winnie told me that it was far more serious than any film I'd been in before, I started to make notes on the scenario to help me better understand my character, the country bumpkin wife of a man who begins having an affair with a visiting woman from the city, then visualizes killing the wife.

With George and I co-starring again, we could easily repeat the success of *3 Bad Men*. If *Fig Leaves* did well too. *Sunrise* would be boffo business.

WINFIELD SHEEHAN'S OFFICE, FOX STUDIOS, *July 1926*

"What I'm trying to say, Olive, is that we need you to stop being so friendly. You're making this difficult," Winnie said.

"Making what difficult?" I said.

"When we signed your contract, we told you about the persona. We discussed that with you, and you agreed to it."

"I did, and I've tried to do all that."

"Then no fraternizing with the crew," he said.

"What are you talking about?"

"Your constant chats with the hair stylists, the makeup people, the extras...you talk to *everyone*."

"Sadie is my makeup person, but she's also my friend."

"That's not the impression we want to create."

"Jesus, Winnie. I've already brought on a chauffeur, four maids, a personal secretary, and a gardener, and I have Mystikum sprayed everywhere I walk. I'm doing my best."

"That's being ostentatious, not elegant. I'm saying *be a little unreachable*. Mysterious, for God's sake."

"I'm not Greta Garbo. I like meeting people and I like getting to know them, even if they aren't royalty or members of the Beverly Hills Country Club. If someone says good morning to me, I'm not going to turn my nose up and not respond."

"You *can* respond. Give them a cordial good morning, and that's it. Back to business. Pretend you're an empress."

"I'm not an empress."

"No, but you *are* under contract, with the terms that we laid out for you when you signed. We expect you to honor them. Do I make myself clear?"

I nodded. My mistake had been trying to do this myself. Momma and Ben were better at it than I was.

The next morning at the studio, I snubbed three of the crew who tried chatting with me. I said my good mornings, then acted preoccupied and ignored them. It hurt like hell, and I felt bad for days afterward. Sometimes, this business was the pits.

CHAPTER SEVEN

COCOANUT GROVE, AMBASSADOR HOTEL, LOS ANGELES, CALIFORNIA, *Early June 1926*

Gus Arnheim and his band were playing "Hard-Hearted Hannah, the Vamp of Savannah" when we arrived. George and I quickly found a table near one of the gold palm trees, and I ordered the squabs with currant jelly. George had the English mutton chop.

"Well, well, well!" said Claire Windsor, pausing as she passed. "How *are* you two? It's been ages!"

Like me, Claire had been a WAMPAS baby star. While my birth name had been good enough to use in Hollywood, Claire had been christened with the unfortunate "Ola Cronk," and I had no doubt why they'd changed it to something far more elegant. Her blonde hair was bobbed and tucked under a lace picture hat, and she wore a lace dress with matching shawl.

"Claire, it's so good to see you! Sit!" I said, pulling out the chair out next to me.

"Hi Claire," George said, smiling as he tapped his foot to the music.

"George, what happened?" she said, gesturing to the bandage on his forehead.

He touched the bandage and chuckled. "Testing with F.W. Murnau. A plank fell on me. Had a couple of nails in it."

"You're lucky you didn't take out an eye!" she observed.

"It's all right, I've got another one," George joked.

"Where's Bert?" I asked. Claire had married Bert Lytell the year before.

"Over there, chatting with Richard Dix." She caught his eye and they gave each other little waves from across the room. "It's been so nice getting a night out. I've been going non-stop for weeks!"

"What are you working on now?"

"*Money Talks* with Owen Moore." She lit a cigarette and placed it in a holder. "You?"

"I'm heading to Canada soon for *The Country Beyond*, and George and I are supposed to be starting *Sunrise* soon. Oh, George, have you heard any more from that Murnau fellow about when shooting starts?" I asked. "I haven't heard anything for weeks."

George looked uncomfortable. His face flushed and he wouldn't meet my eyes.

"What's going on?" I asked.

"Ollie," he said. "I'm sorry. I've been trying to figure out the best way to tell you, but I didn't know how."

"Tell me what, exactly?"

"He replaced you with Janet Gaynor." He exhaled, evidently relieved to have it off his chest.

Claire looked down, trying to hide her discomfort, and suddenly became very interested in checking the hem of her dress for pulled threads.

"He *what*?" I said. "Who the hell does he think he is? He

doesn't call the shots! Winnie and Sol do!" I said.

"They're doing whatever it takes to keep him happy," George said. He took my hand. "He says The Man and The Wife can't be involved in real life. He's afraid the romance will affect our performances, and that it won't be as believable. He wants it to come from the heart and soul."

"What about my performances doesn't come from my heart and soul, George?"

"I'm sorry, Olive. He says you're not a strong enough actress to be believable in the role."

"That no-good Kraut bastard," I muttered.

"It's a role. There will be other roles, honey. Good roles."

"How do *you* know?"

"I just know.

Claire glanced back and forth between us, her blue eyes looking more uncomfortable the more heated things got.

"Oh, look! There's Betty Bronson and I haven't said hello!" She tittered nervously. "Call me soon, Olive. We can have lunch at Montmartre." She slipped away into the crowd, and I turned back to George.

"I can't believe he's doing this," I said, still reeling.

"I hate to say more, but it gets worse," George said. "Fred wants me to spend some time seeing nobody but him—no friends, no parents...*no one*. I have to completely lose myself in this character. 'The Man' is so dark and conflicted that I have to stop being George completely and be *him* instead. This is the most important role of my career. I want it to be something I can be proud of."

"So...me wanting to be proud of *my* role in it...that doesn't mean anything?"

George cast his eyes down, embarrassed.

"I have to become this tormented character for at least two weeks—no interruptions and no distractions from friends or family. He needs for me to begin thinking like The Man. That means no lovey-dovey stuff for a while."

"Then pretend I'm not the wife. Pretend I'm The Woman From The City instead."

"Olive, I *can't*. We know each other too well—like a married couple. The Woman From the City embodies temptation and sin and everything bad. You're not that. You're just...Olive."

"You make me sound like a pair of old shoes."

He sighed and ran his hand through his hair.

"Honey, this part could make my career. More than any other part I've ever had. I want you to realize how important this film is to me. Think of it like if I got called for jury duty and they had to sequester us. It's like that. They've booked me a room at the Alex so I'll have everything I need. I won't be able to see you that whole time."

He kissed the hand he held. "You know I love you more than anything in the world." He was quiet for a moment. I didn't say anything, so he continued. "There's something else. Since you've already studied the role, I was wondering if you could help Janet with learning the part."

"*You* were wondering, or Murnau was?" I said.

He didn't answer me.

I blinked back tears. The giant lump in my throat made speaking nearly impossible.

"I'd like to go home now," I whispered. I'd barely touched my squabs.

"Sure, honey."

That night, George hadn't even pulled his Willys to a complete stop before I jumped out and ran inside.

"Olive, wait!" he called after me. I didn't respond.

OLIVE'S BUNGALOW, FOX STUDIOS LOT, HOLLYWOOD, CALIFORNIA, *June 15, 1926*

The next week, there was a hesitant knock on the door. Lila was brushing out my hair, so I lightly touched her hand to make her pause. "Come in," I called.

Janet Gaynor stepped inside, smiled warmly, and introduced herself. She was pretty, with dark eyes and chestnut curls. A real girl next door.

"Hello, Olive. I hope I'm not disturbing you. George said you'd been studying to become The Wife in *Sunrise*. He let me know you might be able to give me some tips."

"Of course," I said. "That will be all for now, Lila."

Lila nodded. "I'll go get a quick bite at Munchers," she said, before retreating outside.

I rose from my dressing table and crossed to the bookshelf, where I'd been keeping all the notes I'd made. "Have a seat," I said, thumbing through the pages.

"Thanks," Janet said, sitting on the edge of the chair like I'd bite her if she took up any more space.

"I'm sorry about you being replaced. It seems so unfair, simply for being George's sweetheart. I don't understand it at all. You deserve to have this part after *3 Bad Men* did so well.

You and George were wonderful together. I wouldn't blame you for being angry."

I let out a frothy laugh, as if I hadn't a care in the world. "That's Hollywood, isn't it?" I said nonchalantly. "Not really much I can do about it. The important thing is that you've got the part now, and we must figure out how you and George can make it a perfect picture."

"You really are as wonderful as he says," she said. Then she smiled again.

George had been talking to her about me? One part of my brain was angry at him, but the other part wanted to know exactly what he'd said.

"He's quite the fella, my George." I said. We hadn't spoken since our night out at the Cocoanut Grove, Murnau's orders. I sat down near her and sorted through the papers.

"Here's the scenario," I said, sliding it towards her. "I made some notes in the margins and on the facing pages of some things I could do to make her more believable. There are also some suggestions I was going to make to Mr. Murnau for my costume."

She flipped through a few pages and nodded.

"And here," I said, passing her some scribblings, "Are some more notes I made on characterization. It's a back story I was writing for her to help me understand her more."

She looked impressed. "That's unusual."

"Well, this part was going to be so much meatier than the whipped cream I've been in the last few years. I wanted to be more thoughtful. More somber. The poor woman has a cheating husband who wants to bump her off. I wanted to do her justice, that's all."

"You deserve this part so much more than me," she said.

"Pfffft," I dismissed the sentiment with a wave of my hand as she shuffled through it all. I wanted to dislike Janet. I wanted to hold a grudge until I died, thinking of her in *my* role, starring with *my* George, but she was too damned nice. "If you'll excuse me, I need to be on set in a few minutes," I fibbed. "Please ask if you have any questions."

"Of course!" she said, apologizing again and gathering up everything. "I didn't mean to make you run late. Thank you for all of this. I so appreciate it."

She gave a little wave as she closed the door behind herself. After she left, I finally gave myself permission to let the façade drop. I rarely cried, ever. Instead, I got angry and frustrated, unable to talk, but fully intent on slamming and breaking things. I sank onto my daybed, wishing I could just cry and get it out, but nothing came.

When I crossed the lot to Munchers around noon, I saw Murnau and fought the urge to punch him. Because he was so freakishly tall, the most damage I could do would be to kick him in the shins. He was unmissable at 6'5", with a shock of reddish hair and a ruddy complexion. He studied me like a scientist analyzing the subject of an experiment. I glared back, resenting him for throwing a giant monkeywrench into my career and my life.

Several weeks later, I left for Alberta, Canada to shoot *The Country Beyond*. George still hadn't called.

DINING CAR, GREAT NORTHERN TRAIN OUTSIDE
GREAT FALLS, MONTANA, *Late June 1926*

"Hi, Olive," said Ralph Graves, taking a seat across from me. "Mind if I join you?"

I looked up from my copy of *The Constant Nymph.* "Would it matter if I did?"

Ralph and I had starred together in *Good Morning, Nurse* the previous year for Sennett. I liked Ralph, and he'd been through the wringer the last few years. His wife, Marjorie Seaman, had passed away during the birth of their little boy, Ralph, Jr., in '23, so I'd kept in touch with him, sometimes bringing by a hot meal or babysitting Little Ralphie.

He laughed. "I suppose not. I can never resist a beautiful woman sitting by herself."

"Well, Momma's taking a nap, but don't worry, she'll probably be along any minute."

"Then we have some time to catch up." He leaned across the table and leered. "I've scored a bottle of Gordon's from the porter. Why don't you come back to my compartment and help me drain it?"

"I don't think that's a good idea," I said.

"Can't blame a guy for trying."

"I'm taken, Ralph." *Was I, when things with George had hit such a sour note?*

"I'll believe it when I see a rock on your left hand. Whatsamatter? Georgie-Boy too cheap?"

"Can it, huh? I told you I'm taken. He's shooting in Lake Arrowhead." I was trying to be understanding. He had to be climbing the walls after three years without, and he was definitely on the make. "How's little Ralphie?" I asked, to douse the fire.

"He's fine," Ralph said, lighting a cigarette.

"That's it? 'He's fine?'"

"What should I say? He's three years old. He plays with trucks and stuff."

"Ralph, he doesn't have a mother. That's got to be hard on a kid."

"I got him a nanny. She takes care of him real good."

"He's such a sweet little boy, and I love kids. Sorry I haven't been by for a while. I'd like to come and spend some time with him again, if that's all right. I'm sure he's lonely."

"You spend time with him, you gotta spend time with me too," he said.

I bit my lip as he grabbed the menu and examined it.

"What's good today?"

"The waiter said the beefsteak."

"I'll take your word for it," he said. When the waiter arrived, he ordered the beefsteak and vegetables. "But no beets," he qualified. "Can't stand the things."

"Yessuh," the waiter said, hurrying to the kitchen.

"Excited about seeing Canada?" Ralph asked, placing the menu back between the salt and pepper shakers and taking a long drag on the gasper.

"Sure," I said. "I love visiting new places."

"I hear this lodge we're staying at is supposed to be the Banff Biltmore," he said, browsing the travel brochure for Alberta that lay on the table.

"Not Banff. Jasper," I corrected him.

"Same difference," he said, taking another puff.

"Not really. They're several hundred miles apart," said a man sitting behind us.

"Mooses, maple syrup, and mounties. That's all I know about Canada, and all I *care* to know," Ralph replied.

Obviously an offended Canadian, the man made a face of annoyance and turned back to his plate of fish.

"Bastards sided with the British during the Revolution anyway," Ralph muttered.

"Oh come on. That was a hundred and fifty years ago," I said. "They were on the right side in the Great War."

"I know how to hold a grudge." Ralph said with a grin.

We arrived in Jasper after another day's worth of travel, and a series of hired cars retrieved us from the depot. A rough road took us through town and out to our destination. A scenic lake lay to our right. Like a picture postcard, it mirrored the bright blue sky above and the mountains surrounding it. Motorboats putted across it, and canoes glided by.

A wooden sign flanked by stone columns announced the lodge. Thick branches formed the word:

JASPER

Guests clustered around a swimming pool with wisps of steam rising from it, and past the entrance, a sign directed golfers to the green.

"That's why *I'm* here," Ralph said, pointing. "Best eighteen holes in the world, or so I've been told. First thing I'm doing is trying it out."

Our car pulled up in front of the main building and a series of bellhops collected our trunks, piling them onto carts.

The lodge was exactly the way I'd pictured it. Thick, rough-hewn logs formed the veranda. Rustic rocking chairs and potted palms sat at intervals along its length, and hanging baskets full of fuchsia, geraniums, and ferns dangled across the front. Inside the main lounge, a cozy stone fireplace dominated one wall. Guests in wicker chairs sat around it, involved in animated conversation. Momma and I checked in, and after a bellhop showed us to Cabin 6, we began to unpack.

The Country Beyond was adapted from a novel by James Oliver Curwood, and Irving Cummings was directing us. I played Valencia, a French-Canadian orphan girl from the Canadian backwoods who ended up on Broadway. Gertrude Astor played a character named Mrs. Andrews, Ralph had the part of Roger McKay, one of my suitors; and Mac, my buddy from *3 Bad Men*, played "Singing" Cassidy of the Northwest Mounted Police. There were also a romantic fugitive from justice and an avenging dog to liven things up.

Irving insisted on shooting rough, so the next day, a guide named Gordon graciously gave us a tour of the park before we went full force into the bush. Crowded into two jalopies, we set out, circling the edge of Maligne Lake, then following a trail that had been carved out of the poplar and spruce.

"That is Mount Edith Cavell," Gordon said, pointing to one of the peaks. As we rounded a curve, he lowered his voice. "If you look to the right ahead, you'll see a moose cow emerging from that stand of jack pine."

A tall gawky creature with impossibly long legs and a prominent head glanced at us, then moved back into the trees.

"They're usually quite shy," Gordon murmured. "But you must be careful during rutting season."

"When is that?" I asked nervously.

"Not until the end of August or so," Gordon said. "You have plenty of time."

We breathed a sigh of relief. Everywhere we looked, there was more wildlife: hares hopping through the brush, little black porcupines waddling through meadows of sunny yellow buttercups and bright purple wild pea vine. The tiny white flowers of native strawberries ran rampant. Overhead, an eagle swirled and dipped.

The unpleasant part was that anytime the cars stopped, swarms of mosquitoes and gnats descended on us. When Gertrude complained, our guide apologized.

"I'm sorry," he said. "It's the melting snowpack and the muskeg. The standing water attracts them."

"All roses have thorns," Ralph quipped.

"What's a musk egg?" I asked.

"Muskeg," the guide repeated, being sure to enunciate. "It's a Cree word. It's what we use to describe a marsh here. You can imagine that with all the snow we get, the spring thaw leaves a lot of stagnant water laying around. So that brings our pesky friends. I'll get us back to the lodge now, but I hope you've enjoyed the tour."

For exteriors, we set up tents and made campfires and smudge pots, and Momma said she would be filing an official complaint with Winnie, since Ben had negotiated for no more roughing it in my contract. After a while, her complaining became louder and more annoying than the mosquitoes, and I was relieved when we returned to the lodge. It turned out that the Canadians enjoyed having me there so much they even dedicated a mountain to me—Borden Peak—on Dominion Day.

Despite his initial attempts to make our relationship more of a romance, Ralph and I settled back into a comfortable friendship during the shoot. We chatted about roles and films and Hollywood, and then shared confidences about love or the lack of it.

One night, after a long day of filming, we enjoyed dinner in the rustic dining room. I tried elk for the first time, and Ralph and Momma sampled caribou. Then after Saskatoon berry cobbler for dessert, Momma retired. Ralph and I ordered drinks and retired to the veranda for the fresh mountain air.

Our rocking chairs creaked as we chatted. Ralph savored his Canadian rye, lamenting the sixth endless year of Prohibition back home. Maybe I was lonely, or maybe the booze loosened my tongue, but I dared to open up about the previous few months.

"It was *my* role," I continued. "Murnau gave it away. It's not fair. I would have *killed* to play The Wife."

"Maybe he didn't think it was right for you," Ralph said gently.

"It had nothing to do with that. I was fine until Murnau found out George and I were involved in real life. Then, suddenly, I was replaced. I'd already been chosen, and I would have done an amazing job," I snapped.

"What does George think of all this?"

"I honestly don't think he cares," I said. "He's become another person since he got this role. Murnau doesn't want him spending any time with his family or his friends or with me. Anything that could detract from this persona of 'The Man.'"

"I have an easy solution," he said.

"What's that?"

"Break up with George. Then you can go out with me. Everybody's happy."

"Ralph, you know I care about you. I do. And little Ralphie..."

"That's why it's so perfect, Ollie. You care about us. I care about you."

I stood to go and wobbled a little. "I need to go to bed."

"Ollie, I..." He stood too, then placed his hands on my shoulders and planted a forceful kiss on me. I pulled away and used the sleeve of my jacket to wipe my lips.

"He doesn't care about you the way I do," Ralph said, the pain in his eyes truly palpable.

"I could never feel for you the way I feel about George. I wish I could make you see that. Goodnight, Ralph." My boots echoed over the planks of the veranda.

Despite the beautiful scenery, I wanted to get home. For myself, I wished George could have seen Canada with me. He would have loved the lodge and all the outdoor activities.

When we wrapped the shoot in mid-August, Momma and I spent a few days in Calgary at the Palliser Hotel, then booked a fare home to California.

Winnie and Sol wedged in a publicity trip to San Francisco right before *The Monkey Talks* began production, so I went there instead of going straight home. Momma had to continue to Los Angeles, since my aunt Bessie was ill, so I'd be on my own this time. Despite Momma's cautions and warnings, and trying to find me a chaperone, I looked forward to finding a speakeasy and kicking up my heels.

CHAPTER EIGHT

PALACE HOTEL, SAN FRANCISCO, CALIFORNIA,
August 25, 1926, 3:00 a.m.

W hat had started as a simple case of dyspepsia around dinnertime now seemed far worse. I'd asked the hotel concierge if he could get me some Milk of Magnesia, but that hadn't worked. I'd been back and forth to the toilet, hoping for some relief, but there was none. Now, I was vomiting too, and it felt like I was running a fever.

I could see it now. Once again, I'd be letting down Winnie and Sol. My appearance at the Pantages was scheduled for tonight at seven, but there was no way I would make it. One of the first times Momma wasn't around, and now this happened.

I lay curled up, moaning, and praying for relief. Finally, realizing things wouldn't improve, I picked up the telephone and asked the hotel operator to call for an ambulance. When they arrived, they sped me to Dante Sanitarium on the corner of Broadway and Van Ness. I was seen immediately by a Dr. Weeks, who prodded around my middle. When he reached my right groin area, I nearly catapulted off the bed with a yelp of agony.

"It's as I feared," he said. "Appendicitis." He turned to the nurse. "Prep the patient for surgery immediately."

"Yes, doctor."

"Doctor, wait. Before you knock me out, could someone call my mother down in Los Angeles? Her name is Cecilia Borden, and my sweetheart's family is here in town. His father, Daniel O'Brien, is the chief of police. He can get a message to George." I gave him the names and our telephone number in Los Angeles. Despite the situation between Momma and me lately, I still wanted my mother, and I'd never needed George more than I needed him right now. I hoped he could come.

Around noon, I was back in my room after surgery. The nurse brought me a hand mirror, but I looked as terrible as I felt. My skin had turned a sickly yellow color. I was too weak to do anything other than cower beneath the blankets, shivering. When I finally did upchuck, it was nothing but bile.

As I drifted in and out of consciousness, I finally heard that familiar voice at the door to my room. "Doctor, you must let me in immediately. I am Mrs. Borden, Olive's mother. She needs me." Momma had arrived at last.

The doctor's lowered voice followed. "Mrs. Borden, her condition is grave. Infection has set in, and I'll need to perform another surgery. You must remain calm for her. If she comes to, don't let on how serious this is. It could go either way, and she will be more likely to recover if she has hope."

"Yes, of course," Momma said. "Please help my baby." She held tightly to my hand until they wheeled me away. In the operating room, they gave me something to control the vomiting, then put me under. That was all I knew for quite a while.

When I came to again, I had to close my eyes. The blinds in the room were open, and between the sun glinting off the metal bed and the glare off the white sheets, the brightness was too much.

"Water..." I whispered. My mouth was so dry, I could barely speak.

Momma had nodded off in the chair next to the bed, so I tried to reach the water pitcher on the side table myself. The stitches low on my right side protested painfully. My groin was very sore.

"Momma," I said through gritted teeth. She didn't stir.

I tried again to reach, but knocked the full pitcher and all the water in it onto the scuffed linoleum floor, where it smashed into a million pieces.

"Sakes alive," Momma said, nearly jumping a foot in the air. She clutched at her heart, then moved closer to the bed to hug me. "Oh, my darling Baby, you're awake. You do know how to get my attention, don't you, pardner?"

"Water," I repeated softly, gesturing to my neck.

"Of course, honey. Nurse!"

One was already on her way in the door, carrying a mop and bucket.

"I heard the commotion," she said with a chuckle.

"Before you do that, could you please get my daughter some water?" Momma said.

"I'll need to get her some ice chips. She can't have much in case the doctor needs to operate again."

"A *third* surgery?" Momma said. "Did the man go to medical school or not? What is he doing in there?"

"Unfortunately, there is a lot of infection, Mrs. Borden. I'll go get that ice," the nurse said, heading out the door.

"I've never heard anything so ridiculous," Momma drawled,

turning back to me. "This doctor is a quack. I'm taking you home to Los Angeles. I've already made the arrangements. It will be easier for me to care for you with a private nurse."

"It was that bad?" I rasped, my throat raw.

"The quack said it was one of the worst cases of appendicitis he'd ever seen. Evidently, that was the only thing he did correctly—diagnose you."

The nurse brought the ice, swept for glass, then mopped the linoleum. When she'd gone, Momma plumped up the pillows behind me and helped me to a sitting position, then offered me the cup full of ice chips.

"How long have I been here?" I asked, sucking a chip.

"Over a week."

"I can't remember anything. Did I make the appearances at the Pantages?"

"No, Baby. You got sick the morning before the first one, I'm sad to say. I personally think this is because of that brute that threw you during *3 Bad Men*. I asked the doctor if it was possible that could have caused your condition. He said he couldn't rule it out."

"Do the papers know?" I asked.

"Yes. We tried to keep it quiet, but someone leaked the story. You're not out of the woods yet, so we must be very careful and keep a close eye on you. George's father is playing liaison with the reporters for us. I thought that was very generous of him," she said, tucking the sheet around my legs.

"How about George?"

"He's been here as often as he can. He told Fox he would not be dictated to when the woman he loved was in such grave danger."

"Where is he?"

"At his parents' place. He went to get some rest. The poor dear was exhausted. He's barely left your side. The O'Briens have been kind enough to offer me their guest room while I was in town, but I can't keep imposing on them like this. I bought us two sleeper compartment tickets on The Lark. You can lie down until your stitches heal, and I can bring you your meals."

I wondered what happened to George's sequestering. Now he wanted to be near me constantly, but I was unconscious.

"I spoke to Mr. Sheehan and Mr. Wurtzel myself, and I'm keeping them apprised of your condition," Momma continued. "If we play this right, you'll be up and at 'em and ready to go by the night of the premiere."

"Which premiere?" I asked, my mind a blur.

"*3 Bad Men*, darling. It's scheduled for the 10th at the Figueroa back home. I told them I'd have you home and well by then."

On the third, Momma found a gurney and a nurse to move me downstairs to the hospital lobby, then out to the street, where an ambulance waited. The driver hurried through the busy streets, Hyde to 8th to Brannan, then pulled up in front of the Southern Pacific depot at Third and Townsend. Momma helped me out of the car and I sat down on a bench while she found a porter to take care of our trunks.

True to her word, Momma catered to my every need onboard the train, but I felt sicker and sicker by the minute. I was still in pain, and I was starting to shiver again. My forehead seemed hot, but I didn't want to worry her. I didn't want to miss the premiere, but by the time we reached Los Angeles, I was delirious.

ST. VINCENT'S HOSPITAL, SUNSET AT BEAUDRY, LOS ANGELES, CALIFORNIA, *October 30, 1926*

"Olive. Olive, wake up, Baby."

The darkness was warm and soft, and I wanted to stay there, but someone kept saying my name and trying to get me to open my eyes. I didn't want to.

"Come on, Baby. Open your eyes for Momma. I've been so worried. You try, George."

"Olive, it's me, George. Wake up, won't ya?" His calloused hand clasped mine, and at last the darkness released me. I opened my eyes.

"Baby, you're back!" Momma squealed.

George rubbed my hand with his, then lowered his face to kiss my forehead.

Once they flicked the light switch off and adjusted the angle of the Venetian blinds, I could focus on them.

"We've been so worried," Momma said.

George was sitting on the edge of the bed, nestled up against my leg. His smile made me warm all over. Behind him appeared to be at least a hundred floral arrangements of various sizes, varieties, and color combinations. The room smelled wonderful.

"How do you feel?" he asked.

"Like I've been rode hard and put away wet," I said, using an expression I'd heard Tom Mix use.

"Your mom has been frantic," George said.

"How long was I out?" I asked.

"You've been on the critical list for weeks. We almost lost you," Momma said. "I got Reverend McHugh from Blessed Sacrament to come and give you last rites." At this, she broke down and edged George out, planting herself in front of him on the mattress.

"Why was I still so sick if they removed my appendix already?" I asked.

"Your doctor called it stump appendicitis. Not all the infected part was removed up in San Francisco, and it became inflamed again. The infection had started to spread, and they were worried about peritonitis. I'm furious at that Doctor Weeks for his ineptitude."

"Momma," I whispered hoarsely. "The studio...my appearance...I let everyone down. They'll be so mad at me."

"Don't you worry about that, Baby. George's father called another press conference and spoke to the reporters. Everyone knows how sick you are, and they're all praying for you. Look!"

She pointed at a huge hospital linen hamper that was overflowing with letters and postcards.

"How did they know where I was?"

"Everyone knows where the police department is, and the trades announced it," George replied. "Cap and mom shipped them to us. I wanted you to see them when you woke up."

"Can I read one?" I asked, holding out my hand.

Momma placed one of the letters in it, and I tried to find a comfortable sitting position, with Momma plumping the pillows behind me.

The letter was from Mrs. Prudence Netherington of Toms River, New Jersey:

Dear Miss Borden-

We heard from the newspaper that you are ill. I do hope this letter finds you in better health, and that you will be making more films soon. We so enjoyed The Dressmaker From Paris and The Yankee Senor.

PS- I do wish you would wear more clothes in your films.

Sincerely,

Prudence Netherington

"Me too, Prudence. Me too," I muttered.

"What, Baby?"

"Nothing, Momma," I said, tucking it back in its envelope and reaching for another. George handed me the next one, with perfect penmanship, from North Platte, Nebraska.

Dear Miss Borden—

I am writing you to tell you of my deep admiration for you and your movies. I have seen all of them that come through our town, and would love to meet you in person someday. I'll bet you are as sweet and lovely as you are in your films. I hope that you recuperate soon from your surgery.

Much affection,

Dickie Hansell

Momma shared a few more, then she and George told me I needed to rest, but that they'd be available if I needed anything.

A week after I was released and finally given a clean bill of health with my incisions healed, I began filming *The Monkey Talks* at the studio. I played a French circus performer, Olivette, with multiple admirers. One was a dwarf who was disguised as a monkey, billed as "Jocko, the monkey who talks." Jacques Lerner had originated the role of Jocko on the Paris stage. Three weeks into shooting, I was training with a slack wire expert and attempting tight-wire walking. Momma was horrified, but I insisted I was healed enough and had a job to do.

Because I played a circus performer, Fox once again had an excuse to dress me in more skimpy outfits, so once again, my part consisted of a minimal acting and major amounts of skin. When I arrived at the costume department and saw my wardrobe (or lack of it), I blew my top. Maurice would be exhausted taking me back and forth between my bungalow and the stages every day. I complained to Winnie again, but he laughed and told me that Fox was just giving the public what it wanted.

The Monkey Talks was another hit. According to Winnie, theater owners nationwide were reporting its popularity with young male viewers. No surprise there, but Winnie and Sol cautioned me again that I wasn't playing as distant as I'd been instructed to do.

"Olive, you're not being remote enough. Remember our deal. Empress. Ice queen," Sol said as I rolled my eyes.

I'm *not* an ice queen!" I said. "I'm a well-paid artists' model who says a few lines between changes of underwear."

"A very *well-paid* artists' model in very expensive, *money-making* underwear," he corrected me.

"Sol, did you even read the reviews for *Yellow Fingers*? I doubt anyone noticed my performance. They were too busy saying how great I looked in my sarong. For *Fig Leaves*, it was lingerie, for *Monkey Talks* it's a tutu. I want to wear some clothes and do some real acting! How about a nice mystery or a melodrama?"

"Those little outfits kept the lights on here for a few months, and you have a contract," he said. "Do we understand each other?"

I fumed for a minute and he raised an eyebrow. I finally nodded and got up to leave, the resentment stinging like acid. They wanted me to be something I wasn't, and I had no idea how to do it.

After *The Monkey Talks*, they moved me into something called *The Secret Studio*. It was my first real flapper role, and I hoped I could enter those ranks, along with Clara Bow and Colleen Moore. Flappers were known for their short skirts and outrageous behavior, but at least they wore clothes. To be a *real* flapper, I'd have to bob my hair, but I simply wasn't ready for that.

One night after a long day at the studio, George came over to take me to dinner at the Mayfair Club at the Biltmore, which was held the second Saturday of the month. Since my illness, he'd been much sweeter and downright romantic again. We had a lively conversation in the car, and when we were seated and listening to the orchestra, George turned to me.

"Honey, I have some bad news for you," he said. "I'm being pulled off *Pajamas*."

"You what? Why?"

"I can't do that and *Sunrise*," he said. "Scheduling conflict."

I glared at him. "Fox is caving to Murnau again, isn't it? What about *my* picture?! He wouldn't deign to have me in *Sunrise*, and now he wants to ruin *Pajamas*?! It was supposed to be another *Fig Leaves*, George! *Our* picture, remember? It would have been a surefire hit!"

"I'm sorry, honey. I really am. Shooting has run over, and there's no way I can do both."

I could feel my face flaming red, and my Irish temper, usually kept in check, began boiling.

God damn F. W. Murnau to hell.

"I didn't want you to be sore, so I got you this," he said. He pulled a velvet box out of his pocket and set it on the tablecloth near my hand. "Please don't be angry. I love you. We can star together in something else soon. I'll make sure of it."

I reached for the box and opened it. Inside was a gorgeous linked bracelet of princess-cut rubies, my birthstone. I lifted it out and held it over my wrist. George fastened the clasp.

"I love it," I said softly.

"Really?" he asked eagerly. "I wanted to cushion the blow."

"You did," I said. How could I tell him that inside, my heart was still breaking? How could we be the Hollywood glamour couple when we always worked separately? His star was rising, but I would forever be modeling lingerie.

IN FLORIDA
AMONG THE PALMS

CHAPTER NINE

GRAND CENTRAL STATION, NEW YORK CITY,
January 1927

"Olive, the minute we arrive, Mr. Dexter wants you at the costumers," Allan Dwan said. "The tailor worked late to finish your dresses, but I want to see them on you. They may need taking in. The hats too. There was a little miscommunication with the milliner."

Allan Dwan was one of the most respected directors in Hollywood. He had a prominent nose and ears, and he usually wore a hat pulled low over his face. His sense of humor was dry and hilarious, and his directorial style, if you could call it that, was very hands off. When I asked him how he preferred to direct, he said, "Depends on what I had for breakfast." So he let his players improvise, and when he liked what he saw, he simply let us keep going. I liked him immediately.

That winter had been hectic. I'd filled my time in California with holiday shopping, when I wasn't promoting *The Monkey Talks*. The critics were mostly complimentary.

George bought me a beautiful set of ruby earrings for Christmas, and after a quick kiss and a celebratory glass of illicit champagne to ring in 1927, Fox rushed me east to star as Jewel Courage in *The Joy Girl.*

Jewel was another flapper role, which I loved. My wardrobe was stunning, and I didn't even mind playing clothes horse this time, because I got to wear more than lingerie.

When we arrived in New York, the train chuff-chuffed into Grand Central, and Mr. Dwan took the lead at shepherding Momma and me off the train and into the company of Mr. Dexter, the assistant to Joseph Engel, one of Fox's east coast bigwhigs. The platform was freezing, with ice and blowing snow besides. I pulled my new Hudson seal coat closed and buttoned it up against the cold. Despite the weather, the press and the fans clustered on the platform, calling my name and trying to get my attention. I smiled and waved as Momma and Mr. Dwan guided me away. Lila and Inez stuck close to our heels.

"Miss Borden! Preston Douglas of the *New Brunswick News*! What are you doing in town?"

I gave a haughty, polite wave. That was it.

"Miss Borden! Perry Hall of *The World*! Can you tell us what you're working on right now?"

"How's your health, Olive?"

Momma frowned at them and at the fans waving autograph books and ushered me into the depot. Outside, a limousine waited at the curb. Mr. Dexter helped to get us all checked in at the Park Central, which wasn't far from Fox's New York studio.

Despite wanting to get me to wardrobe as quickly as possible, he had to back down when Momma flicked into protective mode. No one could argue with her, because she did it very politely, but her iron will was like a fluffy marshmallow coating around a barbed wire core.

"Surely tomorrow is soon enough for Olive to be fitted, Mr. Dexter. My daughter is exhausted from traveling and she needs her rest."

"Of course, Mrs. Borden. I meant no disrespect. I merely thought..."

"You thought incorrectly. Now, if you'll leave us to our unpacking, I'm sure you have a nice dinner date somewhere. You may come and call for us at nine tomorrow morning. No earlier. Olive has been running herself ragged, and she needs her beauty sleep."

"Then we'll see you both at nine tomorrow. Good evening, ladies."

"Y'all have a good night," Momma said, guiding them toward the door, then shutting it after them. Times like these, I could be relieved she was around. "Baby, I'm going to order an early supper from room service. Shall I get you some broth and a salad?"

"No. I'd like some Chicken Piccata."

She frowned and opened her mouth to protest.

"Momma, I'm too tired to argue right now. Please do it."

"Well, you did lose some weight while you were sick," she said. "I suppose if it's only this once..."

After dinner, Lila helped me undress and I tumbled into bed after surreptitiously eating the chocolate that had been placed on my pillow, knowing Momma would disapprove. I slept like a rock.

The next morning, Lila woke me so I could have my bath, then helped me dress in my black watch wool plaid suit. Momma ordered me grapefruit and farina, while she feasted on French toast with strawberry compote.

Mr. Dexter arrived at exactly 8:58. When he walked in the door, he looked me up and down and puckered his mouth.

"Is that what you're going to wear?"

"Why?" I said, looking down in confusion. "It's a costume fitting. It's freezing outside and I was dressing for warmth. Why does it matter what I wear?"

"We've also thrown an afternoon tea together at the Ritz to promote *The Joy Girl*."

I could be dying from a wasting disease and these guys would still want one more promotional appearance.

"Do you have anything dressier?" he pressed.

I sighed. "Sure," I said, wiping my mouth. I was done with the farina anyway. I couldn't stand the stuff.

When I returned to the suite's living room from the bedroom, I wore my silver taffeta with platinum fox trim at the collar and cuffs.

"That's more like it!" Dexter said. We collected Lila and Inez and Dexter ushered us down to the limousine and gave the driver instructions to Fox. "Tenth Avenue and 55th Street," he said.

"Very good, sir."

We pulled up out front to the sight of several autograph hounds near the entrance, and I obliged them, signing their books before Dexter guided us inside. Winnie and Sol couldn't stop me every time.

When we arrived, Dexter went to see to some other Fox business. Momma set up in the corner with Lila and Inez, and I was introduced to the East Coast costumer, Emory Herrett. Like Adrian, Emory gave me the impression I was working with a favorite girlfriend.

"Olive Borden, my *stars* it's good to meet you!" he said. "I have a couple of doozies I think you'll like. But between you, me and this three-way, the studio really blew their wad on Jewel's hats this go 'round."

We spent the morning taking in over ten frocks. My favorite was a filmy pale yellow gown worn under a canary coat with a mandarin collar and seed stitching.

"This coat is utterly outrageous," he said, pinning the cuffs on it. "I bought it on my last trip to Paris. It's over three-hundred years old! Poiret had it in his collection, but they were selling it at a loss."

I gulped. The coat was in remarkable condition for its age. It needed to be in a museum. I'd have to practice great care wearing it. When we finished, I was already dragging. I stepped exhaustedly off the platform, ready for lunch, then a nap.

"Don't forget the tea," Momma said when I yawned.

I groaned, having forgotten it already. One of the worst things about this business was constantly being thrown into large groups of strangers and expected to act witty, urbane, and completely at ease— like they were old friends. It was especially awful because of this person Winnie and Sol wanted me to be. We braved the autograph seekers again and crawled into a waiting limousine.

"Madison and Forty-Sixth," Mr. Dexter said. "The Ritz-Carlton."

"Stop fidgeting," Momma told me as the car approached the hotel. We were dropped in front, then seen to the ballroom.

The Joy Girl had been a *Saturday Evening Post* story by May Edington. I played Jewel, whose parents wanted her to find a rich husband. She met a rich man posing as a chauffeur to avoid mercenary husband hunters, but she avoided him, thinking he was poor. Then, she met his chauffeur who pretended to be a millionaire. Neil Hamilton played John Jeffrey Fleet, my eventual choice. Marie Dressler played Mrs. Heath, a buyer in Jewel's hat shop, and Helen Chandler played a friend named Flora.

In the ballroom, three posters announcing *The Joy Girl* hung behind the podium. A variety of hats on stands were jauntily placed on tables as centerpieces, surrounded by colorful china teapots and tiered serving dishes of bright-colored petits-fours. Large publicity photos of Neil, Marie, Helen, and me were hung around the room. The tables around the room were already full.

"We're an hour late," Mr. Dexter muttered, as an attendant helped me off with my coat. He nudged me toward the raised platform. "Somebody got their wires crossed. Try to smooth things over."

"What?" I said. "What do I say?"

"You'll think of something."

Am I the guest of honor here or am I merely a co-star? What should I do?

Mr. Engel, the head of Fox's east coast office, stepped to the podium, and in a big booming voice, he announced, "Ladies and gentlemen, may I present the star of *The Joy Girl*, Fox sensation, Miss Olive Borden!"

I climbed the stairs of the podium, then looked out at the crowd. To my horror, I discovered that my mouth had gone completely dry. I swallowed frantically before beginning.

"Respected studio heads, members of the press, honored guests, ladies and gentlemen," I began, hoping to God that covered everyone. I nodded to various faces in the crowd as I spoke.

"Thank you for attending today," I continued. "I've been told to say a few words about the production, and I can't say how pleased I am about my director, Allan Dwan, the cast, and the crew. It's been a supreme pleasure working with them all."

Helen Chandler gave me a little wave from her table. Marie Dressler, who sat with Allan and Mr. Dexter, gave me an encouraging wink. Norbert Lusk, the *L.A. Times* New York correspondent, sat near the front, rolling his eyes. He was prematurely bald and used his glasses to look down his nose at those he considered unworthy. Like me.

Distracted, I fumbled my next few words, trying to sound respectful and dignified, but figuring I was royally blowing it somehow.

"If you glance outside, you can see why we're looking forward to our upcoming time in Palm Beach so much. I'm sure *The Joy Girl* will be Fox's next big hit. In other words, *orange* you glad we'll be swimming in profits soon?" So much for elegant and dignified. I got a few claps and laughs, along with a few groans. "Again, thank you for being here today, and I hope you enjoy yourselves!" Enthusiastic applause followed.

I smiled and nodded at several members of the audience as Mr. Engel helped me down from the dais and took his place back at the podium.

As I hurried back to the table that had been designated for Momma and me, I caught the eye of Norbert Lusk, who was lighting a cigarette. He made a noise like a snort, and the expression on his face looked vaguely like disgust. He did not applaud.

"They all leave tomorrow, ladies and gentlemen," Mr. Engel continued. "I've been reliably informed that the Atlantic Coast Line have rechristened their Florida Special train *The Joy Girl Special*! That sounds like a trip you wouldn't want to miss! Again, thank you for joining us! Now, I'll leave you to your tea and refreshments." He stepped to one side and applauded.

After a lukewarm cup of Earl Grey and a couple lemon bars, I let Momma shepherd me back to the hotel. I was too tired to argue. I even ate broth and salad for dinner. The next day, we all met at Penn Station to catch our train. As expected, autograph hounds crowded onto the platform. Feeling rebellious, I obliged as many as I could before I climbed aboard.

Momma found our compartment, and we settled in for the trip, but she bemoaned the fact that we'd only have a quick stopover in Richmond with no time to visit anyone. When we arrived at the depot in Palm Beach, we were met with a group of limousines parked on Tamarind Avenue. They took us through town, past the lagoon and into the driveway of the Alba Hotel. Its two towers, topped by red roof tiles, rose above the water, grandiosely welcoming us to Florida.

Nature seemed to be bursting forth everywhere—glorious jewel-like hibiscus, exotic bird-of-paradise, gaudy poincianas, and tiny geckos darting along the tree trunks.

We shot at The Breakers and the casino, and also at Via Mizner, a charming area on Worth Avenue across from the Everglades Club. The El Patio restaurant served as a backdrop for another scene, and Al nearly pulled out his hair trying to get the local extras not to look at the camera, so entranced were they with the thought of being onscreen.

When I wasn't busy shooting, Momma and I spent our

time at the beach, shopping at the Saks Fifth Avenue in the hotel, or enjoying luncheon with Marie Dressler on the balcony of the Isabella dining room. A quartet, Paul Whiteman's Piccadilly Players, serenaded us with Jerome Kern's "Sunny," Romberg's "Student Prince," and "No, No, Nanette."

We were in Florida for three glorious weeks, and then it was back to New York for shooting interiors. While we were there, I got to see my name in lights in Times Square—the thrill of a lifetime.

By the time we headed back to California, my tan was starting to fade, but my craving for attention from George was stronger than ever. I missed him desperately. It had been so long since we'd been able to enjoy a night out. The last time had been to the Café Montmartre right after Christmas. However, my homecoming was a letdown. I gave George a huge hug and kiss when I saw him, but contrary to his sweetness after my appendicitis, he seemed distracted.

Before, George had been sweet, thoughtful, and friendly, but now he was quiet and distant. I missed the George I'd fallen in love with, and my dislike for Murnau had now become intense loathing. George and I had once discussed how physical our relationship was getting, but we'd both agreed to wait until we were married for anything to happen, since we were both Catholic and it seemed wisest to wait. Now, it was like he never thought about romance at all. He was in the process of filming *East Side, West Side* and since it was about a prizefighter, he was in his element. He spent most of his time reading *Physical Culture* magazine or sparring with his boxing trainer, Leo Houck, who was glued to his side like I had been once.

On the rare night that George and I *were* able to squeeze in some time alone, we quarreled because I wanted more time together and he couldn't spare it. As spring turned to summer, Los Angeles sweltered under a nasty heatwave, and we both wanted to get away, so I mentioned that a change of scenery would be good, maybe to the shore or the mountains.

"I've booked passage to Europe next month," he said over teacups of disguised Canadian rye at the Café Montmartre. "Mom and Cap want to go, and there's a Legion conference in Paris."

"That's perfect!" I squealed. "I've got a break between *Joy Girl* and *Pajamas*. I'd love to see Paris and Rome. France is so cheap now since the war."

"We want to see Germany too. We have a special invitation," he said, his face unreadable for a moment.

"We can all have a marvelous time!" I said. "We can see the Eiffel Tower and the Coliseum, and..."

"Olive, you're not coming."

"What?" I was at a complete loss, then it dawned on me who his special invitation must be from. "It's that damned Kraut again, isn't it? *Murnau* invited you to Germany!"

"Stop calling him that," George said softly.

"So he's coming with you?"

"That's not the point."

"*Is he*?!"

"We're meeting him in Berlin."

"That's perfect," I said, stabbing at my steak, pretending it was Murnau's face. "Why can't *I* come?" I asked, hurt replacing the anger in my voice. "I'm your sweetheart, aren't I?"

"Of course you are, but he invited the *family*. My father's heart condition is worsening. He's retired, and we want to spend some *family* time together. When Fred found out we were thinking of going to Germany, he insisted that we let him show us around. Mom and Cap and I may not be able to go abroad together ever again. We want to make this time special. I'm jumping into *Noah's Ark* after this, and I'm not sure we'll get the chance again."

"That means no me."

"Honey, there will be other trips to Europe. I promise."

"How do you know? I'll be leaving for Canada in July. My train could derail. I don't think you'd even care."

"Of course I care." He took my hand, but I shook it loose.

"I've lost my appetite," I said. "I'd like to go home now." I tossed my napkin on the table and went to the coat check to get my wrap. We were silent on the ride home until we pulled into the circular drive at my house.

"I'll take you to Europe soon. I promise," he said.

I looked over at him for a moment and couldn't say anything. The lump in my throat made it impossible. I got out and slammed the door. George sighed and put the car in gear. I watched as he drove away down Hillcrest.

CHAPTER TEN

LAKE LOUISE, ALBERTA, CANADA, *July 6, 1927*

It was good to be back in Alberta. I'd enjoyed myself so much during *The Country Beyond*, I was happy to return. Everyone we encountered in Calgary and our shooting site was friendly and welcoming, which helped my mood.

I was still sour about George being pulled off the project, but I was also determined to make *Pajamas* the best it could be, even without him. At the moment, I was nearly as angry at George as I was at Murnau, so maybe it was for the best.

In *Pajamas*, I played Angela Wade, the spoiled brat daughter of a loaded Seattle lumberman. Lawrence Gray took George's place playing John Weston, a good-looking young man who came to Angela's home for a business transaction with her father. When Angela lured him and his business plans into the swimming pool and they were ruined, he took her over his knee. To get her revenge, she put flying garb over her silk lounging pajamas, tucked her hair under a cap, and pretended to be the pilot of his flight back to his headquarters. Of course, the plane went down in the Canadian Rockies, and they were forced to live by their wits to make it through three weeks in the wilderness, eating berries and fish. And of course, they ended up falling in love. John Blystone would be directing us. He'd also directed me in *My Own Pal* with Tom Mix a few years before, so we were happy to be working together again.

The cast was staying at the beautiful Chateau Lake Louise, one of the castle-like Canadian Pacific hotels that had been built across the country, as our local guide, Bob, explained. He also told us how the lake had developed its gorgeous aqua blue color, from glaciers rubbing against bedrock and the fine dust being suspended in the water. The mountain air felt cool and bracing, since back home, Hollywood was still baking.

The welcome reception was held in the Lakeview Lounge, then we were escorted to the dining room, where we were served typical north-of-the-border treats like elk, candied salmon, and Alberta beef tenderloin with a tart rhubarb sauce. For dessert, we were served something called butter tarts, which were scrumptious.

"We have a special celebration to wind up the afternoon!" called Mr. Blystone. "Everyone please join us on the front lawn!"

We filed to the exits, and at the sound of buzzing above, we looked up to see two Curtiss-Jenny biplanes swooping through the stretch of sky between mountain peaks. First, they did some coordinated loops, then turns, which became barrel rolls. We gasped in delight as one, then the other dropped into cork-screw spins. At last, they both aimed their planes vertically— up up up—until the buzzing stopped. Terrified for them, I held my breath, along with the other hotel guests, who were standing slack-jawed on the lawn. The planes rotated 180 degrees, until they pointed straight down, then they raced past each other and flew directly over our heads. We applauded, then to our surprise, two mushroom shapes bloomed out from them as they zoomed away.

"Parachutes!" someone called.

In a moment, the parachutists were in our midst, surrounded by yards and yards of dun-colored silk. Congratulated and clapped on the back for their derring-do, they freed themselves from their parachutes and raised their goggles. When they pulled off their leather flying caps, their hair was plastered to their heads, except for small cowlicks that refused to cooperate. Silk scarves lent them an extra air of bravado. One was blonde and fair, while the other was darker-complected and taller than his compatriot.

The flyers were escorted into the Lakeview Lounge and offered drinks, then Mr. Blystone led them toward Momma and me.

"Olive, Mrs. Borden, I'd like you to meet Bill Wilson and Edgar Bigelow, our guests of honor this afternoon. They'll be piloting our planes for the aerial shots tomorrow." The next day, we were shooting the scene where Angela and John had their plane crash.

"It's lovely to meet you both," I said, shaking hands with them. These guys had better be good.

"It's an honor, Miss Borden, Mrs. Borden."

"Did you fly all the way from Calgary?" Momma asked.

"Not quite, ma'am. A friend of ours, Fred McCall, is trying to get a flying club going. He's got some land cleared and has a small airfield west of Calgary near the Banff Coach Road."

"I'm a little nervous," I said.

"Don't be," Bigelow said. "We've both been doing this for over ten years."

"*Ten years?*" I said.

"Lafayette Escadrille," Wilson said with a grin and a mock salute, referring to the French unit that had taken international flyers to fight the Hun during the war.

"Me too," said Bigelow with a shy smile. "Lotsa dogfights under our belt. This will be a piece of cake."

"Promise?" I said. I tittered nervously.

"I only crashed once," Wilson joked.

"Come on, everybody knows that's your nickname," Bigelow joked.

Momma paled.

"Mrs. Borden, please don't worry. She'll be as safe as a baby in your arms."

Momma looked unconvinced, and into the evening, she continued to remind me not to forget my parachute. I thought I might scream.

In the morning, we pulled up at the dirt strip that passed for an airfield, with a wooden shed and some metal fuel drums to indicate its purpose. When we arrived, Mr. Blystone was already there, deep in discussion with Mr. Bigelow, Mr. Wilson, and Glen MacWilliams, our cameraman.

Once again, the flyers were suited up in heavy leather jackets, fitted trousers, and silk scarves, with leather caps and goggles.

By contrast, I was in a pair of goldenrod-colored silk lounging pajamas (thus the name of the film), with a flight suit over the top of it. My knees were knocking as my makeup lady applied another layer of orthochromatic pancake makeup and darkened my lips. The winds were chilly, even in July, which surprised me.

Lawrence Gray stood to one side, away from the fuel drums, smoking nervously. Obviously, he'd never flown before either. His face was green. He and I had both been in *The Dressmaker from Paris*, but we hadn't met before now. I'd been a nobody then.

Larry was easy on the eyes, with slicked back brown hair, a looming brow, a ski slope of a nose, and a direct manner that brooked no nonsense. I gave him a little smile to show him that we were in the same boat, and I was scared too.

The aeroplanes sat nearby, hulking and silent. Soon, they would be the only thing between me and an unsurvivable fall to the ground from a mile up. I noticed for the first time how rickety they looked up close.

"Such flimsy little things. How can they possibly stay up?" Momma protested adamantly.

A plane crash would leave a runaway horse in the dust as far as dangerous stunts went, but Mr. Blystone reassured Momma over and over that it was perfectly safe.

"Tell that to Ormer Locklear," she observed. Mr. Locklear had been a stunt flyer who had been killed seven years before while filming *The Skywayman*.

Momma had brought her mothering bag, but today, her knitting was noticeably absent. She was nibbling a fingernail, and kept hugging me, convinced it would be the very last time.

For myself, my heart pounded in my throat. I was excited at the prospect of flying, but also terrified at all the things that could go wrong. I didn't even know what they all were.

"Olive! Larry!" Blystone said with a wave, calling us over. Larry ground his cigarette out with his boot, and we both moved closer. "Here's what's going to happen. Wilson is taking you two up first. Glen is going to film your plane taking off for distance shots. He and I will take off afterwards with Bigelow and fly alongside, me yelling commands at you. The fellas have told me that the air pressure up there blocks your ears pretty good, so it may be hard to hear. Here, chew this. It'll help."

He handed us each a piece of Beech Nut gum.

"Try not to make it obvious, like a cow chewing cud. When you need it, bite down."

We nodded.

"Don't be nervous," he said before retreating. "We'll all be up there together. These guys are professionals."

Larry and I looked at each other, our faces frozen in fear.

"Good luck," Larry said.

"Yeah, you too," I replied.

"All right! Let's move 'em out!" Blystone called.

Wilson hopped up as nimble as a monkey and lowered himself into the rear seating area, then ducked out of sight. They'd carved out extra room for him to sit.

Andy Petri, our take boy, gave me a hand to crawl up into the plane, and I hunkered down in the seat, as Larry crawled into the other with Wilson. We pulled on our goggles and I took a deep breath.

"Try not to touch anything!" Wilson called up to us.

"I'm too afraid to touch anything!" I said.

"Contact!" the fellow on the ground shouted.

"Contact!" yelled a muffled Wilson.

The ground man grabbed the propeller and spun it, and the engine sputtered to life. The propeller whirred, ever faster.

"Dump the chocks!" Wilson shouted.

The man moved the chocks away from the wheels, and in

moments, we inched forward. We bounced over the dirt and gravel, slowly at first, and as we pulled onto the straightaway, faster and faster. Before I realized it, our wheels had lifted off the ground.

I squealed as we rose. It was the most exhilarating feeling I'd ever known. We were weightless, continuing to climb up and up into the sky. I was surprised the air that high up wasn't actually blue the way I'd always thought it was. It was the same as on the ground. The clouds, which seemed so fluffy from below, were little wisps of nothing floating by. Even though we'd been moving fast on the ground, up here out pace seemed lazy and relaxed. The cold wind battered my face, and gusts hit the plane every minute or so, buffeting it about.

I looked around in wonder—at the birds now far below us, at the patchwork of trees and fields, and at the Rocky Mountains to the west.

After they'd had time to take off too, Mr. Blystone and Mr. MacWilliams caught up to us. Mr. Blystone carried a bright red megaphone. Cameras had been fastened to the left, right, front, and rear of Mr. MacWilliams, so he could film from any direction. He reached in front of the camera to slam a clacker, which the wind nearly grabbed out of his hands. He recovered, then stowed it away, cranking the handle of the camera to his right.

"Olive!" Mr. Blystone yelled through his megaphone. I turned at the faint sound. "Don't look at me! Go ahead and start! John is trying to play pilot and Angela is distracting him!"

I wrapped myself around Larry, being as obnoxious as I dared without falling out of the plane.

"That's good! Now, Larry, look more frustrated!"

Larry looked like he would vomit at any moment, but he and I pretended to fight over the controls, dramatically moving back and forth while trying to avoid the control stick in real life. I peeled off the top half of my flight suit, leaving the flight controls unattended. Then I sat back down to "steer" the plane, which Wilson caused to bank to the left. The engines revved with a deep, low-pitched growl. He brought us around again, and Larry and I continued to struggle.

"Good! Good!" Mr. Blystone yelled. Then he paused.

"Larry, now try to—oh shit! Cuuuuuuuuuuuuuuuuuuuuut!"

CHAPTER ELEVEN

t the last moment, I turned my head, and wished I hadn't. The camera plane, with Mr. Blystone, MacWilliams, and Bigelow hurtled straight toward us.

They say that when you're about to die, your life flashes before you. For me, that included Aunt Bessie and Cousin Natalie, my aunties at the Monticello Hotel, school at Mount St. Agnes, moving to California, Momma's candy shop, then climbing through the ranks at Christie, Sennett, and Roach. Mostly, it showed me Momma and George. I'd never been so terrified—literally thinking I'd fall to earth in a flaming wreck—and hoping that my years of catechism and Catholic school would at least let me spend the afterlife up here in the clouds rather than in the fiery pits of hell.

At the last minute, the other plane zoomed past with inches to spare, and Mr. Bigelow didn't regain control until they were several hundred feet below us. Then their plane leveled off and climbed once again.

"What happened?" Larry yelled when the other plane got back alongside us. He looked pale and shaky.

"You didn't feel that gust?!" Blystone demanded. "I thought we were goners! Eddie called it a cross wind! All right, let's try it again!"

"I think I shat myself!" Larry yelled to me. "Remind me never to make another film with aerial shots in it!"

We filmed twenty takes, and when we landed, my legs nearly caved beneath me. I would never take solid ground for granted again. At least, the next day I'd be closer to earth. Still not on it, though. It was July fourteenth, my twenty-first birthday, but I didn't have the luxury of celebrating or sleeping late. Today, we'd be filming the scene where Angela had to hang from her parachute until John grudgingly cut her down.

Because of the near miss in the air, they brought in my stunt double, Margaret Hatfield, but I argued with Mr. Blystone that I should do at least a few of my own stunts, and that was how I spent most of my birthday strung up by a parachute in a tree.

"How's the air up there, Miss Borden?" Andy Petri joked.

"Peachy. How long have I been up here anyway?"

"About two hours or so."

"I can't feel my feet! Somebody cut me down this instant!"

"Are you sure you don't want to stay up a while longer?" Larry said with a grin.

"We're *hanging* on your every word!" Andy chirped.

Larry and Andy laughed uncontrollably as I squirmed in my parachute straps. "Andy Petri, you come cut me down this instant. I have to pee!"

OLIVE'S HOUSE, 627 HILLCREST, BEVERLY HILLS, CALIFORNIA,
Late October 1927

"It's too bad we couldn't stay longer, but Warner's wired me to say they were starting *Noah's Ark* sooner than they'd planned," George said. He reclined against the sofa cushion and stretched his arm across the back of it. He was so popular now, Fox was even loaning him out.

"Yeah, that's a real shame," I said, my voice etched in sarcasm as I mixed up drinks at the bar. Momma didn't like me being a scofflaw, but I'd be damned if I'd do without my gin and ginger ale during George's endless tales of the old country. All this time apart, and he'd kissed me on the cheek and not the lips. I'd hoped we'd be able to celebrate his return properly, but to say he was distracted was putting it mildly.

"It was so perfect," George continued. "I got some liberty in Paris during the war, but seeing it again in peacetime was different. We went to museums and to the opera, we ate delicious meals, and there wasn't all the fear there'd been during the war. Mother bought some new dresses, Cap got to see Napoleon's tomb, and Germany? You've never lived until you've had a proud German tour guide show you his country. I discovered that I love *Konigsberger Klopse* and *Schwarzwalder Kirschtorte.*"

"What the heck is that?" I said, handing him his drink.

"Meatballs with this wonderful lemon sauce, and Black Forest Cake with chocolate, whipped cream and cherries. It was all delicious!"

I pursed my lips. I wanted to tell him that I didn't *care* how his vacation had gone. I didn't care how many dresses his mother had bought. Didn't care about the museums or the opera or how "Fred" had guided them around Germany. When I thought of my fantasies of the two of us sharing candlelight dinners and wine at intimate bistros or taking moonlit walks along the Seine, I could barely restrain my anger.

"What's wrong?" George asked, taking a sip of his drink.

"You have to ask me that?" I said. "You took a European tour and wouldn't let me go along. What do you think?"

"Olive, I told you why. My parents—"

"I know all of that, and I don't care. Am I your sweetheart or not? Ever since *Sunrise*, it's like I'm invisible to you."

"But Fred—"

I gritted my teeth. "Do not mention that man's name to me again. I'm sick of *hearing* about him, and I'm sick of having my career and my life *decided* by him."

"Jesus, Olive. You're still mad about that?"

"You would too if you were me. When I was in Catalina shooting *Come to My House*, I lost one of the ruby earrings you gave me last Christmas. You know what? I didn't even care. It actually seemed symbolic." At least I'd gotten a nice suntan while I was there.

I watched him to see if my barb had hurt.

He ran a hand through his hair frustration. "I really wanted to take you out for a nice dinner and dancing tonight. I'll have to go on location again soon—up to Chatsworth and to Big Basin. Are you going to be like this all night? Because you used to be a lot of fun."

I was quiet for a moment, but my voice broke when I spoke again. "I missed you, George. I've always wanted to go to Europe, and it would have been wonderful to see it with you.

Can't you see how much that hurt, leaving me behind and then babbling on about it?"

He lowered his eyes, everything dawning on him right then. "I'm sorry," he whispered. He held his arms open to me, and I moved to the couch and sat down, cuddling up next to him.

"I'm sorry too," I said.

"For what it's worth, my mother said she wished she'd had another opinion when she was shopping. She said the French flattered her too much. It came off insincere. She said you have such wonderful taste and would have made a good partner in crime at all the fancy boutiques. She also said I have to take you somewhere very special for a honeymoon."

"Honeymoon?"

"You heard me."

"Oh, George. I want us to be close again, like we were in the desert and at Yellowstone."

He laid a kiss on the top of my head, and I nestled into the hollow between his chest and his shoulder, inhaling his scent of Proraso, Hudnut brilliantine and boxing gauze.

"We can be. I love you."

"I love you too, Swabby." We held each other for a few moments, then he looked at me.

"Can we have dinner now?"

"If you promise not to talk about Europe," I said.

He grinned the happy-go-lucky grin that I'd missed so much. It had been so long since I'd seen it. "Deal."

We took his Willys to the Lafayette, found a table close to the dance floor, and danced to three songs in a row until I was giddy and out of breath. He grinned and spun me in a pirouette as the last song ended. We laughed, and I waved to Anna

May Wong, who was having a tête à tête across the room with Richard Dix.

"Heard about the new flicker that opened the other day?" George asked when we returned to the table. "It's called *The Jazz Singer*. Word is, it's a real humdinger!"

"Is that the one with the real singing?" I asked, as he pulled out my chair for me.

"Sure is. The dope at Warner's is that they finally pulled a fast one, and all the other studios will be stuck playing catch-up." I guessed since George was working at Warner's for *Noah's Ark*, he'd have all the goods.

I furrowed my brow. "Why?" I said.

The waiter took our drink order and our teacups arrived discreetly a few minutes later.

"Warner's caught everyone off guard. Suddenly, they've done something no one else is doing. That gives them a big advantage. I bet it'll take some real kale for all that new equipment."

"I hadn't thought of that," I said. "Guess what? I got the news that John Ford wants me for *Hangman's House*. I guess I'm forgiven for the water barrel. Now I know why Ben hired this dialect coach to work with me. I wondered why I needed one."

"That's terrific!" he said.

"Momma's none too happy about the thought of me working for Ford again, but I explained to her that *3 Bad Men* is still my best film. I *acted* in it instead of only wearing lingerie, so of course I'm intrigued."

"You'll be fantastic, of course," George said.

"Winnie and Sol want to see me tomorrow. I think it may have to do with that. Momma's insisting on coming."

"Honey, I think that's a mistake. You should take Ben, but leave Sibbie at home."

"I was out car shopping when the call came, so unfortunately, she took it, and she's insisting on coming. Remember the Lincoln I told you about?"

"The gunmetal one?"

"I special ordered it." I smiled. "It's so sleek and gorgeous, I couldn't resist."

"I can't wait to see it."

"Play your cards right, and I'll let you drive me around." We clinked cups.

The next morning, Momma, Lila, Inez and I made our usual trip across town in the Delage. Maurice dropped us in front of the administration building, where Ben was already waiting. Of course, Momma took charge and I followed. Lila and Inez sat in the waiting room and we entered Winnie's office.

"Come in, Olive, please," Winnie said. "Ben, Mrs. Borden, make yourselves comfortable." He gestured to the chairs in front of his desk.

I lowered myself into a chair, clutching my purse and gloves. Momma sat daintily on the edge of her chair. Ben pulled his pant legs up before sitting.

"All right, we're here," Ben said. "This sounded ominous on the phone."

"Yes, what did you want to see us about, Winnie?" I said.

Sheehan gazed down uncomfortably.

"Mr. Sheehan, my daughter is speaking to you," Momma chided. I glared at her to make her pipe down.

Winnie cleared his throat.

"As you might imagine, the studio is beginning a period of great transition. Since the success of *The Jazz Singer*, we're looking at massive investment in equipment for an eventual sound conversion. We have to test all our stars to make sure their voices are suitable, and we have no idea how many of those tests will be successful. We'll also have to pay out the remainders of contracts for those who aren't, then invest in new talent. All of that costs money."

"So this is about her voice test?" Ben said. "Olive's been working with a voice coach that I recommended. I saw this coming."

"Good. That's good," Winnie said.

"Romeo, Romeo, wherefore art thou, Romeo?" I said, showing off the lack of drawl I'd been aiming for.

"Excellent," Winnie said. "That's what we want to hear."

"But there's more to it than that?" Ben pressed.

"Yes," Sheehan said. "Your current contract is ending soon, and we may have to post a loss on our balance sheet because of these changes. We're asking Olive to take a pay cut until we can get through all this sound conversion business, at least until we can see the light at the end of the tunnel."

"How *much* of a pay cut?" Momma asked, her eyes turning hard and flinty.

"Ten percent, with a forty-week contract."

"But my current contract is fifty-two weeks," I said.

Momma burst out laughing.

"What? What is that laugh?" Winnie asked calmly.

"Why, bless your heart," Momma drawled. "A big fat no is what it is, Mr. Sheehan,"

My neck snapped in her direction, and Ben looked extremely uncomfortable. What the hell was she doing? We should be trying to negotiate.

"Now wait a minute, Sibbie," Ben said. "Let's not be hasty. Mr. Sheehan, I need a little time to confer with my client and her mother. Can you give us a while to consider this?"

"Take all the time you need," Sheehan said. "Within reason."

"Within reason," Ben said, nodding. "Understood. Expect to hear something from us soon." He ushered a protesting Momma and me out of Sheehan's office and out to his Cadillac.

"I can't take a pay cut, Ben. I've worked too hard to get where I am," I said.

"I understand that, Ollie. I do. And I worked hard to get you here. I realize ten percent sounds substantial, and it could be painful for a time, but what happens if they decide to call your bluff?"

Momma snorted. "They wouldn't *dare*. She's one of Fox's biggest commodities right now."

"I wouldn't underestimate them, Sibbie. You don't know how they might react."

"Things are up in the air all over Hollywood. People are panicking. I want to hire an attorney to advise us. Olive will never have any bargaining power again if she backs down on this."

"Let me worry about it. I'll go talk to some lawyers," Ben said. "Why don't you both go home, relax, get some rest, and we'll meet for lunch, say in two days. You may feel differently. Then, we can go back to Sheehan with an answer."

We agreed.

In the meantime, Ben found a team at Evans, Pearce and Campbell to represent me. My number one request was holding fast on salary reduction. "I have a mortgage now," I told him. However, as the days progressed, discussions became testy. I demanded fewer lingerie scenes, they insisted on more. I wanted a choice of better parts, and they said the studio would enforce the roles I was given. It went around and around for weeks. Ben gave us periodic phone updates as negotiations continued, but Fox held firm on their salary demands. I held firmer. Then, Ben called us and said it was time to meet. We decided on lunch at the Tam O'Shanter the following Tuesday.

"The bad news is that the studio isn't budging," Ben said. "They've knuckled under on a few things, but they absolutely will not negotiate on your pay reduction." Then he told us everything that had been discussed—my prime bungalow location, my wardrobe allowance, traveling perqs like snacks on the train and hotel suites, allowances for my maids and servants.

"We're not changing our minds," Momma said, cutting her rarebit.

"I'm going to advise you both against being stubborn, Sibbie. I can't emphasize this more strongly. I have a really bad feeling about this."

"You have your feelings Ben, and I have mine. I think they're all bluster," Momma said.

"How does Olive feel? She's the one who should be making the decision. It's her career."

"There are other studios in town," Momma said. "She's bigger now than when she was at Roach. Paul Bern's doing well now. He loves her. We could call him, couldn't we, pardner?"

"Momma. I think we should listen to Ben, and—"

"You're too young to understand how this business *really* works." She patted my hand. "But we'd still like you next to us at the bargaining table, Ben."

"Of course," he said.

At the end of the week, Winnie's secretary, Miss Murray, announced us and ushered us into his office. I'd worn my dark navy suit with the mink collar—all the better to make me look powerful, confident, and immovable in my resolve.

"Have you had a chance to think any further about what we talked about?" Winnie said. Sol stood behind him, trying to intimidate us. "We thought we'd talk to you in person. Leave the shysters out this time and speak to you as friends and coworkers."

"I have," I said, looking to Momma, who nodded.

"Did Ben go over everything we discussed with the attorneys?"

"He did," I said.

"And?"

"And I'm rejecting your offer," I said. I looked to Momma, and she nodded. Ben's eyes were resigned. He thought I was making a mistake.

"Olive, I wish you'd reconsider. Fox has been good to you," Sheehan said. "We've built you up, we've developed your talent, we've—"

"No compromise, and no cut," Momma said. "You've profited off how good she looks in lingerie, Mr. Sheehan. Her voice is fine, and she brings an enormous amount of money into your studio. She deserves every dollar she earns and will continue to earn in *sound* films. There will be no pay cut."

"The studio..."

Momma leaned forward to further make our point.

"Perhaps you didn't hear me. No pay cut. If you want to cut someone's pay, how about Janet Gaynor? *Sunrise* has been a big hit. Let *her* eat all these sound conversion costs."

Winnie sighed and looked over at Sol. A look passed between them. Sol gave a nod, and Ben watched them carefully.

"Before the meeting, Winnie and I spoke about this, and I assured him that you would be reasonable," Sol said.

"Well, I'm not," I said.

"Eight percent," Winnie said.

"No." I rolled my eyes, tiring of it all.

"Seven and a half."

"What are we doing?" Momma said. "Because *we* can randomly start calling out numbers too."

"You've completely thought this through?" Sol said.

"Yes," we both said with finality.

Ben looked heavenward, like he was praying for strength.

"Then I'm sorry, Olive. Since your current contract expires today, Fox has no choice but to end your contract, effective immediately. Miss Murray will see you out. We'll need you to vacate your bungalow by the end of the week."

CHAPTER TWELVE

"W hat?!" I said, gripping the armrests on my chair. "What?!" Momma said, even louder.

"That will be all. We'll send you your earnings for *Come to My House* when it's released. After that, our working relationship will officially come to an end."

Momma paled, with a look of horror on her face. I felt like I'd been slapped.

"I'm afraid you've given us no choice," Winnie said. "Take care of yourself, Olive. Ben, Mrs. Borden, you know the way out." He turned his chair toward the window with the back to Momma, Ben, and me. He and Sol conferred in low voices.

"You can't do this. Olive is a *star*! She makes a fortune for this studio! She can go to United Artists and make thirty-five hundred a week!" Momma said.

"She's welcome to try," Winnie said, looking back over his shoulder at us.

She paused, then caved in at last. "All right, nine percent."

There was no response. It was too late.

"You'll regret this, Winfield Sheehan." Momma stood, haughtily tossed her fox neckpiece over her shoulder, and stormed out of Winnie's office, with Ben and me close at her heels. Outside, we paused by the fountain behind the administration building. I looked at the statue of Atlas holding up the world, and at that moment, I know exactly how he felt. I paced back and forth as Ben tried to reason with us.

"Have they asked anyone *else* to lower their wages?" Momma protested.

"Evidently so," Ben said. "I checked. Those stars cooperated."

"Who? I want names," she said.

"They wouldn't tell me."

"Hmmmph," Momma replied.

"I've been working with that dialogue coach and everything!" I protested. "She said I'll be as big an earner in talkies as I am in silents!"

"This is ridiculous. It's an intimidation tactic. That's all this is. Sheehan is bluffing."

"Momma, you heard him. That doesn't sound like bluffing to me." I sat down dejectedly on the ledge around the fountain.

"That was definitive, Sibbie," said Ben.

"Then we'll be counting on you to negotiate the best opportunity for Olive at a new studio. One with more taste and appreciation for her talent. We'll expect a report within the week of the new contacts you've made. Come on, pardner." Momma herded me back to the Delage, which was parked at the curb on Western. Maurice sat in the driver's seat finishing a Gauloise. I crawled in back and tried to keep from crying. Momma followed me.

"Where to, Mam'selle Borden?" he asked.

"Home, please," I said in a strangled voice.

"Everything is all right?" he asked.

"Fine," I replied. But any idiot could have seen that it wasn't.

Maurice accelerated west on Sunset to Hillcrest, the trip we'd made so many times, and I realized I'd never be making it again. We passed Warner Brothers, The Garden of Allah, and the nearly finished Chateau Marmont on the hill. Momma babbled on about revenge and how sorry Winnie would be when I went on to be as big as Gloria Swanson. Maurice pulled into the circular drive out front of the house, and the car had barely come to a stop before I leaped out and ran inside.

"Olive, wait!" Momma cried.

I ran to the bar, poured a glass of illicit gin and ginger ale, and retreated to the back terrace. Thank God she didn't follow me. Sitting by the pool always calmed me, and staring into its tranquil turquoise depths lifted my mood. Today, it didn't help. I sat stewing all afternoon, worrying about the mortgage, the bills, and how I would make ends meet. Ben needed to find me a new studio fast. Eventually, Momma came and let me know that it was five p.m., and that dinner was ready. Somehow I'd lost four hours.

To make myself feel better, I had the car dealership drop off my new gunmetal Lincoln. Instead of having Maurice drive me, I sped up the coast to the end of the under-construction Roosevelt Highway and back, letting the wind whip through my hair, enjoying the feeling of being free of Momma for a little while.

A day spent strolling along the shore improved my spirits, but going back to the house filled me with dread. Momma and her big mouth had talked me right out of my contract. Now, George and I would be working at different studios. We wouldn't even get to star together unless one of us was loaned out. I'd been angry at him, but now I felt even greater distance between us.

Every night, I tossed and turned, trying to imagine what I'd do next. The thought of being poor again terrified me. A few years before, being poor had always meant going hungry. But movie stars didn't starve, did they? My world was tilting on its axis, and I wasn't sure what to do. The last few years, I'd used money to make up for the years we'd been poor and Daddy's family had distanced themselves from us. I'd used clothes, jewels, and furs to get back at every snotty brat at Mount St. Agnes who'd poked fun at me for being a scholarship case. Now, I still had those same sad holes in my life, but I had no idea how to fill them.

While I was worried about unemployment, I *did* like being able to sleep late for the time being. Momma was so used to rising early to accompany me to the studio that she kept doing it. She was always up before dawn, and had the paper read and sorted hours before I came to. For two months, I slept late, swam about ten-thousand laps in the pool, and waited for Ben to call with good news. There wasn't any. Then, it came time to pay the piper.

"We can't make this mortgage payment," Momma said one morning, holding up the dunning notice from the bank.

"We? You mean *me*, Momma."

Her mouth puckered as I took a sip of my coffee "We'll have to cut back. What will we do?"

"No more Inez, no more Maurice, no more maids, and I'll sell the Delage."

"The Lincoln isn't even paid for yet."

"I'll sell them and get something cheaper," I snapped.

"That won't be enough to take care of all of these..." Momma began.

"I know!" I fired back. "I *know*, Momma. I'll sell a fur or two, some jewelry, and some of the antiques. Ben's looking for more jobs for me."

"I'll have to go back to work again."

"You might."

I felt a sick sense of glee that her big mouth might have some consequences. We should have listened to Ben. Now we were both paying for it.

"Here you are, Miss Olive," Mandy said, placing some pancakes on my plate.

"Thank you, Mandy."

"Pancakes? You might as well smear those on your hips," Momma observed. "That's where they're going."

"I'm going to enjoy one small thing today," I said, pouring some syrup on them from the little china pitcher.

"This is not a vacation," she insisted. "You must stay slim or you can kiss your career goodbye."

"It's a plate of pancakes!" I yelled. "Leave me be!" I jammed a mouthful sopping with syrup into my mouth, savoring the mushy sweetness. I laid the dunning notice to the side and opened the entertainment section, noticing that Alma Whitaker's column had an interview with George on page 1.

Momma glared at me and stood there, probably waiting for me to apologize. Feeling guilty, I swallowed and took a sip of coffee to wash everything down.

We'd spent a miserable Thanksgiving contemplating our futures, knowing we were now living beyond our means, but all the same, Momma had insisted on a twenty-pound tom with all the fixings. "This will remind us to be truly thankful for what we *do* have. Besides, the leftovers will keep us fed for a few weeks." Sandwiches, soup, and stew. Momma had clicked right back into poor mode like it had never truly left her.

"Baby, trust me, you don't want to read that story," Momma said, looking over my shoulder as I read.

"The one about George? Why not?" I took another bite.

"The last two paragraphs, that's why not," she said. Then she left the room like she was daring me to read it. She knew I would.

I skimmed most of it. It was what I'd expected from George and from one of the *Times'* biggest busybodies. Then I flipped to the continuation on page thirty-three, and my eye was drawn to a quote. It was as bad as Momma said.

"...doing eight pictures a year has kept me too busy to fall in love."

"Too busy to fall in love?" I repeated stupidly.

If he had wanted to hurt me, he hadn't needed a knife or a gun. Those words, coming on top of his relationship with Murnau, his trip to Europe without me, and barely a word while he was in New York for *East Side, West Side* had done the job perfectly well.

Too busy to fall in love.

What was it we'd been doing for two years? Had he been pretending all this time? Was he telling me what I wanted to hear?

Momma returned a few minutes later, wearing her burgundy wool crepe coat frock and matching bicorn hat with black ribbon, and she carried Granny McKenna's tipsy cake. She'd probably dipped into my stash for the booze.

"Where are you off to?" I asked.

"Pola Negri's mother, Mrs. Chalupec, is having a mah-jongg party." She set the cake down and sat for a moment, looking over her shoulder as she lowered her voice. "You should tell them *today*."

"I know, Momma," I said through clenched teeth. I dreaded the prospect of letting the servants know we could no longer afford them. Lila and Mandy were the two I could consider keeping. One housekeeper and a maid. Until I was working again, I hardly needed a social secretary.

With a swish of her dark gray sable neckpiece, Momma headed to the garage, and as soon as I heard the Lincoln's deep rumbling move off down Hillcrest, I finished my pancakes, took a gulp of coffee, and hurled one of my china geegaws across the room in a fury Then I composed myself the best that I could, went to my desk, and prepared envelopes with the servants' final pay.

"Lila, could you call all the servants together in the living room, please?" I asked.

At the panicked look in her eyes, I lowered my voice. "Don't worry. You and Mandy are fine."

Relief flooded her features. She nodded and hurried in the direction of the servants' quarters over the garage.

When Maurice, Inez, the maids, and the gardener were all gathered in the living room, I took a deep breath and stepped forward.

"Hello, everyone. Thank you for meeting with me. I know by now you've all heard the news about me separating from Fox."

There were somber nods from everyone. Then Katie, who was extremely observant, noted that Lila and Mandy weren't there.

"That's true," I admitted. "Unfortunately, no new

contracts have come in for me at another studio, and movie stars have to save money like everyone else. I'm afraid this will be the last week I can pay you. I'm very sorry. Perhaps one day soon, I can bring you back on. But I've calculated your pay to the end of the week, and I can write you all very good references for new positions."

I handed out the envelopes, thanking each one of them for their faithful service, then watched as they filed out, dejected. The truth was, if things didn't improve soon, even Lila and Mandy would be unemployed. When everyone had gone, I called Ben to find out if he'd had any luck yet. I'd see a little coin when *Come to My House* came out near Christmas, but the hard truth was that I needed a new gig now. Christmas was coming, and I had no idea how I'd buy presents for everyone. I'd have to sell my doll collection next.

"Olive! Good to hear from you!" he said.

"Is it? I haven't heard from you in two weeks," I said.

"I've been working for you this whole time, trying to butter up studio heads."

"Anything to report?" I asked.

"I got you an audition for Tiff-Stahl. Something called..." I could hear papers being rustled as he fumbled for the name. *"Albany Night Boat."*

"What's it about?"

"I didn't read the scenario, I only got you the audition. They were the first ones that said yes. I'll have a messenger run this over to you. Screen test's on the fourth."

"Thanks," I said. "I appreciate it." I placed the phone in the cradle. Tiffany-Stahl? Talk about bottom of the barrel. I was still in the doghouse, then.

Momma returned around three, humming 'My Blue Heaven,' and unpinned her hat, placing it on the hall tree in the entry.

"How did it go?" I asked.

"Mrs. Talmadge is ferocious! But Mrs.Chalupec is quite the little devil. She curses in Polish when her suits don't work in her favor. She served caviar on some scrumptious little buckwheat pancakes. Then there were some hors d'oeuvres with—"

"I let the servants go," I said. "Except for Lila and Mandy."

She was quiet for a moment. "Good. Now we have to find buyers for the cars."

"I know. Ben got me a screen test, so I'll hold off on that for the moment."

"Marvelous. Universal? Paramount?"

"Tiffany-Stahl," I said.

Momma sniffed. "That low-budget cracker factory? He could be doing so much better than that for you."

"At this point, beggars can't be choosers," I said.

"You are not a beggar. You're between jobs at the moment. That's all."

There was a knock, and my first impulse was to let Katie answer it. Then I remembered, no more Katie. Might as well get used to opening my own doors.

I crossed to the entryway and opened the door as a cab pulled away from the curb out front.

"George!"

George stumbled in the door on crutches, favoring his right foot, his left wrapped in a thick dressing.

"George, what happened?" Momma said, rushing to his side. George had been shooting *Sharp Shooters* at the Fox lot.

He limped to the couch and lowered himself into it, sighing with relief.

"There was a loose board on the platform, and my foot caught on it during a fight scene. Part of the floor gave way."

"Here, put it up," I said. I pulled an ottoman closer to the couch and gently set his foot on it. He winced as I did. "What's the damage?"

"The doc says I sprained my ankle and tore a couple ligaments."

I hadn't seen him for at least a week, and now here he was, all laid up.

"To what do we owe the honor of a visit?" I asked, crossing my arms.

"You're my girl, aren't ya?" He looked confused.

I crossed to the bar for a gin, steeling myself for a fight. I didn't even want ginger ale to go with. I wanted the alcohol to burn away all the anger and resentment I felt.

"Momma, could you go tell Mandy to start on dinner?" I said, giving her a pointed glare.

"Certainly, Baby."

I poured the gin and didn't think to pour George one until he glanced at me and raised his eyebrows. I made him one and handed it to him, then swallowed mine in one gulp.

"I read Alma Whitaker's column this morning," I said.

"I like Alma," he said amiably. "I feel like she really understood me. She didn't gush like some reporters. But did you see all the adjectives? She said I have poise and polish now. I mean, I usually get 'muscular' and 'brawny' and all that. But she called me 'cultured.' Can you believe it?"

"Oh, I can believe it all right." *Could he really be this dense?*

He babbled along about Alma Whitaker until I wanted to scream.

"...anyway, I hadn't heard from you for a little while, and I wanted to make sure we're still on for Tuesday night. Obviously, I couldn't drive like this." He gestured to the crutches.

"What's Tuesday night?" I said, my irritation barely kept in check.

"The premiere, Olive. For *Sunrise*, remember? I told you a few weeks ago."

I'd forgotten, even though I'd bought a new frock for it. Off the sale rack.

"I had to miss the east coast one because we were still at sea, so Winnie let me know that this one is non-negotiable," George continued with a chuckle, gesturing to the crutches. "I'm gonna make a hell of an impression with these."

Finally, I could stand it no longer. "There's one part of that interview you neglected to mention," I said.

He wrinkled his brow in confusion.

"'Too busy to fall in love,' I believe, was how you phrased it," I said.

"I can't believe you're taking that seriously. You know how it is when you're talking to the papers. Alma Whitaker doesn't need to know all our business and neither does anyone else."

I stood with my hand on my hip, unwilling to let him off so easy. Not after what I'd been through the last month.

"Ollie, I love you. You *know* that."

"I do? Between your kowtowing to Murnau, your going to Europe without me, and now this? How am I supposed to know that, George? How?!"

He sighed. "I'm sorry, honey. I really am. I was so concerned about my career that I neglected you. I wish..."

"What?"

"I see fellas like Chaplin and Barrymore being called geniuses and showing all this depth of emotion. I was tired of everyone always bringing up my muscles and my boxing and how athletic I was. Now, they're finally talking about my depth and my range instead of my brawn or my war record. It's like you not wanting to wear skimpy underdrawers all the time. Wanting to be taken seriously. You understand, don't you?"

"A little." I wanted to stay angry, but I couldn't. He was right, but it was so unfair that the same film that had sent his career sky high had scuttled mine, and that it continued to erode our relationship.

"I'm sorry. I was a Grade A clod, wasn't I? I promise things will be different."

"I need more from you, George, starting right now." I sat down next to him. He took my hand and kissed it.

He gestured to his foot. "I'm afraid I'm going to be the center of attention Tuesday, whether I want to be or not."

"Well, it's your big night," I said, trying to be gracious.

"You forgive me, don't you?" he asked.

"Of course," I said. I could never stay mad when I loved him so much. "Guess dancing's out for a while, huh?"

"I know other things we can do to keep ourselves amused," he said. He leaned over and kissed me.

CHAPTER THIRTEEN

SUNRISE PREMIERE, CARTHAY CIRCLE THEATRE,
LOS ANGELES, CALIFORNIA, *November 29, 1927*

The spotlights criss-crossed in the night sky, and the line of limousines snaked down San Vicente. As ours pulled to a stop, George was helped out first with his crutches, then an usher assisted me out. Cap and Maggie had been worried when George told them about his foot, so they'd taken the Lark down from San Francisco. They were in a limousine several cars behind us.

My snug white satin gown made moving difficult. Along with the dress, I'd worn my red satin slippers with rhinestone buckles. Over it, I'd draped my white ermine coat with the fox collar that George had bought me for my twentieth birthday. This would be its last wearing before I took it to a furrier downtown. There were oohs and aahs from the spectators behind the maroon velvet cordon ropes when I stood on the red carpet, But tonight, all the applause was for George. He smiled as he limped along beside me, and we paused to speak to the announcer for KHJ.

"Here's George O'Brien, one of the stars of the film with his lovely sweetheart, Olive Borden! George, what happened to lay you up?"

George chuckled in his infinitely likable way. "Little accident on set as we were shooting," he said. "I'm fine, but a little wobbly right now."

"I'm sure your fans are very relieved about that, aren't we ladies and gentlemen?" A cheer burst from the crowd. "Do you have anything to say about the film?

"I do," George said. "Working with Herr Murnau was one of the most rewarding experiences of my life. He taught me so much about emotion and tapping into my personal feelings so that I could portray a more realistic character onscreen. His ideas on lighting and mood are terrific!"

I continued to stand by his side, trying to look enthusiastic. I'd heard all this before about the German Expressionistic style, the artful juxtaposition of light and dark, and the morals tale of good over evil. The next limousine dropped off Janet Gaynor, and I tried not to let resentment roil up in my gut.

When the announcer came up for air, I guided George toward the entrance, where an usher led us into the auditorium and to our seats. In a few moments, the lights went down, and the orchestra launched into the discordant main theme as the curtain went up.

I wanted to hate *Sunrise*. I wanted to despise it with every fiber of my being—the dramatic shadows and dim lighting, the simple story of temptation, innocence, threatened violence, and love rediscovered—and George was masterful in it. His face registered every tortured thought of killing his wife and every conflicted glance in her direction. Janet did a good job too, it pained me to admit. When the curtain fell, there wasn't a dry eye in the house.

The lights came up, and all around us, the applause was

deafening. George, Janet, Murnau, and Margaret Livingston all waved to the audience from their seats. I blinked back tears, and while George socialized in the lobby, I went to the ladies room to check my makeup. When I returned to George's side, he gave me a kiss on the cheek.

"I know I already told you how beautiful you look tonight, but I wanted to tell you again."

"Oh, George." I gave him a kiss on the cheek, lit up with new optimism.

The day after the premiere, I hopped in the Lincoln and headed out to Santa Monica to find a cheaper place to live until more offers came in. It would be any day, I could feel it. Although there were mutterings in the trades that Fox was talking about taking me back, I put no stock in them.

I found a sweet cottage on Ocean Front Walk, and with help from Mr. Danziger the realtor, I regretfully put the house on Hillcrest up for sale. Thanks to Lila's husband, a big burly man who worked for Consolidated Moving Company, we were able to get the most important furnishings across town with a minimum of fuss. The pieces that weren't paid off were sacrificed, including my Lalique crystal collection, my doll collection, my Louis XIV loveseat, and my 12-seater Hepplewhite dining table and chairs, which wouldn't fit in the new place anyway. I put a story out in the trades that Momma and I were headed out on a European sojourn to relax for a while, but the truth was that I needed every nickel to cover my debts. I sold the Lincoln to an assistant director at Metro who wanted to impress his wife. Bebe Daniels bought the Delage. I found a serviceable used Ford, which although not glamorous, was the most practical choice. George usually drove when we went out anyway.

Fox had begun a blacklisting campaign in the trades, branding me difficult. Ben told me what he was hearing through the grapevine from the other studios he contacted. At this rate, I despaired of ever working again.

When I walked in the front door of the little bungalow, I set down the box I was carrying and opened one of the casements to circulate a little air into the dark musty room. Momma followed me in.

"This is nice," she said, pulling open the shade on one of the other windows. "Lovely light. And the floors are in good shape. There's even a little garden. Look at that."

I surveyed the back patio and the flowerbeds, overgrown with untrimmed bougainvillea, plumbago, roses, and weeds. All it would take was a little work to make it a nice space to relax, but it paled beside the terrace and swimming pool on Hillcrest.

After a week or two, we'd unpacked most of the boxes and settled in. Although I dreaded it, I attacked the walnut secretary desk that took up one whole corner of the living room. In my office on Hillcrest, it had been there to look respectable. All offices had desks, but I'd never even used the thing before now. Every drawer was stuffed full of bills from the furriers, the jewelers, Bullock's, Hamburger's, The May Company, Barker Brothers, C'est Jolie Antiques, Ralph's, and the Bureau of Power and Light. There were others, but those were the largest.

I poured a stiff drink from my secret stash, sat down, and pulled out my checkbook, sending partial payments to the highest, then writing letters begging for more time on the others. When I was done, I combed the newspaper ads for jobs, in case Hollywood was done with me. Momma did the same. All at once, I saw an ad for a commercial block on LaBrea and had a brainstorm. Ben had once told me about the profitability of real estate. Buying a home, not for a residence, but for renting it out to others.

The house on Hillcrest sold pretty quickly, and with the equity, I bought some business properties in Boyle Heights that were self-supporting. While Fox continued badmouthing me to the press for being "difficult," the rent on those properties kept me from losing my shirt. I stashed income from each to begin rebuilding a nest egg. Momma found a job as a saleslady at the Wilshire Jewelry Boutique to help out. George was busy with *Honor Bound*, so he couldn't even spend Christmas with us, but when he could, he finally popped by for a weekend visit after New Year's.

"I like the new place," George said, walking in and glancing around. "It's small, but it suits you."

"It *suits* me? What's that supposed to mean? A rundown cottage for a rundown career?"

"I mean...you like decorating. Your furniture looks good here. That's all. Honest, honey."

I grimaced and bit my tongue. Another nasty remark I shouldn't have made. Lately I couldn't help myself. Everything he said and did seemed like a barbed insult, even if he didn't mean it that way.

"I'm sorry," I said. "I hate that I'm having to step back down again. I'm jealous of your success, and it's not fair of me."

"Darling, I understand, and I support you. You know how I feel about the Fox business, but that's all done with. We'll have to move past it and find you some new opportunities. There are plenty of studios in this town. Even if nothing happens now, when we're married, I'll still treat you like a queen. This isn't poverty. It's temporary."

He moved closer and tipped my face up, then kissed my nose, like an older brother.

"I love you," I said. "You're right. Let's enjoy ourselves tonight."

He was getting ready to leave for San Francisco to visit Maggie and Cap, and then he would jump into *Noah's Ark*, filming in Big Basin State Park up in Santa Cruz County. Once again, it might be months before we saw each other.

We went to the Miramar for dinner. George had flounder en papillote and I had the sand dabs. The candlelight flickered over his chiseled face, showing me once again how incredibly handsome he was.

"We'll find you a new contract soon, guaranteed," he said. "I know you're still sore about the thing with Fred, but things will be better now."

"I know you like Murnau, but I want you to realize how completely he ruined my life, simply by picking you for *Sunrise* and not me. It's affected every part of my life. I want you back the way it was in the desert and in Yellowstone, but you're getting more and more famous. Meanwhile, Fox is turning my name to mud. I'm scared, George." Nervously, I picked petals off the daisy in the bud vase on our table.

"Hey, I've got an idea," he said, gesturing with his fork. "Remember that writer from *Motion Picture Classic* we ran into the last time we were at the Cocoanut Grove? Hal Wells? You said he liked you. Why don't you contact him? Sling a little mud back at Fox *and* Norbert Lusk."

"You know what?" I said. "That's a good idea. No one has been able to see my side, but they should."

I finished my sand dabs, then told George I wanted a chocolate phosphate at the Sunrise Sweet Shoppe for dessert. After that, we took a long walk on the beach. I leaned my head on his shoulder and things were good again. The next morning, I phoned Hal Wells and asked him if he'd consider an interview. He agreed.

OLIVE'S COTTAGE, OCEAN FRONT WALK, SANTA MONICA, CALIFORNIA, *February 1928*

When Mr. Wells arrived, I answered the door myself. Seemed like the best way to show him I wasn't high hat.

"Mr. Wells, so good to see you again. Won't you please come in."

He wore a gray suit with a red bowtie and pocket square. He kept his light brown hair short, and it appeared that if he let it grow, the cowlicks would overwhelm his head. Wells was a columnist and sometime screenwriter who was always up for a good story. If Winnie was after me to play ice queen, he was about to see how frosty I could get. Toward *him*.

Wells smiled and looked around at the tiny bungalow, stuffed to the gills with expensive furniture that didn't seem to match its humble surroundings.

"We can go out in the garden if you like," I said. "I can bring us some iced tea."

"Tea would be nice, thank you," he said, removing his hat.

"Go on out and make yourself comfortable. I won't be a moment."

He did, and I pulled the pitcher from the icebox, pouring two glasses. Then I cut two pieces of the lemon cake Momma had made the previous day, and placed everything on a tray, letting the screen bang shut behind me.

Wells had planted himself in the shade of the fan palm and taken off his jacket. I set the tea and cake on the wrought iron table, and he gulped thirstily from his glass. Then, he pulled a pad from his jacket pocket. I cleared my throat, trying to steel my courage.

"You were so kind the last time I spoke to you," I said. "I'd like this interview to counteract the bad publicity Fox keeps spreading about me. I'm *not* difficult, and I'm tired of them giving me a black eye in the press."

He nodded. "You said you're misunderstood. Let's start there. I'd like to make that the focus of this article. There's been so much gossip the last six months that it would be good to clear the air and hear things from your viewpoint. I'm glad you called."

I smiled and took a sip of my own tea. This would mean an all-out war against Fox. No going back now. Fire with fire. I was determined to preserve my good name. "I would really like to set the record straight."

"Tell me how it started."

"Well, firstly, I hated the fact that every role I had at Fox required me to wear fewer and fewer clothes. *Monkey Talks*? *Yellow Fingers*? And those publicity photos for *Fig Leaves* with George? My God, I was practically naked. I loathed it.

I despised the parts, but I'm a go-along to get-along girl, so I kept doing it."

He nodded as he scribbled away.

"The higher ups in management were obsessed with giving me this persona—very hoity toity and classy. I wasn't to speak to any of the crew. That was beneath me, they said. I was to keep my nose firmly in the air. Elegant, an empress. A real ice queen, with perfume sprayed wherever I went."

"They wanted you to play a snob then."

"Not *play* one. *Be* one," I corrected him.

"Did it work?"

"I thought so, but they didn't. I hated it, because I'm not like that at all."

I told him about needing the Delage to take me back to my dressing room from the set and being called high-hat.

"What were you wearing?" he asked.

"A tiny peignoir. Cut up to here, and down to there. There was no way I would cross Western in that getup."

"That seems terribly unfair."

"Now you know why I called you."

"What else has made you feel misunderstood?"

I focused on a hummingbird who was buzzing around the garden near the back door. "I know it must seem hard to believe with the roles I play, but I'm very shy around strangers, and I was constantly thrown into events where I'd have to wear 'the persona' and be elegant and witty and perfect, but I was terrified, so I'd clam up. Once again, everyone would say what a snob I was."

I told him about *The Joy Girl* tea and the nasty reaction from Norbert Lusk, and then how he had ripped me to shreds not long after.

"Enormously cruel," he said, taking a bite of his cake.

"Thank you. I thought so too. It wasn't my fault we were late from the costumers. We were working very hard and I was exhausted when we arrived. Then they wanted me to be charming and gorgeous and act like a duchess."

"Anything else?"

"Yes," I said, taking a drink of my tea because I felt my mouth going dry. "Did you know I was supposed to be in *Sunrise*?"

He looked up from his scribbling. "You were?"

"It was announced by Fox and everything." I told him about my studying and all the notes I'd taken, and how I'd graciously handed them over to Janet Gaynor and watched the movie walk away with accolade after accolade without me in it.

With this off my chest, I sighed. I hadn't realized how much of it I'd been keeping pent up for so long. "I'm afraid this will make me come off like a sore loser. You won't write it that way, will you?"

"Of course not. I can see they dealt you a raw deal and I'd like to see if we can repair things."

We chatted more about everything under the sun, and as the shadows started to lengthen over the flagstones, I thought again of how I might look. "I don't want to sound desperate. If anyone asks, you didn't get all this content directly from me, all right?"

"Your wish is my command. If anyone asks, I'll say you didn't know about it. I got all of it second-hand."

"I can't thank you enough, Mr. Wells. Truly."

"It's been my pleasure, Miss Borden."

George and I were only able to spend a precious week together before he had to travel to Chatsworth for exteriors on *Noah's Ark*. He'd be gone for seven long weeks.

Mr. Wells' article came out in the July issue of *Motion Picture Classic*. He'd called it "The Most Misunderstood Girl in Hollywood," which I thought was quite fitting. He hadn't brought a photographer with him, so they reused some old pictures of me.

Despite my hopes that the article would help salvage my reputation, I got a strongly worded letter from Ben Rothwell not long after its publication, severing our professional relationship, citing the article as the final straw, and saying it was obvious I was behind it and it sounded like sour grapes. Instead of getting angry, I went on the offensive again, screen testing for anything I could. Unfortunately, I couldn't stave off the inevitable and had to tell Lila and Mandy I could no longer afford their services.

Low-rent studio Columbia came through in a pinch with something they were calling *Caught in a Whirlpool* with John Boles, directed by Elmer Clifton. I played a dancer who was lured to a Central American country with the prospect of a gig, but was then held against her will. Boles played my savior, a flying ace. He was incredibly handsome, with a Texan accent that made me purr like a kitten, but I stayed faithful to George. Besides, Boles was happily married, and had been for at least ten years. Columbia ended up changing the name of the film to *Virgin Lips*.

After that, other budget lots took notice, RKO and FBO in particular. Since I was now like a pogo stick, back and forth between them, I realized how inconvenient Santa Monica had become. I found a place at the Romanesque Villa apartments on North Harper, and against Momma's protests, I moved us back across town.

Delighted to be working again, I did whatever I had to do to look like the perfect, compliant star, but I needed more. At this point, nearly every woman under fifty in America had bobbed her hair except me. I fingered the strands of my long mop and finally decided the time for a change had come.

CHAPTER FOURTEEN

DELIA'S BEAUTY SHOP, 3RD STREET, LOS ANGELES, CALIFORNIA,
September 1928

"**D**o you like it?" the stylist asked hesitantly. I'd told her what I wanted, but when the scissor blades closed above my shoulder, and I glanced down to see my curls laying on the linoleum, I almost passed out. She continued chopping and shaping until at last she handed me a mirror. I closed my eyes, afraid to look. But when I opened them, I was pleasantly surprised. Colleen Moore had nothing on this bob!

"I love it!" I squealed. Then noticing the sensation, I turned my head from side to side. "My head feels so light!"

Now I can screen test for all the flapper parts I'm not getting, I thought.

"Heavens to Betsy, what did you do to your hair!?" Momma cried when I got home.

"I got it bobbed," I said.

"George will be over to get you in an hour!" she said. "What do you suppose *he'll* say about this?"

I laughed. "I doubt he'll notice."

Oh, he noticed all right. And not in a good way.

"What'd you do to your hair?!" he said, in that tone of voice that told me he was wondering how long it would take before it grew back.

"I needed a change," I said, casually running my hand over it. "There were flapper parts I wasn't getting, and I thought it would help. Everyone's doing it, George."

"It's awfully short."

"Awfully *short*? Or just awful?" I said.

"You look fine. I'm surprised, that's all," he stammered, but I caught him glancing at me when he thought I wasn't looking. I assumed it was because of the hair. We did our usual dinner and dancing at the Lafayette that night. We talked about my new film, about his shoot in Chatsworth, and his experiences working with his eccentric new Hungarian director, Michael Curtiz.

In *Gang War*, I played Flowers, a taxi dancer. She was in love with Clyde, played by Jack Pickford, but she was forced into an unhappy marriage with a gang lord, played by Eddie Gribbon.

"Japheth's eyes are supposed to be put out," George said. "I mean, I know he wants realism, but I'd never been so afraid in my life!"

"What happened?" I said, taking a bite of my lemon soufflé.

He lifted the lock of hair over his eye. "See that?"

"Your eyebrow!"

"Yep. Practically singed off. Look how red it is! They'll have to use plenty of makeup this week. That guy held the spear so close, I could feel the heat of the thing. You've never heard anyone scream quite so loud. I was convinced he'd do it." He shook his head. "My eyes are killing me. Feels like I'm getting a stye. Or seven."

When he dropped me off, I made him come up. He did, and I prepared some warm compresses. He lay with his head on my lap while we chatted.

"Something big is going on. I'm not sure what," George said, playing with my fingers, letting the compress do its work. "There was a lot of arguing. Jack Warner was there on the set, and he and Curtiz got into it with our cinematographer, Hal Mohr. Curtiz was in a fury. It's hard to understand him at the best of times, but he was raging in Hungarian too. He kept saying *seggfej*. I'm curious what it means, but it can't be good. Mohr quit."

"He quit?! George, that Curtiz sounds absolutely bats. I'm worried about you. It's only a movie."

"Oh, Curtiz isn't crazy, he's brilliant. It doesn't mean he doesn't scare the hell out of me though. Fred is dedicated to his art and his realism. This guy is one-hundred times more than that. More *real*, more *genuine*, more *everything*. When you're in that audience, he wants you to jump. Part of me admires him, and the other part is cowering, wondering what's next!"

I lifted the compress a little. "How's that feeling?"

"A little better. Thanks, honey."

A week later, we'd agreed on dinner at the Mayfair, and when I went to hug him, I felt a large bulge around his middle.

"George, what in the world?" I backed up and he lifted his shirt to show me the large bandage wrapping his side. "Curtiz again?!"

"Yup. Anders had to throw a spear at me, and...he missed."

"Oh my God! Come here and sit down. Are you all right?"

"The medical staff took care of me at the studio. I'm fine. Can I beg off dinner tonight?"

"Of course, of course."

"I didn't get blood on your frock did I?" He looked down at the bandage where it was seeping.

"No, no. My dress is fine. I'm more worried about you." I caressed his cheek. "This guy scares me, George. I don't want you to end up like Red Thompson."

Red Thompson had been a stuntman who'd been killed the previous year working on *The Trail of '98*, about the Klondike Gold Rush.

"I'll be fine. Don't worry about me. I'm plenty tough." He leaned down and kissed me. That night, I made soup and sandwiches, and we played pinochle. It was one of the most special dates I could remember having in a while. Sweet and innocent, with simple fun, as it had been when we'd first met.

A few days later, I got an unexpected call from George around midafternoon. It was earlier than he usually finished shooting, but I wasn't filming anything at the moment, even a low budgeter.

"Hi, honey. Could you possibly come get me?"

"Where are you?" I asked.

"I'm at St. Vincent's," he said. I could hear commotion in the background.

"George, what are you doing at the hospital? It's Curtiz again, isn't it?"

"Please come. I'll be out front waiting. I gotta go. They need the phone."

Fortunately, I was already dressed and decent. I fired up the Ford and sped across town to the hospital. George was outside on a bench next to a wax myrtle, with a pair of crutches leaning against his leg. Both feet were bandaged, and he was covered in cuts and bruises. I pulled the car to a stop at the curb in front of him.

"George! What in God's name did he do this time?" He leaned on me to rise and stand unsteadily. I handed his crutches back, and he hobbled across the scrubby grass to the car, where I helped him in. He closed his eyes as I put the car in gear and glided out onto Sunset.

"I can't believe what happened today. I honestly can't. Remember I told you I didn't think Curtiz was crazy? I'm not sure about that anymore."

"What the hell happened on that set?"

"He brought in extras. Hundreds of them. Coulda been thousands, even. Not stuntmen. *Extras.* Most of 'em probably couldn't even swim. He had the carpenters build real structures, then mixed 'em with breakaways. He knew where the real parts *and* the breakaways were and he even *marked* them, but he put the humans next to the real stuff and the mannequins next to the breakaways! Then, he had them empty the dunk tanks. Fifty of the damned things!"

I gasped. Fifty dunk tanks was an unbelievable amount of water.

"It was chaos," George said as we sat waiting for a Red Car to pass. "Animals and people, all trying to save themselves in the water. Heavy chunks of scenery are falling on them, and there's Curtiz, yelling, 'Don't stand!' and hurling two by fours at them! I saw at least thirty ambulances leave the lot. It was a nightmare come to life."

"What happened to your feet?"

"Both my big toenails are gone. It hurts like crazy. When Curtiz had em open the sluices, a statue fell right across my feet. I'm lucky I didn't lose a leg! Sorry, honey. I'm afraid it'll be a while before we get to do any dancing again."

"That's the last thing I'm worried about right now. I swear, we need to insure your feet for a couple grand. I know you don't want a stunt double, but..."

"That's rich, coming from you, Miss 'I can't let my stunt double get hurt.'" He chuckled.

"I know. I know. I'm the last person to talk to about that. Let's get you home to rest."

"You don't mind, do you, honey?"

"Of course not. You had quite a day."

I pulled the Ford to a stop on Sunset in front of the Hollywood Athletic Club, where George lived in the adjacent residential tower. I helped him inside and into the elevator, then heated some soup on his hot plate.

Poor George. Thanks to Curtiz's carelessness, they had to shoot him from the shins up for a few weeks until the bandages came off. We couldn't go anywhere because the only shoes he could stand to wear were the Roman sandals he wore for his part as Japheth.

One nice thing was that we could sit in the lounge at the athletic club and play cards or talk about everything under the sun. We got to know each other again, and had long talks like we used to. George let me know that several of those who had been hospitalized during the flood scene died. Everyone kept mum about it, but insiders knew.

NOAH'S ARK PREMIERE, GRAUMAN'S CHINESE THEATRE, HOLLYWOOD, CALIFORNIA, *November 1, 1928*

George sat forward in the backseat of the limousine, as excited as a boy with his first fire engine. He looked so handsome in his tux, and for once, he wasn't on crutches for a foot injury.

I tried to get comfortable in my snug purple velvet gown without crushing the garland of gardenias that draped over my shoulder and halfway down my back. I wore my diamond and amethyst earrings and my slippers with violet sequins and rhinestones on them.

When we reached the curb in front of Grauman's, we were helped out of the car, and I took George's arm.

In the forecourt, KFWB was broadcasting the premiere live over the radio, and we stopped to chat with the announcer before entering the lobby. Grauman had really outdone himself on this place. The columns, the huge stone dragon between them, and the heaven dog statues were all works of art.

Inside, we stood in front of one of the murals, chatting with William Mong and Anders Randolf, who was still bereft about injuring George with the spear during the shoot. George pooh-poohed him with a clap on the back while I waved at Louise Fazenda across the room.

Eventually, an usher saw us to our seats in the auditorium under the giant starburst medallion. It was strange not to see a full orchestra as we'd always experienced in the past, but a piano and organ were the only instruments that were visible.

Conrad Nagel stepped to the stage, acting as our master of ceremonies. "Ladies and gentlemen!" he began. "Let me introduce tonight's prologue, brought to you by our host, Mister Sid

Grauman!" He stepped to the side of the stage, applauding as he did so, and the audience followed his lead.

The curtains parted, and in a moment, we were surrounded by otherworldly voices, and one, a boy soprano, rose high and strong above the others. I recognized "Hear My Prayer" by Mendelssohn from Catholic school choir practice. This segued into a dramatic choral number I didn't recognize. The program said it was Gounod's "Unfold Ye Portals" from "Redemption."

Using blue lighting and theater scrim placed in front of the singers, Grauman had made it seem that massive waves were spraying over the singers. The lighting gradually adjusted and the fabric shifted to reveal the effect of wooden beams and shadows behind the singers, like the inside of an ark. At last came the masterful conclusion. Somehow, Grauman had found zebras, elephants, buffalos, and other zoo creatures. The music crescendoed, then gradually faded, and the animals were briefly visible through the scrim before the auditorium faded to black. More blue wave effects washed over the singers, and then the curtains closed.

Mr. Nagel reappeared, enthusiastically applauding, and stepped to a microphone, which had been placed onstage for him. "Now, ladies and gentlemen, our talking picture subject, Mr. Albert Spaulding!"

Mr. Spaulding played violin onscreen, and it sounded exactly like he was in the theater with us. I realized for the first time how much I would need to work at losing my accent if I wanted to keep going in Hollywood. After a spectacle like this, no one would ever want to see a silent film again.

Noah's Ark didn't begin as I thought it would, in biblical times. George had mentioned that it used a parallel timeline—one in the Old Testament, and one during the Great War. It turned out to be a parable against war and evil.

When it ended, the applause was thunderous. George and I filed out to the lobby with everyone else, and I excused myself to go to the ladies toilet to freshen up.

"Hey," George said when I returned to his side. "There's a party at Bess Meredyth's house after everything wraps here. You up for it?"

"Of course," I said. Maybe I could scare up some new connections at Warner Brothers.

George laughed. "That's my girl."

I have to admit I was curious. Everything George told me suggested that Curtiz was crazy as a bedbug. I wanted to see for myself.

Bess Meredyth was a screenwriter who'd been in Hollywood for positively ages. She wasn't glamorous—far from it, in fact—but she was a smart cookie who threw wonderful parties, and she happened to be Curtiz's fiancée. Her house was a boxy, cream stucco two-story on North Roxbury Drive, a hop, skip, and a jump from my old house.

"Welcome! Welcome!" Bess cried when she saw us. "Mike! Look who's here! It's George and Olive!" She swept me into an Arpège-scented embrace.

"George. Iss good you came. Come, I get you drink. Olive, drink for you?" Curtiz said.

"Yes, thank you," I said. Funny, he seemed so normal here.

"Bessky, Miss Lili iss out of cigarettes."

"I'll find her some, darling," Bess replied.

"You must meet her," Curtiz said to George and me. "Lili Damita. Is beautiful and sweet. Have made three film together."

He showed us to the bar, where Bess had gotten hold of some prized liquors, obviously from a quality bootlegger. Then he grabbed a bottle with Hungarian writing on it, and generously poured each of us a glass.

"Drink! Iss delicious!"

"What is it?" I asked, dubiously looking at the tinted clear liquid.

"Pálinka. Hungarian fire water. You try."

"Bottoms up," said George, fearlessly knocking his back. He coughed, and his eyes bugged a little. "Good stuff..." he rasped.

Curtiz watched me eagerly, so I had to drink it. I sipped instead of gulping, which was a mistake, as it allowed me to taste more of the plum spirit burning its way through my gut. George was right about Curtiz. The man was a sadist. I kept the smile glued to my face while silently cursing him.

"Lili! Come!" he said, gesturing to a gorgeous brunette who was flirting with an entire group of men. I doubted she would desert such a fawning circle of admirers. She waved her cigarette with a disaffected air and a bubbly trill of a laugh.

"Michel! *Mon petit chou!*" She tore herself from her fans and enveloped us in a cloud of Chanel #5.

"Lili, George O'Brien, Olive Borden," said Curtiz.

"*Oui*! From ze feelm! *Enchanté*! So *merveilleux*!" She took hold of George's hands and gave him a European kiss on each cheek.

"Olive is love of George," Curtiz continued.

"*Enchanté*," she said again. The hug and the cheek kisses she gave me were nearly romantic. If I'd been jealous of her caress of George's arm and the way she fondled his bicep, it seemed she was nearly as attracted to me. She caressed my cheek, saying "*Tu es si belle.*"

I swallowed hard, never having received this kind of attention before. "*Merci*," I whispered, falling back on my one year of French at Mount St. Agnes.

Lili engaged us in conversation, asking us all about Hollywood about where to go for fun, as she'd recently arrived from Paree.

"We like the Lafayette for dancing," George said.

"Ze Lafayette? Is zis ze real name? I think Hollywood likes very much *le francais. Oui?*"

"*Beaucoup*," I said.

"*Parlez francais?*" Lili asked me, enthusiastic to have someone to talk to.

"*Un peut*," I said. "*En école.*"

"*Dommage*," she said. "But zis way I can practice my English, *n'est ce pas?*"

I nodded.

Curtiz, while obviously quite fond of Lili, had been drawn into conversation with Victor Varconi and his wife, and they were all chattering away in Hungarian, so I was happy to see Bess approach once again.

"Everyone, we have a late buffet supper in the dining room!" she announced. She herded us all in the direction she was moving.

The dining room contained a Chippendale dining suite set with porcelain serving dishes etched with gold rims. As many of the dishes looked vaguely Eastern European, Bess had kindly created placards with their English and Hungarian names—cheese spread, cheese puffs, tiny sausages, meatballs, and stuffed peppers.

"Help yourselves. Step right up!" Bess said. "Come on, Merv. You go first and everyone else will follow you."

Mervyn LeRoy and his wife, Edna Murphy, stepped up and took some cocktail plates to begin filling them. As they did, there was a commotion from the entry hall, and I looked up to see that Dolores Costello had finally arrived on the arm of a guy I didn't know. Dolores was George's costar in *Noah's Ark*—a stunning blonde with a face so angelic, you expected to see wings sprouting behind her. She wore a slinky seafoam green gown and full-length white fur, which she handed to the maid to place in the closet.

"Dolores, you look beautiful," I said.

"Olive, hello!" she said. "Let me introduce my date. This is Arthur Lake."

Arthur had one of those earnest, friendly faces that were so good for college boy roles. You could imagine him wearing argyle sweater vests and knickerbockers and saying "23 Skidoo" a lot.

"Nice to meet you, Arthur," I said. "Where's John tonight, Dolores?" Her paramour was John Barrymore, who, although completely swoon-worthy, was more than twice her age. I wondered if she might have told him to stay home to keep tongues from clucking so much.

"They've been keeping him hopping, working on *Eternal Love* at UA."

As we blended into a line behind Merv for supper plates, Dolores and I caught up. Her bare lisp of a voice was even hoarser than usual, and she was discreetly coughing into a handkerchief.

"Are you all right?" I asked her.

"I'm still fighting this damned cough from Mr. Curtiz's swim meet," she quipped. "Did George tell you I caught pneumonia?"

"No," I said. "But I think I heard about everything else. Broken bones, cuts and bruises, and George lost two toenails."

"Along with however many people died," Arthur muttered.

"Ssshhhhhh," I said. "You'll get us kicked out of here."

"It was horrible," Dolores said. "I called the shoot mud, blood, and flood." She lowered her voice even more. "I was so frightened. Sure I'd end up dead by the end of it."

"I think George was too," I whispered back. "Personally, I'm convinced the man is nuts."

"Off topic, I loved you in *Fig Leaves*, Olive," Arthur offered. "You were terrific! Seems to me Fox gave you a raw deal, sending you out the door the way they did."

"Thank you," I said. "And bless you for saying so." Dolores had been drawn into conversation with Warner Oland. When we were finished filling our plates, Arthur and I found a spot on a nearby couch to chat. It felt so good to have someone listen and sympathize.

"I've been reading the trades, and they're overly harsh," Arthur continued.

"That's how I feel. I don't think I'll ever make it to the top of the pile again, thanks to Fox blackballing me," I said.

"Well, you know I'm just some nobody right now, only starting out, but if I get the chance to help you, I will. Guaranteed."

"Thanks, Arthur. I appreciate that."

A shadow loomed over me.

"There you are," George said, caressing my hair. "Hi, Arthur. You don't mind if I steal my girl away, do ya?"

"Of course not. It was nice chatting with you, Olive."

"Where were you?" I asked, as I rose.

"Catching up with Lois," he said. Lois Moran waved from across the room.

"Guess what? Arthur said he'd put in a good word for me for any of his roles at RKO."

"That's great news, honey."

I hoped it was.

CHAPTER FIFTEEN

COCOANUT GROVE, AMBASSADOR HOTEL, *January 1929*

"George, you're a card! An absolute card!"

"You think this is fun, you should see me on horseback," George said with a chuckle.

"Oh, but I have! We've seen all of your films, haven't we Nicky?"

In a few days, George was leaving for Monterey and Carmel to work on *Son of Anak*, a Ben Ames Williams story. I'd begged him for some time together before he left, and though I'd hoped for some time alone, he'd persuaded me to accompany him to dinner to get to know his new co-star, Sue Carol, and her fiancé, Nick Stuart.

"Come on, honey, it'll be fun!" he said.

I'd gotten used to coming in second to his film roles ever since *Sunrise*. But now, with the loss of my Fox contract, I'd become extra sensitive to other changes in George. He'd always been charming and thoughtful and courted his leading ladies before jumping into a new role. Heck, he'd done it with me. Then Virginia Valli for *Paid to Love* and *East Side, West Side*, Dolores in *Noah's Ark*, and most recently, Lois Moran for *Blindfold*. He said it made the romance more believable if there was real friendship between the leads, but sometimes it could be misconstrued. The previous fall, I'd had a cold, and George and his friend, Larry Kent, had gone to a party at June Collyer's place. George paid so much attention to June that it had made the trades. Right now, this Sue Carol person made me nervous.

Sue gushed over our shared Baby WAMPAS titles, but she kept touching George's arm when she laughed at his jokes. I glanced over at Nicky, and he didn't seem any more amused than I did.

"Olive, what are you working on now?" Sue asked. "It was so awful what Fox did to you. I don't know how you still have such a wonderful attitude about everything."

"Actually, RKO signed me for a two-picture deal, with an option for two more," I said with a bright smile that I used to disguise my clenched teeth. Arthur had come through like a champion, like he'd promised.

"That's marvelous. I suppose all work is good work these days, even if it *is* on Poverty Row."

I had to fight not to punch her, and after an hour or so, Sue's nasal Chicago accent started grating on my nerves. I spent the evening pretending to be interested in Nicky's conversation about how, if the Hollywood thing didn't work out, he'd open a shop selling menswear. And did I know the differences between Kuppenheimer and Hart, Schaffner and Marx suits? It was all in the stitchery and the pocket design. He'd been studying.

I nodded and feigned interest with a smile plastered to my face, but I wanted to toss my plate of chicken Lyonnaise in Sue's lap, then dump my filbert pudding over her head for dessert.

After a particularly tiring Black Bottom, I hurried to the ladies' toilet. On my way back to our table, I happened to see Ralph Graves under one of the decorative gold palms, billing and cooing with a woman I didn't recognize. I realized how long it had been since I'd paid him and little Ralphie a visit. When the couple came up for air, I gave a little wave.

"Ralph! How are you?" I asked.

"Ollie!" He stood up and offered me the third chair at the table, but I shook my head.

"I can't stay, only wanted to say a quick hello."

"Of course. Olive, this is my wife, Virginia. Virginia, Olive."

"Nice to meet you. And congratulations!" I said, taking in her burnished curls and intelligent gaze. She wasn't a raving beauty, but she was pretty, and I hoped she'd be a good step-mother to little Ralphie. I suspected she had money, because the silver cuff bracelet on her left wrist looked like it cost as much as a new Packard.

"Likewise," she said, holding out her hand and looking me up and down. I think she was trying to figure out if Ralph and I had slept together.

"How's little Ralphie?" I said. "I'm sorry I haven't been by for a visit lately."

"He's fine. Growing like a weed. Hey, you working now?" Leave it to Ralph not to mince words.

"I'm back and forth these days. FBO mostly. I signed a short contract at RKO. Why?"

"I'm over at Columbia. Our leading lady on *The Eternal Woman* fell through. You should come test for it."

I thought a moment. "Of course. I can always use the work these days. Put in a good word for me?"

"You know I will."

"You're a prince. I gotta get back to George. Nice to meet you, Virginia."

"You as well."

When I returned to the table, Ruth Roland had stopped by for a chat. Ruth had been the darling of serial fans in *The Red Circle* at Balboa Studios, with her chestnut curls and self-satisfied smirk. Now she had her own production company, distributed through Pathé. She'd married Ben Bard the previous year. She and Ben and George and I had been on a few double dates.

"There you are, Olive," she said. She stood to give me a hug.

"Ruth, it's been ages. Positively ages. How are you? How's married life?"

"It's good. George and I were catching up and I was getting to know Sue and Nick. How's Sibbie?" Ruth said.

I rolled my eyes. "Sibbie's Sibbie."

Nick drew George into a conversation about the cut of his suit, and Sue watched Ruth and I as we chatted. I purposely turned my back to not include her.

"Was that Ralph Graves I saw you talking to?" Ruth asked.

"Yes, and the lovely new Mrs. Graves," I said. "Ralph's working at Columbia. He wants me to test for *The Eternal Woman*."

"What's it about?" Ruth asked.

"I didn't even ask. You know, two years ago, I would have been making demands all over the place. Now I'm simply happy to get work."

"I get that," Sue said.

I glared at her. Ruth lit a cigarette and slipped it into a

holder. Ben called her from across the room, and she looked up and waved. "Have to go, kids. Ben's getting restless. See you soon."

"Of course!" I said. "Lunch at Montmartre this week?"

"Definitely! I'll phone you!" she shouted over Gus Arnheim and the orchestra as she waved and disappeared into the crowd.

On the way home, I was quiet.

"Sue's a lotta fun, huh?" George said, downshifting as he rounded the corner on Rossmore.

"Laugh riot," I said.

George glanced over. "What's wrong?"

"Other than Nicky and I having to sit and watch his fiancé flirt shamelessly with you all night? Not a damned thing."

George snorted in surprise. "You're jealous? Ollie, come on. There's nothing to worry about."

"From you, maybe. But it's a different story with Sue, and you're blind if you don't see it." Three hours of watching Sue try to winningly beguile George right in front of me had been too much.

"It's a lark, that's all. She told me." He sounded perfectly calm.

My head whipped around. "What?"

"She's been divorced a few months. She started dating Nick, and she wants to be sure that she's not making another mistake. She told me she's having a ball right now. Drinking, dancing, flirting, all of it."

"Well, she'd better back off," I said. "You're taken and she knows it."

"Ollie, I have no intention of throwing you over for some

woman I barely know, co-star or not. We had a couple drinks and a dance in full view of you and Nick, all right? I love you."

"A year ago, you told Alma Whitaker that you were too busy for that."

"You're still holding that against me? Jesus, you hold a grudge like a Corsican." He shook his head.

"If anything gets back to me about shenanigans on that set, there will be hell to pay. I know *you're* an altar boy, but I don't trust her as far as I can toss her across the goal line at USC stadium."

"Honey, trust me. You have nothing to worry about."

I was torn. Accompany them out to dinner where I had to gnash my teeth and watch it all? Or refuse to go and wonder if George might actually respond in kind? I didn't want to seem disagreeable—men hated that—but the alternative might be worse.

George left for Monterey, and he'd been gone a little over a week when I received a telegram from a boy in a Western Union uniform and a pillbox hat.

WESTERN UNION

OLIVE STOP THINK YOU WERE RIGHT ABOUT MY FEET STOP BROKE MY BIG TOE YESTERDAY STOP LAID UP AGAIN STOP DON'T BE MAD WILL BE DANCING AGAIN SOON STOP LOVE GEORGE

I shook my head. The man needed to be swaddled in cotton batting. I wondered how he'd hurt himself this time. Due to his injury, he was home far sooner than we'd hoped, and we planned on attending a party he'd heard about, even if he wouldn't be doing any dancing. That night, he showed up looking as handsome as ever, if a little wind-burned and ruddy-cheeked.

I poured him a drink when he arrived.

"Remind me who this shindig is for?" I asked.

"Mary Duncan. She's a Broadway actress. This is her 'welcome to Hollywood' party."

"Who's throwing it?"

He avoided my question. "It's an open house so she can say hello and meet everyone. Fred wants to use her in a picture sometime soon, he says. She's from Virginia, and I thought you'd like to meet her—you'd have something in common."

I sighed, reading between the lines. "It's Fox, isn't it? It's a Fox party."

"The studio heads are the ones who brought her out here," he said.

"Sol and Winnie."

"Yes, Sol and Winnie."

"So they'll be there." My face grew hot and I felt faint. "I can't face them, George. I can't. Everyone from Fox will be there. Looking down their noses at me and laughing."

"Olive, it'll be fine."

"It *won't* be fine, George! After the Wells article, I'd be as welcome there as a pork chop at a bar mitzvah."

"She won't have a bouncer at the door, for Christ's sake."

"That's not the point!"

"It's not the job of everyone else in Hollywood to kowtow to you," he said, looking exasperated.

"I'm not asking that," I said, trying to talk over the lump in my throat. "I've eaten a lot of humble pie the last few months. I'm a different person, but all they see is the spoiled rotten brat I used to be, getting served a huge portion of crow. I'd like for you to understand. That's all."

"You shouldn't come with me if it will upset you so much," he finally said.

I looked up from my handkerchief. "You're still going?"

"I have a career to think about," he said. "I'll go, and I'll make up something. I'll tell them you have a cold."

"No one will believe it." These people had destroyed my career, and he still wanted to socialize with them. Unbelievable.

"I'm sorry if it hurts you, but I'm going."

My face flushed and my throat closed up. I couldn't cry, but I could hardly speak either. "You know the way out," I said.

"Ollie, don't be like this."

I turned and went into the kitchen before he could finish. Momma was at the table playing solitaire, trying very hard to look like she hadn't been eavesdropping. From the living room came the noise of the door slamming.

"Was that George?" she asked nonchalantly.

"You know it was. He's gone," I said, reaching into the icebox for some orange juice, I added gin from the flask in my garter.

"Oh?" Momma asked.

"Stop it, Momma. You're a terrible actress."

"Why were you so awful to him? If you want to keep a man, you mustn't be so disagreeable."

I gulped my drink, mindless of the burning as it went

down. "You and daddy were married, what, a whopping year and a half? That's a wealth of experience with men right there."

"What has gotten into you? No man wants to be with someone so waspish, Baby."

"I won't go to his damned Fox party," I said. "I'm going to bed. Goodnight."

George called two days later to apologize, and I told him I wasn't angry, but it still stung. I wondered who'd been at the party and what they'd talked about. We went to the Cocoanut Grove to smooth things over. Dancing always made things better, even if I did have to wear a frock from last season.

Ralph turned out to be a lifesaver. *The Eternal Woman* would stereotype me as another "exotic type," this time an Argentine girl named Anita. Having dealt with Harry Cohn for *Virgin Lips* and *Stool Pigeon*, I made sure to have Momma accompany me, as a convenient and necessary chaperone.

In early summer, Arthur Lake made good on his promise again and got me a screen test for *Dance Hall* at RKO with him. I got that part too. In keeping with the theme, they wanted Arthur and I to take real ballroom dancing classes, so they sent us to school. RKO didn't have the big budget of the other top drawer-studios, so we took our instruction after hours at the nearby Wills-Cunningham Studio of Stage Dancing on Hollywood Boulevard.

We studied all the steps, since we didn't know what our director, Melville Brown, would want to use. We tangoed, we foxtrotted, we waltzed, we quickstepped, and we did the Charleston. George and I had always liked going out dancing, but now I had a whole new repertoire, and he had to stop me from leading.

The studio also decided to completely break with my usual look, since my hair was already short. The salon turned me honey blonde, and I hated it. I couldn't wait to dye it back. The critics sure sat up and took notice though. Most of the reviews barely talked about my performance, only my hair.

I played Gracie Nolan, a taxi dancer who's in love with a pilot, but wins dance contests with Tommy Flynn, played by Arthur. When she discovers the pilot is really living with another woman, she returns to Tommy and a happy ending. I'd had a few lines in *Gang War* and *Love in the Desert*, but this would be my first full-length sound film. Despite my nerves, my voice was fine. The dialogue coach had taught me some useful techniques, and they worked, so I could still find work in talkies if I did my vocal exercises.

My bob had grown shaggy, and I wanted to ditch the blonde, so I went back to Delia's. When she was done with my cut this time, my hair was at most, around two inches long all over. It molded to my head becomingly and formed two spit curls near my ears. This time, there could be no doubt about my flapper status.

When I was done with *Dance Hall*, RKO moved me into *Half Marriage*, another talkie.

GEORGE'S BOAT, THE IRON HORSE, IN THE WATERS
OFF CATALINA ISLAND, *November 1929*

The sun had lulled me into a relaxed stupor as I lay on the deck. The breeze was perfect, and it felt good on my skin, which was drying off after a quick swim.

"Hey Ollie!" George called from his place at the wheel.

I looked up and shaded my eyes with my hand. "What is it?"

"You should put some suntan stain on. You don't want to get burnt. Come below deck with me."

"I'm fine," I said, feeling far too lazy to move from my comfortable spot.

"But you know how painful they can be. Remember in the desert you got a little red on your face, and—"

"I'm all right, really," I said.

"Honestly, you can be so gosh-darned stubborn sometimes," he said. He went below for a moment, and then he was back.

"I don't know why you're so sore," I said. That was when he sat down beside me, and pulled open a small velvet box.

"Olive Borden, will you marry me?" he said with a big smile.

"Oh, George! I squealed.

Inside was a gorgeous rock in a classic marquise setting. Surrounding the main diamond were a series of tiny rubies, my birthstones. I shut the lid and grabbed him in a hug, clutching the box carefully. "You are the sweetest, most wonderful man ever," I said, kissing him.

He laughed and kissed me back. "Put it on," he said. "I want to see how my investment looks on you."

"Not out here," I said. "What if it slips off? That would be a disaster. After being patient for nearly four years, I'm going to be extra cautious with it."

"So you like it then?"

"Like it? I love it!"

"Good. I saw it at the jeweler and knew it would be perfect. When should we plan the wedding?"

"We'll have to see when Blessed Sacrament is free, won't we? June brides are traditional, but maybe we could aim for spring. Momma will want to be my maid-of-honor. I'm not sure where to have the reception, but I suppose there's time for all that."

George looked deep into my eyes. "I'm sorry things have been rough lately, honey. I know it's been hard for you and I'm sorry. I love you so much."

For months, this was all I had wanted to hear. The Murnau thing, the trip to Europe, the interview saying he'd been too busy for love, Sue Carol... each one had seemed like a new wound. At last, it seemed like things were changing.

"I know. I love you too. More than anything in the world," I said snuggling up close. He was a true sailor, who smelled of canvas and salt spray and perspiration—a manly combination I'd come to adore. When he smiled at me with that puppy dog grin, I was smitten all over again. I was his, he was mine, and we were going to be fine.

"Put this back in your pocket to keep it safe until we get back to land," I said.

"Whaddya say I put us in at Avalon and we can grab some grub and celebrate?" he said as he pocketed the velvet box.

"Perfect," I said.

When we docked, I put on the ring. At the Shoreline Cafe, we dressed our fresh flounder with lemon, fed each other bites of orange soufflé for dessert, and I told him all about what to see at Lake Louise, since Fox had announced that they were sending his company there for *The Girl Who Wasn't Wanted.*

When we got back to Los Angeles later that night, George dropped me off before he returned to the Athletic Club, and we shared a sweet kiss in the car.

"Soon, we won't have to do this anymore, in the car away from Momma" I said. "We'll be together for real, with a house of our own, and kids..."

He touched my cheek and looked into my eyes. "I'm crazy about you, Olive Borden."

"Not as crazy as I am about you."

Reluctantly, I dragged myself out of the Willys, then stood and waved as he drove away. I had a huge smile on my face as I went back inside. I'd no sooner closed the door behind myself when Momma confronted me in the front hallway. Her quilted robe was tightly sashed, and her hair was in curlers.

"Where have you been? I've been worried sick! I was about to summon the entire Los Angeles police department to search for you!" She enveloped me in one of her overwrought hugs, but I put my arms up and extricated myself.

"Momma, I left you a note. George and I went for a sail, and then he took me to dinner on Catalina. By the way, congratulate me." I held out my right hand with my new ring on it. "George and I are engaged."

All the color drained from her face.

"You're engaged? But...but I thought..."

"What? That I'd forego a life of my own forever? No. I'm

in love with George and he's in love with me. We're going to make a life together."

"I suppose he'll go sailing off anytime he wants, to Europe with that Hun," she said. Something like a smirk played across her face. She knew her little barb would hit home.

"We talked about it, and everything's fine now," I said.

"Until next time," she said. "Then you'll be running home to me." She turned on her heel and went back to her room.

I went to bed seething. This should have been the most amazing day of my life, and she'd ruined it. Our feud continued over Christmas, with a tense gift exchange, and very little warmth. Every day I thought of George's ring, and the prospect of escape from Momma.

CHAPTER SIXTEEN

OLIVE AND SIBBIE'S APARTMENT, ROMANESQUE VILLA, HOLLYWOOD, CALIFORNIA, *January 1930*

The friction continued into the new year. Momma acted like a guard dog on the set, not letting anyone come near me. It was like she couldn't stand to watch me drifting away. The harder I pulled, the harder she tried to keep me tethered to her side. Engagement or not, she was holding on for dear life. I finally confronted her one morning before we headed to the Goldwyn lot in Culver City, where I was working on *Hello Sister*. Even my director, Walter Lang, had had it with her, and had demanded I talk to her.

"Momma, this overprotectiveness has got to stop. You follow me to the ladies' room, for goodness sakes! You interrogate George anytime we go anywhere. Your overprotectiveness has gone too far."

"I am your mother, and I will not be spoken to this—"

"Walter has told me he will ask for a closed set because of *you*! Are you listening? I am finally starting to rebuild my career after I was stupid enough to listen to you at Fox. I'm not knuckling under to you anymore about my career. Starting tomorrow, I'm going to the lot without you. You can stay here and knit."

"Olive, I can't believe that you're—"

"You need help," I said.

She sniffed. "Fiddlesticks. It is not wrong to worry about one's daughter."

"Caring and worrying is one thing. You've always done that. Making me a prisoner is different. I won't live like this. I won't."

She looked offended. "What do you propose?"

"I'm not sure. I'm working on it."

"What do you mean you're *working* on it? You make it sound like I'm a problem to be dealt with."

"I'm not arguing about this. You are not coming to the set with me again. That's that."

"I'll let Mr. Lang tell me himself, thank you very much."

"No, you won't. He told me to lay down the law to you. I've been far too lax about letting you be in charge, and you're not anymore. This is *my* life, and *my* film. If my co-star wants to chat, or if my director needs to give me some guidance, they will."

"I am trying to protect you from—"

"*I don't need protecting*! I'm twenty-four years old. Why can't you just *love* me like other mothers do? Why is smothering the only thing you know how to do?"

Her face turned that flushed red that true Irishwomen have, and she harrumphed away. On my next day off, I spoke to my physician, Dr. Siegel, to see if he could offer any suggestions.

"I honestly don't know what's gotten into her, doctor," I said. "She's always been overprotective, but lately, it's like living with a prison guard or a Doberman pinscher in a hat. Do you have any advice for me? I'm at the end of my rope."

He listened thoughtfully, playing with his pen. "Have you considered one of the nearby facilities for psychiatric disorders?"

"She'd never consider it. You know how small the Hollywood grapevine is. If I did send her somewhere, it would need to be further away. That way, she could claim she needed a vacation. But where?" I pulled out a handkerchief and worried it with my fingers.

"I have an idea," he said. "I'm not sure how receptive she'll be, but..."

"Let's hear it. I'm desperate."

"I have a colleague from medical school who has opened a private clinic. It's so exclusive that very few people know about it, but I can vouch for his methods, and he says he's doing well."

"Where is this clinic?" I asked.

"In Hawaii."

"You said 'exclusive.' I'm smart enough to know that means pricy," I said.

"Unfortunately, yes."

"I'll have to come up with the fee, whatever it is. I need my sanity back."

"I'll send a wire to Dr. Tedford right away, then."

"Thank you, Doctor."

Within weeks, it was arranged. Momma was so excited about seeing Hawaii that she nearly forgot about the clinic part. I imagined that the lure of the islands could do that to a person. She boarded the *City of Honolulu* on March 22nd. The clinic assured me they would send a private car to pick her up at the dock in Hawaii.

As I'd been planning Mommas's hospital stay, I got a line

on *The Social Lion* at Paramount with Jack Oakie, and they liked my screen test. I got to play snobby Gloria Stanton to Jack's polo-playing hero. Eventually I was revealed as a lying opportunist, and lost him to Mary Brian.

One evening after filming, I stopped by the Athletic Club to see George. I pulled up out front, then took the elevator to his place, ready to launch myself into his arms.

I gave a quick knock, and when he opened the door, he got a confused look on his face.

"Hi, honey. Did we have a date? Did I forget?"

I looked him up and down. He was wearing a white dress shirt and gray flannel trousers, and his hair was pomaded. He usually didn't wear pomade unless he was going out.

"Going somewhere?" I asked.

"Well, if you want to know the truth..."

"The truth would be nice, yes."

"It's a small get together at Winnie's place for some of the talent."

"How small?" I said.

He shrugged. "I don't know. Forty people, maybe? He didn't really specify."

"Why didn't you tell me?"

"Come on, Olive. Remember how sore you got the last time I wanted to go to a Fox party? I thought it would be best not to say anything because I didn't want to hurt your feelings. That's all."

"Who's going to this party?" I asked.

"I didn't ask him for the guest list. I don't know who's RSVP'd."

"Sue?"

"Probably."

"Probably? Come on. She's said something to you about whether she's going or not,"

"Yes, she's probably going. Do we have to do this right now?"

"Do what?" I asked with innocent eyes. "Is Nick going?"

"I don't know. I assume so," he said.

"You're not sure?" I stood with my arms crossed.

"They're married now, Olive."

"Yeah, and she's already been divorced once. Why do I feel like that band of gold isn't something she takes seriously?"

"I get it. You don't like Sue. But I'm still a Fox employee, and she and I could still co-star in something, so you'll either have to learn to live with it, or..."

"Or what?" I asked.

"Or can the complaints."

"I don't like either of those choices," I said.

"Then say it straight out. If you have a beef, don't beat around the bush."

I took a deep breath. "If you go, that's it. We're through."

George raised his eyebrows and shook his head. "Olive, you can't do this every time I go to a Fox party. The person who destroyed your career was you. Yeah, Sibbie got you into hot water, but you could have bucked her! You could have listened to Ben and taken the damned pay cut. The rest of us took a pay cut. Why was it so hard for you to do? You want to be an adult so bad, then take some responsibility for yourself! I love you, but I don't like ultimatums." He walked away from me, grabbed his hat from the hall tree, and shoved it on his head.

"Don't go," I said. I hated the desperate pleading tone in my voice, and followed him to the door, as it was obvious he was going, despite my begging. We stood in the hall outside his apartment for a minute.

"My life is my own," he said. "If you put me in a corral like a horse, I'll bust it down. Let me know if you ever grow up."

He turned on his heel and headed to the elevator. When it arrived, he got in and gazed at me as the doors closed. I felt like I'd been slapped. For the first time in a very long time, I felt tears in my eyes. I stood there a moment, trying to collect myself.

After a minute or two, I turned and furiously stabbed at the button for the elevator before catching it and hurrying to the lobby. By the time I got there, George was gone.

Back home, I crawled under the covers and tried to block it all out. What he'd said had cut me to the bone. By refusing to budge in the negotiations, Momma had signed my death warrant at Fox, and stupid me, I'd listened to her. I should have followed George's advice and let Ben negotiate. I should have been flexible. Now I was persona non grata in this town. The shoestring studios would still give me work, but my name was mud at the larger ones since Fox's media machine had gone to work.

Thoughts assailed me. Sweet days in mountain meadows with George, him bringing me oranges during my typhoid, showing me how to tie a dry fly for fishing, fox trotting at the Lafayette and the Cocoanut Grove, afternoons on his boat, or stealing soft gentle kisses under the Yellowstone moonlight. That night, I didn't get much sleep.

The next morning, I awoke newly determined to make

some major changes. A change of scenery was tops on the list.

Mary Brian, who was starring with me in *The Social Lion*, was as pure as milk, with a heart to match. She'd also been a WAMPAS baby star the year after me. We'd developed a great working relationship, and everyone loved her. I thought I'd see if she knew anyone who might be able to help me. I rang her up after breakfast.

"Olive! How are you, dear?"

"It's so kind of you to ask, Mary. I'm not at my best right now, I'm afraid. George and I have called it quits."

"You what? Oh, no. Olive, it can't be true. You're the cutest couple in Hollywood!"

"Unfortunately, it happened, but I'm hoping you can help me."

"Anything. Name it."

"I'm wondering if you know anyone with connections in New York. Unfortunately, the ones I'm acquainted with all work for Fox, and that ended so badly, that..."

"Of course, of course. Well, there's Mr. Brenon."

"Herb Brenon?" I thought a moment. "That makes sense."

"He directed me in *Peter Pan* and also in *The Street of Forgotten Men*. Before he came out here, he worked in vaudeville and did a little for IMP in the east. I could listen to that Irish accent of his all day, couldn't you? Besides... Fox fired him too. You'd have something in common. You can commiserate."

"Oh, Mary, do you really think so?"

"I'm positive. I'll try to get hold of him. He finished that *Sergeant Grischa* thing for RKO a while back. I have his private number. I'm sure he'd love to help. What is it that you need?"

"Connections. All mine are in Hollywood. I'm thinking

about trying Broadway or vaude, and I have no idea how to get started."

"Then you relax. I'll take care of everything," she said.

"You're so kind."

"You'd do the same for me. I know it."

Not long after that, Herb Brenon called to reassure me that he'd wired several contacts and was waiting to hear back. Mary was right. That lilting Irish accent was the cat's whiskers.

"You're not the only one heading east," he told me. "California has lost its charm for plenty of us. Between talkies and the stock market crash, greener pastures are on everyone's mind."

"I so appreciate you trying to help," I said.

"I'll let you know if I get a line on something," he said.

As it happened, leads began trickling in right before Momma's stay in Hawaii was due to end. One part of me would have been happy to have her stay a while longer. The other knew it wasn't realistic, and there was no way I could continue to pay for the expensive clinic. At least my bank account would be getting a break. A Broadway producer, A. H. Woods, wanted to talk to me about a part in his upcoming play, *On the Spot*.

The day Momma's ship, the *S.S. Calawaii*, was due to dock, I drove down to Wilmington and waited for her to emerge from the debarkation area. She had on a new magenta frock, sported a hibiscus behind one ear, and wore a new fragrance— something exotic and overpowering. Usually, it was her hugs that were overwhelming. This time, it was both.

"Welcome home, Momma. How do you feel?"

"Marvelous!" she said, turning and snapping her fingers at the porter who brought her trunk on a wheeled cart. "I have to admit—I was quite resentful at first, but Dr. Tedford turned me around. He made me see how unreasonable I was being."

"Really?" I did a double-take. Thank God the investment might have worked. "How did he do that?"

"He asked me how long I planned on holding you hostage. That you are in your mid-twenties now, and that I must learn to let you go."

I took the first deep breath I'd taken in a very long time.

"He made me see that I was trying to protect you because I couldn't protect your daddy or baby Frankie, and he was right. I'm sorry, pardner. I really am, and the next time George comes over, I'll apologize to him too. He's such a wonderful man, and he'll make an outstanding son-in-law."

My silence loomed as wide as the Grand Canyon as I tried to think of something to say.

"Baby, what is it? Oh." She patted her own hand in a pretend display of discipline. "Doctor Tedford says I am not to call you Baby anymore, because it is disrespectful to you, and I apologize."

Wow. This guy was *good*.

I sighed. "Momma, George and I broke up."

"You what? Why?"

"We got into an argument, and we both said some harsh things."

"Fiddlesticks. George is the most understanding fellow there is, and I was a fool to doubt his motives all this time. If you both apologize, everything will be fine."

I shook my head, blinking back the stinging in my eyes

that signaled possible tears. I didn't want to wreck the car. I pulled to the side of the road, and all the emotion I'd been holding back burst loose like the St. Francis dam.

"It's been three weeks, Momma. Usually, he'll call or stop by. He hasn't. I ruined it. I drove him away."

I let the tears fly, and for the first time ever, Momma seemed unsure how to react. I was trying to be mature and independent, and now that I was showing need for the first time in years, she seemed shocked—not sure if she should hug me or not, thanks to Dr. Tedford. Finally, she did what came most naturally, and allowed me to soak the front of her blindingly vivid frock.

"I'm so sorry, darling. What happened?" She tipped my chin up and looked me in the face.

"There was a party—Fox people again—and I told him I didn't want him to go."

To her credit, she didn't say, "I told you so," even though I knew it had to be difficult. She simply let me bawl some more and get it out of my system.

"Shall I drive us home? I don't think you're up to it."

I nodded, and we got out of our seats and changed, right on Western Avenue in front of the Richfield service station.

When we got home, she put me to bed, and all of Dr. Tedford's advice was temporarily put on hold. She called Aunt Bessie and Natalie, and they came over and joined us for dinner. I swore Nat to secrecy—no talking to the trades. I wouldn't make a big announcement. Once Grace Kingsley and Louella Parsons realized they hadn't seen George and me at the Lafayette in a couple months, they'd realize the engagement was off. That reminded me. I looked down at the beautiful ring on my finger, and knew the time had come. The next morning, I called George.

CAFÉ MONTMARTRE, HOLLYWOOD, CALIFORNIA,
Spring 1930

The luncheon rush was hectic as usual. Our favorite waiter, Hector, quickly brought my Filet of Sole Mornay and George's Ravioli Genovese. We nodded our thanks as he retreated.

"How've you been? George asked, tucking his napkin into his collar.

"Fine," I lied. "You?"

"Great," he said, without enthusiasm. "You look good."

"Thanks. You too."

"What did you want to talk about?" he asked.

"Oh." I reached into my bag and set the ring box on the table between the salt and pepper shakers and the dish of butter pats so it wasn't as immediately visible to those around us. This was hard enough as it was. I'd purposely chosen a busy restaurant so we could do it quietly without it making a big scene.

"You don't have to give it back," he said. "I gave it to you."

"It's probably bad luck to wear an engagement ring for a broken engagement," I said.

He shrugged. "It didn't have to be," he said.

"No, it didn't, but it is," I said, annoyed at how this was turning into an argument anyway. "You'll socialize with who you want, and I'm a jealous scold, right?"

I looked up and our eyes met. I saw genuine pain and heartache in his.

"I still love you, Olive. I do." The ring sat on the table. He showed no signs of picking it up.

"I love you too," I whispered.

"Hollywood is a small town. There will always be one more party, one more co-star, one more studio head I have to deal with. I just want to do my job, get paid, and enjoy some of the fringe benefits that go along with it. I don't understand why it has to be such an issue with you. You've been gone from Fox nearly three years now."

I closed my eyes for a moment, and I knew he'd never understand the shame of being on top of the world, then getting too big for your britches and falling from that perch. Everyone loved him, and they always would.

"I don't know why I'm like this, George, but I am. I burned that bridge, and there's no going back for me. Can't you get it?"

"No, I can't. You shit the bed at Fox, but that doesn't mean I have to lie in it with you."

"It's a small sacrifice," I said.

"Not when they pay *my* bills, it isn't!" Heads turned at our raised voices. George eyeballed an assistant director from FBO who was glancing over at us. I'd seen him around, but didn't know his name.

"I don't know why you had to ruin things," he said. "I thought we were happy."

"We were," I said. "But I expect any man I'm with to support me, through thick and thin."

"I support you, but I'm your fiancé, not a foundation garment," he muttered.

"You *were* my fiancé," I said quietly.

"You're dead set on this?"

I nodded.

He set his napkin on the table. "I'd hoped that we could fix things today, but I can see that won't happen." He grabbed the ring and stuffed it in the pocket of his jacket, tossed a couple bills on the table for lunch, then stood and walked out.

"Bye, George," I whispered.

CHAPTER SEVENTEEN

ROMANESQUE VILLA APARTMENTS, 1301 NORTH HARPER
AVENUE, HOLLYWOOD, CALIFORNIA, *Spring 1930*

"**T**hat you, pardner?" Momma said. Her voice was muffled, and when I found her, she was at the door of her closet, tossing clothes into a colorful pile on the floor.

"What are you doing?" I asked.

"I'm getting rid of some of these old dresses and donating them to charity." The clothes had been her favorite perq from my success, since we'd never been able to have anything nice when I was young. My mouth fell open in shock.

"I met the most marvelous woman in line at the bank today. She calls herself Sister Essie. We got to chatting, and she told me about a charity she runs downtown for destitute women and children. I don't have any children's clothes, but I have plenty of frocks for ladies. They're all from last season anyway. Remember when we were happy to have a dress, even if it was a hand-me-down? Anyway, she was so inspiring that I decided these needed a better home than my closet."

Did I mention Dr. Tedford was good? With Momma suddenly less clingy and now full of the milk of human kindness, it seemed like a good time for a chat.

"I remember," I said. Things had been simpler then, because we'd both been more concerned with keeping ourselves fed and a roof over our head. For one year, I'd barely eaten a thing when the candy store had closed. If Hollywood hadn't started taking notice at last, I wasn't sure what we would have done.

"Why don't you take a break? I'll make us a cup of tea," I said. Any excuse to pull out Granny Shields' prized Spode tea set with the gold handle and spout. For years, it had been the only thing of value we owned.

"That sounds lovely," she said, eyeing me warily. Hawaii had changed her for the better, but the breakup had changed me for the worse. I was being extra nice to compensate.

I boiled the water for some oolong, and placed some Nilla wafers on a plate. When I was a little girl and we could make cookies, this was our little ritual. We'd set a place for my only doll, Audrey, and have a tea party.

"Something tells me you have something important to say," she said. She poured from the pitcher into her cup and added cream and sugar.

"I do, Momma."

"What is it?" she bit into her cookie.

I was quiet for a moment, but let her swallow before I hit her with the news. I'd been trying to figure out how to do it ever since she got back.

"Well, since George and I broke up, I've been taking stock, and I think I need a change of scenery," I said.

"How much of a change?" she asked.

"The biggest."

"Europe?!"

"Well," I countered. "Not quite that big. New York. I want to try Broadway for a while."

"Do you know anyone back east?" she said. "Anyone who doesn't work for Fox, I mean."

"Mary Brian is helping me. She knows Herb Brenon. He got fired from Fox too, so he's already gotten me a line on a show. I really want to get away from California. It all reminds me of George right now, and..."

"What about me?" she asked. To her credit, she didn't immediately turn hysterical like she might have a few months before.

"The properties are doing well. They're bringing in enough to keep you. The apartment is paid up for the next two months. You can stay and let it yourself, or you can move somewhere else. There are plenty of sweet little apartment courts around town with nice neighbors. I have to go be independent for a while. Please understand."

She sighed, which was far better than the tantrum she might have had previously.

"If you're going to New York, I'll come too."

My stomach rolled over.

"You'll hate the winter," I said, grasping at anything to deter her.

"We had winter in Virginia, for goodness sakes. I liked New York when we were there. You forget...your daddy took me to Boston to meet his family. It was nice seeing the seasons change, and the snow looks like a thick white blanket. Perhaps I'm tired of the sun and sea too."

"We are not living together there. I want that understood."

"Fine," was her quiet response. I was curious what was

going on in that head of hers, and where she planned on living, if not with me.

Over the next few days, I began packing my trunk and booked my ticket on the California Limited to Chicago, then the Twentieth Century to New York. I found a room at the Hotel Jackson on West 45th Street, a block from Times Square.

Mr. Woods' office was in the Graybar Building on Lexington, and I made an appointment for the day after I arrived. Mr. Woods had obviously anglicized his name, because he had the same sort of guttural accent as Mr. Curtiz. Unlike Curtiz, he was remarkably composed. I didn't sense any of the restrained craziness I had from Curtiz. Woods welcomed me into an office that was cluttered with librettos and scripts, tossed haphazardly onto every surface. He had to clear off a chair so I could sit down.

"Glad to zee you! Glad to zee you!" he said. He repeated himself a lot, but I didn't mind if it meant a steady, paying gig. Broadway beckoned like some bright shining beacon in the distance. I looked forward to showing everyone I wasn't just a bratty lingerie model.

I leaned forward, interested in what Mr. Woods had to say. I couldn't wait to get started.

"I like your look. Ve can do great things together," he said. "Great things!"

"I'd love that," I said. "I've been eager to do some stage work."

"Good to hear, good to hear. Movink from California?"

"That depends," I said. "Right now, I'm discovering the lay of the land, making contacts, and getting set up with work. If all looks good, I'll make the move."

"Make the moof. Make the moof," he said. "Dis play is a hit, and ve can put your name in lights again."

"I like the sound of that. As long as I don't have to wear lingerie, I'm in," I said.

"Good. Good. Dis play? Surefire winner."

"Can you tell me more about it?"

"Sure, sure. Fellow who wrote it… Edgar Wallace, English. His view of the gang wars in Chicago. Head guy, Tony Perelli, is head of beer rackets. He runs out de competition, and does okay, until he falls for rival's girl. Then, his own chippy commits suicide. Policeman who has been out to get him burns her suicide note, so he's trapped. Trapped!"

It sounded suspenseful. "So I'd play the rival's gal?" I asked.

"Nah, chippy. Star-making role. Star-making!"

"I'm already a star, Mr. Woods," I said.

"So we help everyone remember," he said with a grin.

"What do I need to do?" I asked.

He thought a moment. "Show up for audition Tuesday at ten at Forrest Theatre. Make plans to come to New York. We open in fall, so you have plenty of time, while I get rest of cast."

"All right. It looks like I'm becoming a New Yorker!" I said with a laugh. I resolved to stay at the Jackson until I found the perfect place, then I could arrange for moving my things from Hollywood.

When the time came, I hopped the Twentieth Century back to Chicago. That summer was chaotic—trying to pack and plan my move while continuing to try to drum up work. June Clyde and I got paid a nominal fee and free lodging to say we were "vacationing" at Breezy Point Lodge in Minnesota. There were more mosquitoes than there were guests at the lodge. After Skeeter Central, it was on to Portland, where I appeared at Jantzen Beach Amusement Park, announcing the jazz combos that played. When I got home, I did a quick traveling vaudeville sketch down in Long Beach. The best I could say for traveling vaude was that it was better than breadlines and soup kitchens. Considering that a good chunk of the population were selling apples on street corners since the crash, I could be doing far worse. But I missed making real movies with a real budget. I missed traveling first class, I missed my house, and I still missed George.

In September, I was in Los Angeles to take care of the last details before the move when I received a call from Mr. Woods. In conversation, he dropped some details he hadn't mentioned before.

"She's what?"

"Chinese," Mr. Woods said. I had thought it was the crackly connection playing tricks with my ears, but no. He'd really said that.

"Chinese? But the script never mentioned that, Mr. Woods."

"We thought about changing to white girl, but dis is closer to original story."

"You couldn't have mentioned it before now? Why didn't you tell me?"

"You not ask," he said. "Hate Chinese people or something?"

"Of course I don't. But I don't want to be typecast. I'm very sensitive about it. I've already played a Malaysian, a Mexican, an Argentinian, a 'native' girl, and an Arabian."

"You have exotic look. You can be anything."

"But I'm *not* exotic. I'm Black Irish for God's sake! I'm the least exotic person there is. You should hire someone Chinese to play it. My friend, Anna May Wong, is actually Chinese. There aren't many roles like this and she could use the work."

"You should thank your lucky stars for dis part," he said.

"I'm sorry, but I'm not interested in it. Let me call Anna May for you."

We parted company about the production, but fortunately, I happened upon a small-time production for a producer named Lew Cantor that would pay the bills a while longer.

I finally made the big move the second week of September, and was so excited, I could hardly sleep on the train. I bought papers from a couple of newsies, then found a diner at Gay Street and Waverly Place to look through the ads for places to rent, then spent time viewing places and learning about New York.

I saw one or two that I liked, but nothing really grabbed me until I saw 59 W. 10 Street. The red brick and white trim didn't look exceptional from outside, but the interior made up for it, and the price was right. I felt comfortable the minute I walked in. It had bay windows and a doorman, and French doors inside, which lent it a classy touch. I spoke to the land-lord and paid three months advance rent to hold it for me until I could have the rest of my things shipped east.

CHAPTER EIGHTEEN

BRANDT'S BOULEVARD THEATRE, JACKSON HEIGHTS, QUEENS, NEW YORK, *December 23, 1930*

I smeared cold cream on my face to remove my makeup, contemplating the Christmas shopping I still needed to finish. I'd been so busy with rehearsals, I hadn't even had a chance to get a tree this year.

There was a sharp knock at the door.

"Come in!" I said.

Jimmy Palmer, the theater gofer, poked his head inside.

"Miss Borden, there's a fan outside who would like to come say hello."

I sighed. "Can you give her my apologies, please? All I want is to go home and have a hot bath."

"It's a man, actually."

"Regardless, I'm in no shape to meet anyone. I'm exhausted."

"I'll give him your regrets."

"Thank you," I said, making another pass over my nose with the Pond's.

The Devil Is a Lady wasn't a flop, but it wasn't *MacBeth* either. It was a mystery, set in an English manor home, and most of the reviews, while not being especially kind to the show itself, at least gave me credit for expanding my repertoire. My co-star, Frieda Inescort, was a lovely Scottish actress who'd originated the role of Sorel Bliss in Noel Coward's *Hay Fever* at Maxine Elliott's Theatre in '25.

New York wasn't producing the results I'd hoped, but this was work, at least. The papers were calling the crummy economy a Depression. As it worsened, stage productions were harder to find for everyone. When no one was working, no one went to the theater. I was reduced to doing advertising for Delica Brow Cake and Kissproof Lipstick on the side to make ends meet.

As she'd promised, Momma had followed me to New York and gotten a place a few blocks from me. When I didn't want to see her, I simply pretended I wasn't home. I made sure to never play the Victrola loudly. For the first time in my life, I felt like we had a healthy relationship.

After changing into street clothes and grabbing my bag, I said goodnight to everyone at the theater and headed for the stage door to the alley. Outside, I glanced around to see a figure striding toward me. I was instantly on my guard, until the streetlight illuminated him more.

"Miss Borden," the man said. "I was hopin' you'd leave this way. I really wanted to meet ya."

"Sir, I'm sorry. I'm very tired, and I—"

My voice trailed off as the shadows receded to reveal a man with a strong, handsome face and eyes that glowed warm and dark, like a welcoming cup of well-brewed coffee. His nose was slim and aquiline, and his hair had the slightest bit of brilliantine. He wore it naturally brushed back. His smile was the kicker—perfectly white and dazzling, with unbelievable dimples and a slight cleft in his chin.

George who?

"Name's Teddy Stewart. I liked your show a lot."

"Thank you, Mr. Stewart."

"I'd hoped I could tell ya somewhere nicer than this dark alley."

"As I mentioned, I'm quite tired. Between rehearsals and shows, I'm done in." I hid a yawn behind my hand so he'd know I was serious.

"I understand. Sorry for bothering ya, but I been a fan of yours for years."

I smiled. Thank goodness someone still was.

"Was *The Social Lion* your last film? I look for 'em all."

"Yes. I did some traveling over the summer, to Oregon and Minnesota for publicity events."

"In New York for a while then?" he asked.

"As long as they'll have me," I joked.

"I'd love to take ya out for a late dinner or a drink," he said with a wink-wink sort of attitude. It was Prohibition, after all. He was awfully handsome, and I'd been so lonely since the split with George.

"All right," I said. "We do a matinee on Saturdays, and after two p.m. I can make plans."

"That sounds terrific," he said.

I opened my bag, found a pen, and scribbled the number down for him.

"I'll call ya tomorrow, then."

"I'll look forward to it."

Teddy called at three p.m. the next day, and we made plans to go for an early dinner. He'd pick me up at my place. I buzzed him up, and greeted him at the door.

"You look stunning," he said of my slinky navy frock and navy cloak sewn with teal peacock appliques. The cloak was several seasons old, but I still loved it. "These are for you."

He handed me an enormous bouquet of calla lilies. I thanked him and put them in water.

"Say, fancy little crib," he said, looking around, and admiring my WAMPAS loving cup and one or two prints on the walls.

"It suits my needs here. My house in Beverly Hills was much nicer."

I locked up, and we took the elevator down to the lobby. His navy Buick Victoria was parked at the curb.

"Nice car," I said, as he opened the door for me. "What do you do, Mr. Stewart?" I asked.

"Stockbroker," he said, putting the Buick in gear.

That explains the expensive buggy. The leather smells brand new.

"How is that going these days? Stocks?" I asked.

"Rough patch, but things'll turn around any day."

"I've been reading some very worrying things in the paper about stocks and the economy."

"I still got a job and my company's still solvent. That's something," he said.

I nodded. "Do you live here in the city then?"

"No, I commute from New Jersey," he said.

"Isn't it awfully long?"

He shrugged. "I used to take the ferry from Weehawken. Now I can use the Holland Tunnel. Paterson isn't far. You like New York? Compared to Hollywood, I mean?"

"It's all right. It's different. In Hollywood, if you blow your line, they reshoot. Here, if you blow a line, the entire production could be in trouble. Especially now, with the economy not doing well."

"Everyone's hurting," he agreed.

When we arrived at Barbetto's, Teddy parked the car and escorted me inside. The maitre d' saw us to one of the tall banquettes, and Teddy gazed raptly at me. So much that I felt uncomfortable.

"What's good here?" I asked, opening my menu.

"The clams will knock your socks off," he said. I studied the options more closely, then agreed they sounded delicious.

"Have we decided?" the waiter asked when he returned.

"The lady will have the clams oreganata. I'll have the sirloin. Medium well."

"Very good, sir." He nodded and returned to the kitchen to deliver our orders.

"How's business for the play?" Teddy asked.

"Not good, but it's the same all over, I've heard."

"You do a great job. Maybe they should get ya to wear those lace drawers you wore in *The Monkey Talks*," he suggested, giving me a little wink.

"My lingerie days are *done*," I said. "You have no idea how hard I fought to be taken seriously as an actress. Ever since the water barrel in *3 Bad Men*."

"Sorry," he said. "I liked that scene. Can't help it if I wanna look at ya. Neither can any other red-blooded American fella."

We chatted more until our food came and we ate in silence for a few moments.

"You're from Virginia originally, right?" he said. "I read everything I could find about ya in the magazines," he said.

"That's very flattering. Yes, Virginia. I spent a lot of time in Baltimore too when I was young. I can't imagine not being near the water. I love it so."

"Hey, me too," he said. "Can't swim real good, but I still like it."

"I'm a good swimmer, but I still had a scare in Catalina when we were shooting *Yellow Fingers*." I told him all about nearly being washed out to sea.

"I got put off swimmin' when I was sixteen. We used to go to the Jersey Shore in the summer. Rent a cottage, ya know? That year? Jersey got itself a man-eating shark. Killed a coupla guys. Scared the sh— I mean scared me to death. I go to the Y instead. Won't go in the ocean anymore."

"Where was this?"

"Near Mattawan. It even got into one of the creeks." Suddenly, he steered the conversation in an unexpected direction. "I think my ma would like you," he said and smiled.

"Yeah? What makes you think so?"

"You got class. Ma always wanted me to find somebody classy."

"That was a studio invention," I said, trying to cover up my bitterness.

"No, you are. Classy, I mean."

"I'm an average girl. I happened to go to Hollywood and get lucky for a few years. They gave me some money and some pretty clothes to wear. That's it. I'm no different, no classier than anyone else."

"Well, ya are to me." He was quiet for a moment. "I gotta friend went out to Hollywood. Says you got sun pretty much all day twelve months of the year," he said. "I'd move out there myself and try flickers, 'cept ma would miss me too much. I'd hear her in my head constantly—'Teddy, you broke my heart. Teddy, you're too far away. Teddy, you were so thin in your last picture. Are you *eating*, Teddy?'"

I laughed. "Sounds like our mothers would get along great. Except mine won't let me eat anything. She used to monitor every morsel." I held up a bite of the cranberry pudding I'd ordered for dessert. "You have no idea how naughty I feel right now."

His eyebrows lifted.

"Does that extend to anything else, or only what you eat?" he asked.

"What do you mean?"

"Well, you and George O'Brien were an item for a long time. I didn't know if..."

I sighed. "I loved George, but we drifted apart. *Sunrise* was it for us, but it took me two years to realize it."

Teddy nodded. "I know I don't measure up in the muscles department, but you've probably guessed I'm a little crazy about ya already."

"You're very sweet," I said. He was a little rough around the edges, but he seemed nice enough.

The orchestra broke into the first few bars of "I Never Knew How Wonderful You Were," and Teddy cocked his head toward the bandstand. I smiled and set my napkin on the table. He took my hand and led me to the parquet dance floor. The restaurant was decorated in red and green Christmas finery, and when I lowered my head to his chest, I felt stirrings of something I hadn't experienced since George. The music was soft and romantic, and with his arms around my waist, I dared to hope again.

As we finished our dance and stepped back toward our table, Teddy pointed up at a sprig of mistletoe that hung above us. I offered my cheek for a sweet peck, but he turned the kiss into something far more passionate, more forceful. It took my breath away. In a good way.

Teddy was attentive. He took me to the Follies and the Scandals, and we went for walks in Central Park and to dinner at the White Swan and Henri's. For a late Christmas gift, he bought me a bracelet of small ruby charms.

I worked on my cooking skills since I was long out of practice, making pork chops with applesauce and baked potatoes for dinner when I had him over, but he had to hide his annoyance. It was then that he confided that his name wasn't actually Stewart, it was Spector.

"You're Jewish?" I asked. "Why did you tell me your name was Stewart?"

"Goys like buying stocks from udder goys, so I use it as my professional name. You gotta problem with it?"

"Well, no, but I wish you'd been honest from the beginning."

"So you could throw me over for some Mick like O'Brien?"

"I wouldn't do that. Half the people in Hollywood are Jewish. My mother might have a problem with it, but I don't."

When spring arrived, we drove up to the Catskills, where we stayed at a hotel called Grossinger's. Everyone thought I was Jewish because I blended right in. At my insistence, we got separate rooms. Teddy was a gentleman, but I could tell he wanted more. He also had a favorite inn where he stayed in Atlantic City, so we took a long Easter weekend and drove down there too.

Our kisses went from sweet and romantic to passionate to

smoldering, and I knew it wouldn't be long before he'd expect me to let him make love to me. I was terrified. George had been an altar boy, but Teddy had been around. I wasn't sure I was ready.

JERSEY BOUNCE

CHAPTER NINETEEN

GYPSY TEA KETTLE, 435 FIFTH AVENUE, MANHATTAN, NEW YORK, *March 27, 1931*

"Come on, Ollie, tell us all about him!" said Betty Blythe, leaning forward eagerly.

"Tall, dark and handsome. What more do you need to know?" replied Ruth Roland.

"Might be enough for you, but I need more details than that," piped up Claire Windsor. "I don't care if the guy is a matinée idol. Once you have to pick up the same pair of dirty socks off the bedroom rug every week, it gets old fast, believe me."

Claire and Bert Lytell had been divorced for four years.

"Hasn't kept you from sampling the goods that are out there though," Anna May Wong noted with sarcasm.

"Don't knock it," Claire tossed out. "Whose business is it anyway?"

"Their wives?" Anna May retorted.

Claire stuck her tongue out as the waiter came to take our orders.

The Gypsy Tea Kettle was a Romani dream plunked down right on Fifth Avenue at West 39th Street. The mint-green upholstered booths and chairs, red accents and giant wall mural of a pastoral scene provided a perfect backdrop for the tea leaf readings and the quartet in the corner playing fiddle, bass, viola, and cimbalom. The five of us had agreed to get together for dinner while we were all in town.

That evening, Ruth and I had starred in a radio program for WEAF that was broadcast from the *Leviathan*, a ship moored at a slip on the North River. Claire was in town making personal appearances, and Anna May had finished her run in *On the Spot* at the Forrest, where she'd taken the role I'd turned down.

We ordered goulash, stuffed peppers, and a Hungarian mixed grill to split. Another thing about the Tea Kettle was that prices were cheap enough for fading actresses to enjoy a fun night out.

All of us were looking at the twilight of our years in film. Anna May had broken ground as the first Chinese-American actress, Ruth had been a queen of serials, Betty's scandalous costume in *The Queen of Sheba* had set tongues wagging nationwide, and Claire had made a career out of playing hoity-toity society girls. Then there was me, the lingerie queen, who'd had more fur coats than all of them. Those fur coats were now at a furrier in Los Angeles, ready to start a second life in someone else's closet.

"I'd still like to know more about the guy," Betty said.

I giggled. "He's very attentive. Remember how I told you George dove into his time with Murnau and I barely saw him after that? How he took his parents to Europe without me? Teddy's not like that. He pays me lots of attention, he's sweet, and..."

"And?" Anna May said, urging me on. She grabbed a

breadstick from the basket and nibbled it with amusement while comically arching an eyebrow.

"He's wonderful in other ways," I said, smiling and blushing. Teddy hadn't been improper, but he'd made me want him to be.

"Marry him!" hooted Ruth. "If he's wonderful in the sack, that means he's generous in other ways too. If he's a selfish lover, then he's a terrible human being. *Fact.*"

"That's the most ridiculous thing I've ever heard," Anna May said, gesturing with her breadstick "A great lover does *not* indicate a great person. Some men have had more experience. That's all."

The waiter brought our food, and we tucked in. Seventy-five cents for all-you-can-eat during these lean days was a steal, especially when you added in the tea leaf reading at the end. We were eager to find out what our futures held.

One of the designated readers for the evening stopped by our table. She wore her hair up in a plum paisley turban, and she wore a billowy blouse and skirt of the same color. "I am Madame Fazenti," she said in a thick Eastern European accent. "Who vill be forst?"

I was eager to see what would happen with Teddy, but I let the other girls go before me. Taking Claire's cup first, Madame Fazenti upended it over the saucer and examined the result carefully, turning to view it from every direction. Then she peered at Claire.

"The leaves say that love has been difficult for you and will continue the same. It may cost you a great deal of money," Madame Fazenti said, as Claire frowned. She placed the cup in its saucer and handed it back to Claire, then moved onto

Betty, upending the cup and smiling at the results.

"You sing like a bird," she deduced. Betty grinned. When she was younger, she'd done vaudeville billed as "The California Nightingale," but she'd lost her money in the stock market and was trying to bounce back. "Your marriage will be a happy one." She set Betty's cup aside.

Taking Anna May's cup, Madame Fazenti looked at it from multiple angles. "Your ancestry calls to you. You will go on a long voyage, but the thing you most desire eludes you." Anna May looked intrigued and signaled to the waiter for another pot of tea.

Madame Fazenti then took Ruth's cup and was barely able to glance at it before shuddering and setting it down

"What is it?" Ruth said.

"So many owls," Madame Fazenti said.

"What the heck does an owl mean?" Ruth asked.

"Sickness. Poverty. Bad luck. Your cup does not bode well, my dear. I'm very sorry."

Anna May put an arm around Ruth. "Come on, honey. Cheer up. Most of this mumbo-jumbo stuff is for the birds anyway."

Madame Fazenti shot her a glare.

"Easy for you to say," Ruth said. She leaned back in her chair, dejected. "You're going on a long voyage. I have all owls."

"Everybody knows it's all malarkey, Ruthie," Betty said, taking her hand across the table.

Madame Fazenti impatiently gestured at me to hand her my cup, which. I did. She wiggled it, dumped the dregs onto the saucer, then peered into it.

"For you, I see—"

"Excuse me, ladies," said the maitre d' as he approached our table. "I hate to disturb you, but there's a telephone call for you, Miss Borden. It's an emergency."

Imagining Momma in the hospital, I followed him to the maitre d' stand, and to my surprise, there stood Teddy instead. The maitre d' looked embarrassed that he'd helped with the ruse.

"Teddy, what are you doing here?" I asked. "I'm out with my friends. I told you."

"I know," Teddy said. "But I couldn't wait, honey." He pulled out a massive pear-shaped diamond in a silver setting, and I gasped at it. "It's an emergency. Marry me. Right now."

I lowered my voice. "Teddy, have you lost your mind? It's too soon. We've only known each other a few months. Not half as long as we should. I can't leave my friends."

"Sure you can. Love makes people do crazy things all the time. I love you. That's all that matters."

"No, it's not. There are practical things to worry about. Where will we live? I'm no housewife."

"You can't live without me," he said with a leer.

I rolled my eyes. "Yeah, I'll throw myself out a fourth floor window if you don't marry me," I said sarcastically.

"I was thinking we could get out of the city," Teddy said, nuzzling my neck and trailing kisses down it. "I've got a friend at the clerk's office in Greenwich."

"I don't even know where that is."

"Connecticut, right over the state line."

My brain now firmly engaged, I considered his proposal. First of all, there was the financial aspect. How dependable were stocks since the crash? Could I retire and relax for a change? Or was this taking a huge risk? I loved him, but Paterson was nowhere to live. Second, if I eloped, would I ever hear the end of it from Momma? That suddenly looked attractive—doing something Momma would hate—something unexpected and impetuous. I let myself be convinced.

"I want a maid and a cook," I said. In addition to having my standard of living back, the main thing I cared about right now was for George to read about the marriage in the paper. The wedding didn't need to be big, but the announcement did. It needed to say 'I'm over you, buddy. Here's the big kiss-off.' "I want a nice announcement though, syndicated, in my dress. Three columns worth, like the society girls get."

"We won't have time, honey. Let's elope. Right now. Let's be rash and impulsive."

"But Teddy, I want the white dress and the train, and the gifts…"

"Think about that," he said. "If we have a big wedding, your mother will want to be there. My mother too. Your mother and my mother in the same place at the same time? The world might never recover."

So much for my three-column announcement.

"That stuff ain't important," Teddy continued. "It's how we feel about each other that counts, right?"

He took my hands and looked at me, all cock-eyed and besotted, and I couldn't very well say no. My life was my own at last, and I would be Mrs. Teddy Stewart. Er…Spector.

"All right, Teddy. I'll marry you," I said. He placed the ring on my right hand until we got where we were going.

He planted kisses all over my face from my forehead to the tip of my nose as the maitre d' chuckled.

"I'm the luckiest sonofabitch alive," Teddy said.

"I won't be a minute," I said. I dashed back to my table, where the girls still sat. Madame Fazenti had moved onto the next group and was looking into a new cup. Claire was having a second reading with a different woman in an emerald green turban, and it didn't appear to be going any better than the first. I gathered up my things, and Anna May was the first to speak.

"What is it? Is it Sibbie?"

I laughed. "No, Momma's fine. It's Teddy. He's *here*!" I held out my hand so they could see the ring.

"Congratulations!" Betty said.

"I have to go," I said. "We're eloping!"

Claire was still involved in her reading, and Ruth was a million miles away, with a vacant expression on her face. But they both turned at my words. Squealing, the girls surrounded me, and all gave me quick hugs before I hurried out the door and down to Teddy's Buick, parked at the curb.

Teddy fired it up, drove to my place, then waited as I dashed inside and packed a quick overnight bag. When we got to Greenwich later that night, Teddy found a large Victorian home near the courthouse with a sign:

ROOMS, $1.00 A NIGHT

Teddy went in for a few minutes, then came back to the car to get his bag. "Come on. I told 'em we just got hitched. Move the ring to your other hand."

"Teddy, isn't it bad luck to—"

"Do it, would ya? It's for five minutes tonight. Then we'll be official."

I did, but the minute we got into the room, I put it back on my right hand, not wanting to tempt fate.

We woke bright and early, and I dressed in the cream frock and cloche that I'd brought along. It wasn't the beautiful white silk with veil and train that I'd hoped for, but it would have to do. Teddy wore his gray pin-striped suit and spats. At eight a.m. on the dot, we pulled up in front of city hall and found the office that issued marriage licenses.

"Harry!" Teddy said, glad-handing the clerk at the counter, who had a weak chin, a pockmarked complexion, and a green eyeshade.

"Teddy!" said the surprised fellow, taking the proffered hand. "What are you doing here?"

"Harry Stein, may I introduce my blushing bride, Miss Olive Borden. Olive, this is Harry. We went to Hebrew school together."

"Blushing bride? Olive Borden? Mazel tov! Congratulations!" Harry said, shaking Teddy's hand and giving me a big smile.

"Well, *future* blushing bride," Teddy qualified. "You remember when you said to look you up if I needed anything? Well, I need something. Olive and I want to get married with a minimum of fuss."

Harry's smile faded. "Have you moved then, Teddy? From Paterson?"

"Nah, still there, but Olive doesn't want to leave the city."

"Sorry, pal. I can't help you. We've got a five-day residency requirement. I can't get around it, unfortunately. They caught me ignoring it a month ago, so now they check every new license I issue. I'm in real hot water."

So much for our plan.

"Come on Harry. You could do it for me, couldn't ya? Ole pal, ole buddy?"

"Teddy, I got this job after being outta work for almost two years. Nothing personal, but I wanna keep it. You'll have to figure something else out."

I sighed and tugged Teddy's sleeve. "Come on, honey. We'll find someplace else."

Harry snapped his fingers. "I know the place. Little town called Harrison right over the state line. There's a fellow there they call the marrying clerk. Name's Bill Wilding. All the Broadway stars go see him. He'll get you in, any time of day or night! Take Route 1 back that way, go past Port Chester, and immediately after Rye, make the turn onto Harrison Avenue, then right at Calvert. Can't miss it."

Teddy's face brightened as he shepherded me toward the door. "Thanks, Harry!" he called back.

We tramped back to the car through the melted snow and mud and Teddy hopped onto Route 1 back toward Rye.

We pulled off at the sign for Harrison Village and steered toward the center of town, looking for something that resembled a government building. The little hamlet was cozy—the type of place for housewives to beat rugs over clotheslines in backyards and pack jars full of preserved apples and pears. I imagined plump children playing tag on lush green lawns and executives making the trip into the city to any jobs that still remained.

"It looks nice," I said. "Homey."

Teddy pulled up in front of town hall, and we went inside, our steps echoing over the marble floor.

"We're looking for the marrying clerk," Teddy said. "We'd

like to get married today." He removed his hat and leaned over the counter, flashing his dark eyes at the bosomy clerk seated at a large Remington typewriter.

"Certainly," the woman said. "I believe he can squeeze you in." She crossed to the door, said a few words to the person inside, and in a moment, she was back. "Go right in."

The sign on the man's counter said William A. Wilding. He was in his mid-50s, with a protuberant nose and big ears. His eyebrows were unkempt and threatened to take over his face. He had us fill out a form, then he entered the information we gave him into a large registry book. Once the license was issued, Teddy leaned over the counter.

"Hey mister, do ya know a good judge you can send us to?"

"I certainly do. Try Winfred Allen. He works from his home. Fifty-four Muchmore Road. Make a left from here and follow 127. You'll see the sign on the left."

Before we left the town center, Teddy stopped at a flower shop and gallantly presented me with a corsage of orange blossom and fern, which he pinned to my dress. He did the same for his matching boutonnière.

We followed the clerk's instructions and rang the bell at 54 Muchmore, which appeared to have an office annex out back. Judge Allen's wife welcomed us in and offered us tea and cake. The judge himself was in his mid 40s, with ice blue eyes and graying brown hair with a balding patch. He donned a simple black robe over his suit and opened his book.

"Do you have any witnesses?" he asked.

I bit my lip. In all the confusion, we'd forgotten.

"Sorry, we don't. Is that a problem?" Teddy said.

"We're prepared for any eventuality here," the judge said

with a chuckle. "Claudia, could you come back in here? And grab Freddie, if you would."

When Teddy raised an eyebrow, Allen chuckled. "My clerk and my page. They're used to it."

Teddy and I laughed nervously as a boyish-looking man of about thirty entered, along with the woman who'd been typing outside his office.

Justice Allen read over our license. Then, as he consulted it, he gently pushed us closer together and had us hold hands.

"Do you, Theodore Irving Spector, take this woman, Olive Borden, to be your lawful wedded wife? To have and to hold, for richer for poorer, in sickness and health, til death do you part?"

"I sure do."

"And do you, Olive Borden, take this man, Theodore Irving Spector, to be your lawful wedded husband? To have and to hold, for richer for poorer, in sickness and health, til death do you part?"

"I do," I said.

"Then by the power vested in me by the state of New York, I do hereby pronounce you husband and wife. You may kiss the bride," said Justice Allen.

Teddy took the opportunity to gently slip his tongue into my mouth. His little joke. Then he slipped Judge Allen something too. A ten-dollar bill. To which the judge smiled and folded the bill into his vest pocket.

"Come on, dollface," Teddy said. "We've got a honeymoon to start."

CHAPTER TWENTY

54 MUCHMORE ROAD, HARRISON, NEW YORK,
March 28, 1931

"I need to get changed out of these clothes," I said. "I'm rumpled."

Teddy grabbed my hand and led me back to the Buick. "Oh, I'll get you out of those clothes, all right," he said with a pointed leer.

"I'll need to call everyone to apologize for last night. I hope they're not too upset."

"You showed em the rock, right?"

"Yes, but you have to admit it was awfully rude to kidnap me away like that," I said.

"Hey, we're married now. You're my *wife*. I call the shots now, and your friends will have to get used to it."

I sat silent as we returned to the inn. Teddy didn't carry me over the threshold, as I'd always imagined my new husband doing. Instead, he laughed. "Nobody really believes that dreck, do they?" he asked when I frowned. He opened the door and followed me in.

"It's a fun tradition, that's all," I said.

"Might be fun for you. My back says otherwise. Sorry, baby," he said.

"Don't call me baby. I told you," I said, irritated. This was a fine how-do-you-do on our wedding day. A tiff already.

"C'mon, let's kiss and make up. I been thinking about this all day. I wanted it to be perfect." He patted the bed next to him.

"Me too," I said, now realizing it wouldn't be, however I looked at it. I started to tremble, and my teeth chattered. Suddenly, I was freezing, and couldn't seem to get warm.

Teddy knelt at my feet.

"It's a little too late to propose the romantic way," I said.

"Shhhhhh..." he said. He slipped off my shoes, then his hands traveled up my legs to the hooks on my stockings. Deftly, he popped them and began sliding them down, one leg at a time. And when that was done, one hand moved back up to the juncture between my thighs.

My breath caught, and I closed my eyes. This was really going to happen, and I wasn't sure if I was ready for it. Teddy's other hand slowly tugged the hem of my skirt until it was up around my waist. He pulled my dress over my head, then lay me down on the bed and began kissing me.

His kisses had always made me a little silly. They made my brain shut off and my heart do little cartwheels, but now he frightened me. George had always been tender and sweet and respectful. But this wasn't like that.

With one hand, Teddy kneaded a breast, rapidly fingering a nipple. I gasped at how good it felt, and when I did, he slid his tongue into my mouth. He took a moment to yank off my step-ins and chemise, and slid two of his fingers into me. Now I knew what Momma had been trying to protect me from all those years. My body lit up, suddenly nothing but a mass of raw nerve endings.

"You're all I've been able to think about for days," he muttered. He moved his hand from my breast and roughly pulled my hand down, making me grip his erection.

"Teddy, I..." I tried saying.

"Take it out," he whispered, his voice a barely there rasp.

I tugged down his suspenders and unfastened his trousers, then I tried doing what he said with my clumsy, beginner's hand. When he pulled down his drawers, I stared in shock, too afraid to touch the thing that was lying there.

"You sure you were an actress? I thought for sure you'd know what to do." He sounded disappointed.

He grabbed my hand and moved it back and forth, showing me what he wanted, then, still half-dressed, he battered into me so roughly that my virginity, for so long a moot topic between George and me, became a relic. It hurt so much. I moaned, and tears slipped into my ears as he kept at me for what seemed like a good twenty minutes. Actually, not a *good* twenty minutes—more like the most awful twenty minutes I'd ever spent. That included typhoid in the desert, my appendectomy, being dragged by Rawhide the horse, and kissing Jack Pickford in *Gang War* after he'd eaten onions for lunch.

When he was done, Teddy at last heaved a long sigh and collapsed on top of me before rolling to one side. Sweat slicked both of our bodies. I wasn't sure if I was supposed to be feeling anything more. Something was missing for me.

"That was terrific, honey," he said.

I pulled the sheet up and rolled over with my back to him, feeling miserable.

I didn't say anything, but I could feel him behind me, the remnants of his erection pressed against my back.

"What is it?" he said. Wasn't it good for you?"

"I was a virgin," I whispered. "It hurt."

Teddy burst out laughing. "A virgin? You gotta be kidding. You can't tell me that you and O'Brien never..."

"No, we never did. We thought about it plenty of times, but we were Catholic. George wanted to wait until we were married. It would have killed both our careers if I..."

"His loss, my gain and all that." Teddy said blithely, moving away and lighting a cigarette. "What a sap."

I quaked silently, trying to hold in the sobs. It was too late now.

"Cheer up," Teddy said, giving my derriere a playful smack. "It gets better."

It didn't. For as much as I'd enjoyed kissing and hugging George and Teddy and thinking how wonderful making love had sounded, sex left me cold. Teddy was always at me, day and night, pawing me and saying how his friends couldn't believe he was married to a movie star. The one that wore all the lingerie. The one with the melon tits and perfect ass.

It became my constant refrain: "Teddy, please not tonight. I have a pounding headache."

"You said that Monday night too," he'd say with a pout.

"Well, it's true."

"This is better than headache powder. It's therapeutic," he'd mutter, continuing his caresses.

"Teddy, no, please..."

In the end, I'd simply lay there, waiting for him to finish, as I had every other time. I desperately looked for work, because the only relief I got was when I was rehearsing. I douched with Lysol like Margaret Sanger's booklet instructed, and I prayed a lot. I loved kids, and I'd wanted a houseful, but I'd wanted them with George. With Teddy, I dreaded the thought.

At last, I found a job. *Moonlight and Cactus* was a short for Educational Films, one of the lowest on the studio rungs. Tom Patricola and Charles Judels starred with me, and Roscoe Arbuckle was directing it.

Poor Roscoe Arbuckle. He'd had his career killed by a horrible lie branding him a rapist and murderer, and now, like me, he was scavenging work wherever he could get it. In his case, he couldn't even use his own name in the credits. He was using an alias, William Goodrich.

Roscoe and I couldn't help but reminisce about the old days. He didn't really direct per se, considering what I'd been used to with John Ford or John Blystone. Roscoe might point to something and calmly make suggestions, but he looked sad and sick. He'd lost so much weight, and he was very pale. Anytime I started feeling sorry for myself, I looked at Roscoe and I didn't feel so bad anymore.

Commuting from Paterson was awful, but I was still acting, and that was what counted. If we'd had two cars, I could have taken the tunnel, but we didn't. The ferry cost was the price for keeping Teddy away from me. At times I would get a hotel room in the city overnight and it was like a vacation. My remaining furniture had made the move east, but it looked very out of place in the suburbs.

On the one hand, Teddy liked the extra income and he loved showing me off to all his friends so he could brag that he was married to an actress. On the other hand, he didn't actually like me working in my chosen profession because he wanted his clothes clean, his house neat, and dinner ready when he got home at night, which wasn't always possible when shooting ran late. Who marries an actress, then gets angry when she acts?

I starred in a couple more shorts for Warner Brothers-Vitaphone. I also made personal appearances at various theaters around New York, New Jersey, and Connecticut. I'd do a little razzle-dazzle before a big film program, introduce it, then thank everyone for coming.

It wasn't much, but it was still my own money. Every time Teddy hassled me about earning it, I gritted my teeth and ignored him, returning to my laundry, my cooking, or my ironing. This marriage had been the biggest mistake of my life, but between trying to drum up work and the exhaustion of constantly fending him off, I let it go on far too long.

A year after we tied the knot, I found a lace-edged handkerchief in Teddy's pocket with the monogram **CM** and the scent of Violette Coquette. I finally had all the excuse I needed to leave, so one afternoon, while he was at work, I found a new apartment on Central Park South, not far from Carnegie Hall. I left him a note with my wedding ring and the culprit set neatly next to it.

Teddy-

Nice hankie. Not my initials, and not my perfume. Things have been going south all year, but this was the last straw. I've moved out. We're done. I'm filing for divorce.

—Olive

Then I spread the word around the theatrical grapevine that I was once again available and actively looking for work. I had to think about what to do next. Did I keep trying the stage or did I see if Hollywood had forgiven me yet?

WHY DON'T YOU DO RIGHT?

CHAPTER TWENTY~ONE

ESSEX HOUSE APARTMENTS, 160 CENTRAL PARK SOUTH, NEW YORK, NEW YORK, *April 25, 1932*

"**M**iss Borden!"

"Miss Borden! What do you have to say about the reports from Buffalo?"

I'd barely stepped out of the lobby on the way to the store when a horde of reporters swarmed around me outside the building. Flashbulbs popped in my face, but with the cacophony, I couldn't hear the questions they were asking.

"One at a time," I said. "I can't understand you."

Finally, one of the reporters in a loud plaid jacket and black fedora won by sheer volume. His voice was much stronger, and the others let him grab the glory for a moment.

"Miss Borden, Norman Hess of the *Buffalo Independent*. What do you have to say about the claim from Mrs. Pearl Spector of Buffalo suggesting that she is the actual legal spouse of Theodore Spector?"

"What?!" I turned toward Hess. He stood ready, pen and pad in hand. I felt faint. "I know nothing about this. Teddy told me he'd never been married before. I had no reason to doubt him."

Teddy, you sonofabitch. As if it wasn't hard enough to get my career back on track.

"Do you have any comments to make?" pushed one of the other reporters.

"No. No comment," I said. "Please excuse me." I hurried back inside the building and summoned the elevator, my mind racing. If it was true, that explained why he'd wanted to elope, with no big announcement.

Benjamin, the doorman, did a little double-take and chuckled. "Short outing," he said.

"I'll be staying in after all," I said. "Benjamin, no one is allowed up to my place right now. Is that understood?"

"Yes, Miss Borden."

The minute the doors opened on the fifth floor, I ran to my apartment and rushed to the telephone.

"Operator, Paterson, New Jersey, please. Eastside-4678."

"Hold one moment. I'll connect you," I was told.

Eventually, there was a click, and then ringing.

"Call from New York City," the operator said, then withdrew as Teddy picked up.

"Teddy, why are there *four* reporters outside my apartment, asking me why I'm married to a *BIGAMIST*?!"

He sighed. "Oh, you heard. Sorry about that. I figured Pearl would divorce me after I'd been gone a while. I didn't realize the stupid cow never filed the papers."

"So it's *her* fault you're not divorced? You married me knowing you were already *were*?! You told the clerk you'd never been married on the license! This could kill my career for good, you rotten bastard!"

"Oh shut up," he said. "You were crazy for me, remember?

'Teddy, I'd throw myself out a fourth-floor window without you.'"

"That was a joke and you know it," I said through clenched teeth. "You arrogant pr—"

"Careful, honey. Don't wanna say something you'll regret."

"That's impossible," I said. "You're a liar and a…a…" I reached for the perfect word, then realized how much Yiddish he'd already taught me. "A…*schmuck*!"

Momma had found a cheaper place out in Islip, and as usual, she could be counted on for phone calls, telling me she wondered what I'd been thinking, eloping with "that Jew."

May was a nightmare, with more newspaper stories being released and more reporters constantly camped outside my apartment building, waiting for a comment. I finally resorted to paying the neighbor lady's son to bring my food from the corner store.

"Thanks, Donny," I said, handing him a five for the $3.50 he'd spent.

"No sweat, Miss Borden. My ma had a friend in Hackensack whose fella tried this business with her. She said, 'Anything we can do to help, we will.'"

"Tell Iris she's a girl's best friend." I took the sack, shut the door, and began unpacking the groceries in the kitchen.

By the end of the month, I could at least leave the apartment with a redheaded wig on. On the twelfth, I'd traveled to White Plains, where Teddy had been indicted for the bigamy charge. Unfortunately, the first Mrs. Spector hadn't brought a photograph of *her* Teddy for the jury to compare to the picture of mine.

We tried again on the 27ᵗʰ. I'd hoped to avoid the newspapermen stationed in and around the entrance, but they still hounded me into the building. I ducked into the ladies room to avoid them. When I emerged, the constant murmurings in the corridor outside the courtroom alerted me to the arrival of Wife #1, and we sized each other up.

The newspapers had stated that Pearl Spector owned a beauty parlor in Buffalo, and it was evident from her geranium shade of nail lacquer to her dark auburn bob what Teddy had seen in her. Her hazel eyes had been artfully shaded with kohl pencil. She wore a deep green frock, matching dyed kid shoes and an emerald velvet beret with sheer veil. A fox stole was slung over her shoulder.

The beauty shop must be doing all right, I thought as we filed into the courtroom.

"Oye oye oye, this Grand Jury is convened," the bailiff said, and the crowd noise quieted.

The District Attorney, Frank Coyne, stood straight and tall next to the prosecution table. He had a head like a half-eaten apple—irregularly-shaped and balding, and his full lips were set in a determined line.

"The prosecution calls Mrs. Pearl Spector to the stand," Coyne said.

Pearl Spector rose from her seat and calmly crossed the room to the witness box. The bailiff approached with the bible.

"State your full name for the record."

"Pauline Haworth Spector." She looked coolly across the room at me. I looked down at my bag and gloves in my lap. I still couldn't believe I was here.

"Do you swear to tell the truth, the whole truth and nothing but the truth so help you God?" the bailiff asked.

"I do."

"Please be seated."

Pearl sat down with care, obviously trying not to wrinkle her frock.

"Mrs. Spector, you are married to the defendant, Theodore Spector?"

"I am, yes."

"When and where were you married?"

"In Buffalo, New York, April the sixth of 1919. I was originally engaged to a boy in the AEF in France, but Teddy swept me off my feet."

"Did you and Mr. Spector spend the last fourteen years together?"

"No, sir, we didn't. Teddy was arrested for grand larceny a week after the wedding."

And here I thought it couldn't get any worse. He's already a criminal in addition to being a bigamist?! I dropped my head into my hand and the pattern of the polished marble floor spun crazily before my eyes. I was sure I would pass out.

"Grand larceny? Could you explain?"

"Teddy stole some stuff from Hengerer's, and I was arrested too, as a...what do you call it."

"An accessory?"

"Yeah, an accessory. I was nineteen. We were married for *a month* before he had to go to prison. Then, when he got out, Teddy left me." Pearl pulled out a handkerchief that had been tucked in her sleeve. "I stuck by him while he was in the joint, but he told me I was too young and immature for him. I'm not sure what else he expected from a nineteen year old."

The gallery tittered.

"Do you remember his exact words?" Coyne asked.

He said, "I've got plenty of brains, and I'm not going to waste them futzing around here."

Murmurs swept through the crowd.

Plenty of brains my sweet patoot, I thought.

"My father told me that Teddy was a bum, and that he'd make my life misery," Pearl continued. "Turns out he was right."

"How did you become aware of Mr. Spector's other marriage?"

"Well, it was in all the papers, wasn't it? I was reading the *Bee* back in April, and there was a story about how Olive Borden, the big Hollywood actress, was divorcing Theodore Spector, a stockbroker from Paterson, New Jersey. I was horrified."

"Why was this such a shock to you?" Coyne continued.

"I figured there couldn't be *that* many Theodore Spectors from Paterson who were stockbrokers. I'd never divorced Teddy, and I certainly never received any papers from him to sign either."

"Meaning you were still married."

"Yes sir, we were still married. I also found out from someone else in town that they'd seen Teddy out with a *third* woman."

The gasps in the courtroom were audible.

"How did you *know* the man in question was your husband, Teddy Spector? Certainly, in New York it might be seen as a common name."

"Because my Teddy *also* uses the last name of Stewart, as this one does," she said.

Coyne looked confused. "Why does he do that?"

"When he meets clients who aren't Jewish, he tries to sound like a Gentile," Pearl said. "Finally one article had a picture of him. Same guy, *my* Teddy.

There were more gasps. Coyne nodded. "Have you brought a photograph to identify Mr. Spector for us?"

"I have."

Pearl produced a photograph of Teddy from her bag and held it up, showing his ersatz charm and dimples. It was handed to the jury members to inspect, and eventually Pearl was dismissed from the witness box. Then it was my turn.

"The state calls Olive Borden to the stand."

I crossed the room on shaking legs and when I reached the witness box, the bailiff produced the bible and I put my hand on it.

"Do you swear to tell the truth, the whole truth and nothing but the truth so help you God?"

"I do."

I was allowed to be seated, and Coyne approached me, his polished oxfords clicking over the marble floor.

"Miss Borden, can you tell us how you met the defendant?"

"He introduced himself outside the Brandt's Boulevard Theatre in Queens two years ago when I was appearing in a play there."

"What happened then?"

"He took me to dinner, and he courted me relentlessly."

"Relentlessly. That's an interesting word choice."

"It's true. He brought me flowers and candy, and he

whispered sweet nothings."

"When did you decide to marry?"

"I didn't really *decide* to marry. Teddy practically kid-napped me."

The courtroom buzz got louder as the outrage gained steam.

"Please tell us more about that."

"I was out to dinner with some friends. Teddy had known where I was going, so he came and found me and made me leave with him in his car. He said we were getting married."

"And Mr. Spector had represented himself to you as a single gentleman?"

"He's hardly a gentleman, but he said he was single, yes. I had no reason to question it."

That drew laughs from the spectators.

"So you eloped. Tell us about that." He leaned against the witness box, looking casual and congenial.

"First we went to Greenwich, where he had a friend at the records office. But we were refused because of the residency requirement there, so we went to Harrison, to the justice of the peace."

"Harrison, New York?"

"Yes, sir."

"And Mr. Spector represented himself as single on your marriage license as well. Is that correct?"

"Yes, sir."

"Thank you, Miss Borden. This witness is dismissed," Coyne said. "The prosecution calls Winfred Allen to the stand."

The Justice of the Peace who married Teddy and me strode to the stand and was walked through the oath by the bailiff.

"State your name for the record."

"Winfred C. Allen, sir."

"And your profession?"

"I am a justice of the peace in the village of Harrison, New York."

"Mr. Allen, were you presiding on March 28, 1931?"

"I was."

"Please tell the court what happened on that day."

"A couple came in around ten a.m. A rather striking couple—both dark-haired and dark eyed and dressed in their best. He wore a gray pin-striped suit, fedora and spats. She wore a cream-colored ensemble and a corsage. What one would expect for tying the knot."

"Do you recognize the woman in this courtroom?"

"I do. That's her right there." He pointed at me.

"And the man?"

"I don't see him," Allen said, surveying the crowd.

Coyne approached the prosecution table and slipped the photograph out of its folder. He held it up for the court.

"I have here Peoples' Exhibit A, which has been entered into the record as a photograph of Theodore Spector, the defendant. Can you confirm that this is the man whom you married to Miss Borden?" He set it on the rail of the witness box.

"That's him all right."

"Thank you, Mr. Allen. No further questions. This witness may be seated," said Coyne. "Next, the prosecution calls William Wilding to the stand."

The man walked to the witness box, raised his hand, and took the oath.

"Please state your name for the record."

Wilding gave it.

"Mr. Wilding, what is your occupation?" Coyne casually placed his hands on the witness box.

"I'm the town clerk in Harrison, New York."

"And did you hold that position on March 28, 1931?"

"I did."

"Did you witness Mr. Spector signing the marriage license?"

"Yes, sir."

"And what did he state on it for his marriage status?"

"In the entry blank for Number of Proposed Marriage, he answered 'first.'"

Coyne placed the photograph in front of him.

"Is this is the man you saw?"

He glanced down at the rail. "Yes, sir."

"Thank you, no further questions. The witness is excused."

Wilding stepped down, and the state wrapped up their case around one p.m. The grand jury voted to indict.

I hope they throw the book at you, you bastard, I thought.

Outside the courtroom, I chatted with my attorney, Fred Boehm, and several newspapermen, while Pearl Spector attracted another set of reporters nearby. It was strange to see her getting more press than me, but as the wronged wife #1, this party was all hers, and I was happy not to be the center of attention at last. Nobody wanted to hear from "the other woman." I was scarlet to the public now.

"I've said it before, and I'll say it again," she stated. "He was a tall, good-looking brute. Six feet, dark and handsome. I fell for him like a ton of bricks. But now I'm through with him. He certainly had a wonderful line."

Had to agree with her there. The reporters rushed off to

file their scoops, leaving Pearl standing alone in the hallway after her attorney said his farewell.

"Coming, Olive?" Boehm asked me.

"One minute," I said. "There's something I have to do."

He frowned as I thrust my shoulders back and crossed that endless expanse of floor. I needed to make amends. Pearl's face went from resentful and angry to amused at my approach. I don't think she knew how to react.

"I don't know if I should call you Mrs. Spector, considering the circumstances and all," I said.

She gave me a wry smile. "Pearl is fine."

"I'm so sorry," I said. "I honestly didn't know about any of this. I'm so furious at him. I...I...I have no words." I shook my head.

"Don't feel bad, honey," she said. "I was young and stupid, and you were gullible. He fed us *both* a line of horse hockey. He wants to get into someone's drawers bad enough, he'll do it again."

I tried to keep myself from laughing. She was right. "How do you figure out what to say at a time like this?" I said.

"You don't," she reassured me. "I still have to call you as a respondent and all, but to show there's no hard feelings, if you get out Buffalo way, come by the shop and I'll give you a free treatment. Color, marcel, haircut, the works."

"That's so generous," I said. "Thank you."

Pearl shrugged and nudged me. "I always intended on divorcing the bastard anyway, but I never got around to it. I couldn't *buy* publicity like this!"

I chuckled in spite of myself.

"I gotta go catch my train," she said, slinging her fox stole tighter around her neck. "But remember, whatever you want. The Rouge Box on Genesee Street. It's on the house."

"Thanks again!" I called after her.

Pearl gave me a wave and kept walking.

Not long after, Teddy was found and hauled to the jail in White Plains for bigamy.

CHAPTER TWENTY-TWO

OFFICE OF DR. GEORGE KOZMAK, GRAMERCY PARK, MANHATTAN, NEW YORK, *August 1932*

"Congratulations, Mrs. Smith!"

Uh-oh. This couldn't be happening.

The doctor removed the earpieces of the stethoscope from his ears and let it hang. His nurse stood by, shaking down a thermometer. She watched me closely. I'd given them a fake name because I'd feared the worst.

"You've been nauseated because you're going to have a baby. You're about three and a half months along, I suspect."

"I can't be pregnant," I said, feeling like I'd eaten a pound of pig iron. I'd tried to be so careful. I'd signed on to star with James Rennie in *The Divorce Racket* for Paradise Pictures, a little shoestring outfit. Considering my impending annulment from Teddy *and* the fact that Pearl's divorce still wasn't official, this was the worst news possible.

"Indeed you are. Make sure you're eating a very healthy diet. Plenty of fruits and vegetables and iron-rich red meat. The little fella will need lots of nutrients to make him strong."

The doctor grinned like a fool. Men were such idiots. No idea how they could ruin a woman's life in only a few minutes.

I wasn't in the papers as often anymore, so I wasn't as recognizable as I once was, but I was still fodder for the gossip columnists. After the bigamy business, I could only imagine what Norbert Lusk would do with this tidbit.

The room started spinning out of control, and it seemed a sure bet that the doctor's white smock would soon be covered in my lunch.

"Mrs. Smith, you look a little pale. Did anyone tell you that you look like that actress? What was her name..." he snapped his fingers. "Olive Borden!"

"I get that a lot," I said.

Dr. Kozmak sent me on my way with the caution that I was eating for two, and my mind raced. Every thought brought me back to the same eventuality. I couldn't go back to Teddy, and I couldn't give up what was left of my career. A baby was the world's biggest monkey wrench right now. Sheer panic set in. As I made my way to the exit, the nurse from the examining room approached me and slipped me a piece of paper.

"I saw the look on your face," she whispered. "If you need help, phone this number." We locked eyes, and I felt a little hope. She was offering me a way out.

In the cab, I pulled out the paper and stared at it. When I got home, I took a chance and called. An older-sounding woman answered.

"Hello. I got this number from a nurse at my doctor's office," I said.

"Which doctor?"

"Kozmak," I said.

"You have money?" The woman said. "It's fifty dollars."

I tried not to audibly gulp, and mentally inventoried the

money I'd squirreled away while I was with Teddy and the few jewels I had remaining. I'd be left with very little but the ability to move past this ridiculous marriage and the continuous chorus of Momma repeating, "I told you so," but I'd be free. If I lived through it.

"Fine," I said.

"Take a cab to 2746 Ocean Avenue, Brooklyn. Then lose the phone number. Tell the cab to leave. We'll call another to take you home. Bring the dough, tomorrow, one o'clock."

"Yes, thank you."

Click.

2746 OCEAN AVENUE, BROOKLYN, NEW YORK,
August 12, 1932

The house was a two-story Cape Cod with faded blue paint and a sagging front porch. I had the cab drop me around the corner and hurried to the entrance, where I knocked twice.

A matronly woman in a flowered navy dress with an apron and black lace-up oxfords answered the door. She gave me an up and down glance, and her eyes behind numont glasses darted back and forth suspiciously. She stood aside to let me in, quickly shutting the door behind me.

"Anyone with you?"

"No," I said. "I came alone."

"Fifty dollars," she said.

I reached into my bag and pulled out the money. She

snatched it and counted it in front of me, then shoved the bills into the pocket of her apron.

"Sit down. He'll be ready in a minute." She pointed to a hideous tan couch. I sank down onto it, nervously looking around. The walls were covered in badly painted amateur landscapes, and a sad side table was the only other furniture.

In five minutes, the woman was back. She led me to another room. In it was a rectangular dining table with a leaf opened for extra real estate. The linoleum below it looked grungy and caked with something I didn't want to try to identify. There was also a large tin bucket in the corner full of God knew what. I shivered and turned back to her. Despite the heat, I was suddenly freezing and couldn't stop shaking.

"Take off your stockings and underwear. Dress too if you don't want anything on it. Put that over you." She pointed to a sheet that might have been white once. Only God knew how many women had used it before me. "Hurry up. We're on a schedule here."

She retreated and closed the door behind her, leaving me alone in the sweltering room. I quickly pulled my dress over my head and folded it up on a chair in the corner. Then I wrapped the sheet around me before unhooking my garters and slipping off my underwear. I sat on the table and shivered until a man entered the room. He wore a gray smock and dark trousers, but I noticed with alarm that the front of the smock was covered with rust-colored stains. My stomach roiled and I closed my eyes.

"Lay back and put your legs up."

I lay back, but there was no room to put my legs.

"Scoot forward on the table."

I did, then lay back again, bending my legs and looking up at the single bare bulb above me.

"Relax," he said.

That won't happen.

I heard him making plenty of noise as he readied his equipment, and he shoved something into me. I clenched my fists and grimaced as what felt like tubing went further and further in. It felt like it would come out my throat. Then he twisted it and manipulated it inside me for a few minutes. It hurt like the dickens.

All those years of Catholicism up in smoke. All the praying, the mass before classes, the catechism, reciting the Angelus before lunch, and saving myself for my future marriage to George—none of it made any difference. Here I lay on an angelmaker's table. There was no way of getting around it. I was going to hell.

"What is that thing?" I asked.

"Hush now," he said. At last he stopped. "All right, you can get dressed."

"That's it?"

"You'll start to miscarry soon, so go straight home. You'll cramp and bleed a *lot*. Get yourself some Kotex and make sure you have plenty of towels on-hand. Stay near the toilet. If it goes on for longer than a week or you develop a fever, go to the hospital. But don't you dare tell anyone about this place. You did this to yourself. Got it?"

I sat up and nodded nervously, feeling a little woozy from looking straight up at the light all that time and then no longer seeing it. The quack retreated into the other room and I quickly pulled on my dress and my underwear, and re-hooked my garters, praying nothing was seeping out.

When I re-entered the main room, the gray-haired woman ushered me out the front door. "Go down to the corner and catch the cab from there. Don't do it out front."

That was it. I was standing in front of this house wondering if I had paid fifty bucks for nothing. My abdomen cramped a little, but I didn't feel much different. Eventually, a cab arrived at the corner of Ocean and Avenue W. I directed him home.

About an hour later, the *real* cramping started. I barely made it to the toilet the first time. And it kept up for hours. Finally, I panicked and called Momma. I dreaded hearing all the Catholic dogma that would come along with it, but dreaded the thought of dying alone and bleeding on the bathroom floor worse.

"Why didn't you call me sooner?" Momma said, helping me to the bathroom once again.

"I was afraid," I said. "I don't know if this is normal or if I'm dying."

"You should never have gone alone, Olive."

"What was I supposed to do, Momma? Teddy and I are kaput. I couldn't have had that baby. I can barely support *myself* right now. Was I going to find some off-Broadway production and come sashaying onstage out-to-here?" I held my hand a foot in front of my stomach.

"Teddy was a good provider, wasn't he? You could have fought the bigamy charge, couldn't you? The Mormons have been doing that for years."

"I'm not staying married to a man who lied about already being married," I said, flinching as another cramp hit me. I doubled over and waved Momma away so I could void my insides again.

"I'm sorry," she said. "I so wish that things could have been different with you and George."

I let out a bitter laugh. "You *do*? You spent a good chunk of your time trying to keep us apart."

"Olive, you were so young and so immature. I needed to make sure that you would be all right. I did my best, pardner, really I did. I've always tried to be a good mother to you. I would do anything for you. You know that..."

The Sibbie Borden chorus. Here it was again. *Olive, you're my entire life. Olive, I'd do anything for you. Olive, do you know how much I have sacrificed so you could live your Hollywood dream? Do you?*

I wanted to scream. Instead, I lowered my head into my hands and winced through another cramp.

Fortunately, Momma didn't have to take me to the emergency room. While I convalesced out of the public eye, trying to repair the damage Teddy had done to my career, I watched from my bedroom window, napping to regain my strength. Momma brought me beef broth and crackers, and for once, she didn't berate me about Teddy, or my disaster of a marriage, or the abortion.

A contact in town let me know about a shoestring production called *Hotel Variety*, so as soon as I could walk upright, I signed on as a singer/dancer who witnesses a murder. Production wrapped on the eighteenth of September, right around the time I officially filed for annulment from Teddy. It was a crazy month.

In mid-November, I received a wire one morning as I was making breakfast, so I slit it open.

BRITISH INT. PICTURES

DEAR MISS BORDEN STOP MOST EAGER FOR YOUR PAR-
TICIPATION IN OUR FILM HELP WITH GENE GERRARD
TO SHOOT AT ELSTREE STUDIOS IN UK STARTING DEC
STOP PLEASE CONTACT US YOUR EARLIEST CONVE-
NIENCE IF INTERESTED STOP WARMLY JOHN MAXWELL
HEAD BIP PICTURES

England? Well, this couldn't have come at a better time. I'd been needing a change of scenery, and now here it was. Here in New York, there were awful reminders of Teddy everywhere, like in Hollywood, there were reminders of George.

I wanted to be somewhere else for a while, and I'd never been to England. I sent off a reply, and soon I heard back that I was in, and could I please arrive by December 2nd. It would be the perfect way to celebrate my annulment, which my lawyer had told me should be complete by the 21st.

I imagined the ocean voyage to be a week at sea in a deck chair with sunny skies, gourmet dining, shuffleboard, and working on my suntan. Instead, the crossing was hellish. The waves were towering giants, and I spent most of the trip below decks, nibbling bland crackers and sipping ginger ale.

When we docked in Plymouth, I donned my older traveling suit of blue angora wool with gray fox collar. I accented it with a new navy merry widow hat and my gray gauntlet gloves. My gray sable was the only nice fur I had left. I wanted to kiss the ground, but unfortunately, it was raining.

I'd thought of England as a place of charming cottages and thatched rooves, rose gardens, quaint pubs, lovely accents, and sunny views of meadows, cows, and rustic bridges over flowing brooks. Instead, it was freezing—a bone-deep, wet cold.

I caught the train into London and learned that it was bustling and dirty, like New York. Cars and double-decker buses whooshed past going the wrong direction. My cabbie helped me unload my trunk in front of the middle-priced hotel that BIP had recommended. I tried not to let myself dwell on the fact that a few years ago, I would have been camped out at the Savoy, but those days were done.

The next day, I headed for St Pancras Station, and from there, to Borehamwood. I'd been told I'd be met at the station.

"Nigel Tavistock at your service," said the man who collected me, touching the brim of his hat. "We found you a charming house near the studio. Hot and cold running water, hot plate, feather bed, and a lovely garden. I hope you'll be very comfortable. I'll be taking you to and from every day."

"Thank you, Nigel," I said, watching out the window as we passed signs for Bird's custard powder and Apollonaris water.

We arrived at a sweet cottage, which looked, from the outside, like something from the era of the Brontës or Jane Austen, so I realized my version of England at last. Nigel escorted me to the door and then inside. It had been thoughtfully modernized, and the décor was cozy and feminine, with floral-print fabrics and chintz, a stone fireplace with plenty of firewood, and thick fluffy throw blankets that would be perfect for curling up with a good book.

"Evenin, miss," Nigel said. "I'll be here at eight tomorrow to collect you." He touched his cap as he departed.

"Goodnight, Nigel," I said. He retreated, leaving me alone to unpack the trunks that he'd brought in. Instead of doing that, I lit a fire, curled up next to it, wrapped myself in one of the blankets, and with the events of the last year finally a memory, I let myself relax at last.

The bedroom contained a dark oak tester bed that I judged to be at least a hundred years old. Fortunately, the mattress was newer than that. That night, I buried myself under layers and layers of eiderdown and wool and fell into the most exhausted, dreamless sleep I'd had in six months.

The next morning, I arose more clear-headed than I'd been for some time. I bathed and changed, and Nigel arrived to get me on the dot. The studio lay down Shenley Road from the depot. A long warehouse-like set of buildings with **British Films International, Ltd** painted in large block letters stood facing the street. Nigel continued past the front gate and dropped me off in front of the main offices so I could get settled.

Help had been rechristened *Leave It to Me* while I was en route from New York. It was originally a PG Wodehouse story called *Leave It to PSmith,* about a fellow named Sebastian Help. He was a Mr. Fix-It type who was asked for help by the Honorable Freddie to figure out the culprit in a would-be jewel heist of his aunt at Castle Blandings. The star, Gene Gerrard, was a stage comedian who'd been called 'The Genie of Laughter.' George Gee and I played Coots and Peavey, the crooks, and I had fun in my first caper comedy.

I'd wanted for so long to be recognized for something other than wearing another bralette and step-ins or another peignoir. Here I was at last, wearing trench coats and getting real laughs, and I wanted more.

In your eye, Norbert Lusk, I thought.

Still, the last few months had thrown me for a loop. After two weeks, the rainy depressing English weather had me climbing the walls. All I could do was pull on my heavy sweaters and galoshes and raincoats and pray for a meager glimpse of sunshine that never came. By late January, most of my scenes had been filmed, but I was still needed for sound recording and retakes. The people themselves were lovely, but I was tired. I wanted to stay under the blankets and not come out. The hours blended together into one long, blur. Despite the comfortable bed, I wasn't sleeping. Everything seemed very hopeless all of a sudden.

"Olive!" Knock-knock-knock. "Olive, are you there?" came the voice at the door.

I dragged myself out of my cocoon and answered the door to see Monty Banks standing there. Despite his very British-sounding name, Monty was thoroughly Italian. His real name was Mario Bianchi, and he was a charmer, with dark hair, big brown eyes, and a brush moustache. We'd commiserated, as he'd recently been divorced, and my annulment was officially final.

"Cara, did you not get the message? They need you on the... say! You look *affaticato*! *Stai bene*? Are you all right?" He furrowed his brow and carefully walked me from the door to the couch in the sitting room. "When was the last time you ate? Or bathed? Or went outside?"

"I don't remember," I said.

"Olive, I must call the studio *dottore*. You do not look well. May I? I worry about you."

I nodded absently. Monty crossed to my phone and I overheard him conversing with someone at BFI.

"Olive, someone comes to examine you. Do not worry."

I wasn't worried. I only wanted to crawl back under the covers. A Dr. Chelmsley arrived shortly, checking my blood pressure and my breathing, and he asked me about my health, and what had been going on in my life. I couldn't tell him about the abortion of course, but I let him know all about eloping with Teddy, then separating, then finding out about the bigamy. Then I told him about feeling my career slipping away since the end of my Fox contract, and my complete lack of sleep.

"This is a case of nervous exhaustion," Chelmsley said. "You've been overwhelmed. This drug is called Nembutal, and it will help you sleep. Better sleep will assist you with the other troubles too. You can take that to the chemist's shop and fill it. In the meantime, here are some to get you started." He pulled a pill bottle from the pocket of his medical smock and handed it to me.

"Thank you, doctor."

"However, I would like to admit you to the local hospital to rule out anything more serious."

I was shaking my head before he even finished. "Whatever it is, treat me here. The Brits may not know me as well as they did a few years ago, but after the bigamy stories about Teddy, I don't need any articles saying I've cracked up and had a nervous breakdown."

"I wouldn't call it that. You've simply—"

"Doc, I know how reporters think. I'm not going to the hospital. If *you* can't do it, find someone to treat me here."

For the next two weeks, that was what happened. Doctor Chelmsley visited every other day or so to check in on me, bringing stability and Nembutal. With enough therapy and rest, I was able to finish the remaining parts of the picture. On February 9th, I boarded the *SS Champlain* to take me back to New York.

When I arrived home, there was a letter waiting from Sun Haven Studios in Weedon Island, Florida with a new opportunity. After freezing my ass off in England, I could now work on my suntan. I accepted and booked a compartment on the ACL for St. Petersburg.

CHAPTER TWENTY~THREE

ATLANTIC COAST LINE DEPOT, ST. PETERSBURG, FLORIDA,
May 18, 1933

"Miss Borden, welcome to Florida! I'm Fred Blair of Kennedy Productions Incorporated."

Blair was probably mid-40s, with slicked back sandy hair, a long face and a prominent Adam's apple. He handed me a bouquet of red roses, then turned to face the group of reporters and photographers who'd gathered for my arrival despite the warm drizzle. We moved under the sheltering palms near the platform, and Blair introduced me to Aubrey Kennedy, our producer; Helen Turner, their chief film cutter; and our director, Mickey Neilan, whom I'd met once at the Cocoanut Grove when George and I were eating dinner. He'd be directing the picture.

"Hello, Mickey," I said, shaking his hand. "Good to see you again."

"Hiya, Olive. Likewise."

"Miss Borden!" one of the reporters called. "How does it feel to be back in Florida?"

"Weather notwithstanding, I'm excited to see another part of this lovely state," I said with a laugh. It was still wet, but after the nagging cold of England, the heat was a welcome change.

I chatted more with the reporters, then Fred took my arm.

"Excuse us, gentlemen. I'm sure Miss Borden is tired from her long journey. We're going to take her to the hotel now."

Blair summoned a porter and his cart, while Kennedy filled me in on the production schedule. The porter wheeled the trunks out to Kennedy's gray-blue Oldsmobile parked outside, and I crawled in as the sprinkle turned into a full-fledged downpour. Kennedy tipped the porter as the others crowded into the car, then he put it in gear and headed out of the lot going east.

"Is Molly here yet?" I asked.

My co-star, Molly O'Day, had been through some bumps in her career too. I was looking forward to meeting her. She and her sister, Sally O'Neil, were both in the same boat as me—starting to feel their stars fading.

"She's gettin' in tomorrow," Mickey said. "Fred's going to get her when the 10:15 comes in. Can't wait to see ole Molls again. When Sally was first starting out, I directed her in *Mike*. Molls used to come visit on the lot. We been buddies ever since. "

Kennedy told me more about the role as he turned left onto Bayshore Drive. Tampa Bay lay sedately in the distance—a blue-green murk pitted with raindrops. I'd forgotten how scenic Florida was.

Eventually, we pulled into the driveway of a blush-colored building surrounded by beautifully landscaped grounds. A sign out front said Vinoy Plaza Hotel. Kennedy pulled under the port-cochère and a bellhop collected my bags. Fred helped me out of the car, then inside to the registration desk.

The interior was styled like a Moorish palace, with wrought

iron chandeliers and banisters, and barrel vaults with rounded arches descending into twisted columns. After I'd freshened up, Kennedy took us to dinner in the hotel dining room and we ordered Terrapin à la Newburg, broiled smelts in butter, and planked shad. When they wheeled the dessert cart past, I passed on the key lime pie. Too much fish and chips and starchy English food had caused me to pack on pounds. Fresh pineapple seemed a more healthy option.

The rain finally stopped, so Aubrey and Mickey took me for a stroll through the hotel grounds and we chatted about the production. The scent of damp Florida was intoxicating. Aubrey promised to show us around town later, but he gave me a copy of the script to begin learning my lines.

The next day, when Aubrey went to pick up Molly, the rest of us were driven to the studio on Weedon Island and given a tour. To say I was disappointed when I saw Sun Haven's setup was an understatement. It was tiny and nearly prehistoric compared to Fox, Columbia, or even FBO or Educational. I tried to hide my dismay. There was one small soundstage and some very basic recording equipment.

"Used to be my club," Fred said with a laugh. "The Narvaez Park Café and Dancing Pavilion. Didn't last too long, but the locals sure had a great time for a while."

Fred introduced me to my co-stars, including Reed Howes, a Wally Reid lookalike who had appeared in a lot of roles that would have gone to Wally, had he still been alive. Philip Ober was a stage actor making his film debut. Mandy, my mother, one of the Negro characters, was played by Georgette Harvey. Georgie was a member of the theater guild in New York. Her character was poor and uneducated, but Georgie could turn her off in a blink, then speak with flawless diction and an impressive vocabulary.

In *Chloe, Love Is Calling*, I'd be playing Chloë, who had mysterious parentage, and might or might not be part Negro. Another exotic role, but this one I couldn't turn down. Along with her mother, Mandy, and manservant Jim, Chloë returned to a cabin near the home of a white man called the Colonel. Mandy planned revenge on the Colonel, whom she held responsible for the lynching death of her husband, Sam.

Chloë fell for Wade Carson, an employee at the Colonel's turpentine plant. However, Jim, who wanted to marry Chloe, vengefully told Wade that Chloe was the daughter of an old voodoo Negress to ruin her chances of happiness with a white man.

Fate intervened when the Colonel saw Chloe and realized that she was the daughter he and his wife had thought drowned years before.

My olive complexion made me believable in the role, but the dialogue was ridiculous. Even as I said the lines, I wanted to laugh. Now I knew why they hadn't sent a shooting script along with the contract.

Fred was so proud of his studio and bragged about it to anyone who would listen, but I didn't have the heart to tell him what a dump it was. We shot in a tropical mangrove jungle, with godawful heat, clouds of mosquitoes, black snakes, and even alligators. There were sentries with shotguns to scare them away, and also attendants, who manned smudge pots to keep the insects at bay. We could shoot for a few hours in the morning, then the heat overwhelmed us and we'd be forced to rest from eleven until five. Otherwise we'd all have passed out from heat exhaustion.

Kennedy had gotten the lights and cameras second-hand from what I guessed were less-reputable equipment houses. One of the lights, which the hands called "Big Bertha," drew every mosquito in the Sunshine State. When *one* hit it, we heard a giant snap. But the effect was constant, so it sounded like bacon sizzling. It didn't give the best light, but boy did that thing provide excellent pest control.

In our second week of shooting, we filmed a night scene at a house in the Hyde Park neighborhood of Tampa. The owner of the house, Mrs. Taliaferro, hovered about. She was proud and excited that she and all her society friends would be making cameos, but she was nervous that one of the fake party-goers would ruin her prize stand of azaleas or that one of the torches might fall and catch the grass on fire.

Red lights flashed, and the heat from twenty-two flood-lights baked the cast and crew even more than Florida's natural temperature.

"All right, we're working!" Mickey called. "Quiet everybody! And...action!"

The party scene came to life under a huge banyan tree. I stood center stage in a slinky v-neck dress. The extras milled around in formal dresses and suits. Paper lanterns hanging from the trees swayed in the breeze.

On the terrace, Georgie, as Mandy, approached Frank and me.

"What'd you do to my baby?" she demanded. "Don't you know no good comes from mixin' white folks with black?"

I let my jaw gape for Chloë's reaction.

"*My* daughter. You're crazy!" Frank protested.

"*You're* crazy!" Georgie threw back. "Just 'cause you found a lil' ole dress that I took from a dead baby they found in the river and gave to my baby, you think it's yours! I *own* mah chile!"

"Shut up! Shut your mouth! Come 'ere!" Frank grabbed Georgie's arm roughly.

I looked distraught and fled the party scene and Mickey kept shooting the others.

"Are you Mandy? You tell the truth!" Frank insisted.

"I done *tole* the truth!" Georgie said.

"Colonel, that ole Mandy is a liar!" Richard, the black butler, said. "Her dead chile sped right by 'er cabin."

"Just a minute, Colonel," said one of the locals. "A dead person's hand never changes. I have a way of telling this affair. Come with me."

"Cut!" Mickey yelled. "I think we can add a little more emotion, Frank. Take it from 'Are you Mandy?'"

We repeated the last part of the scene, and eventually wrapped it. Back on the island the next night, we moved into my scene at the footbridge that supposedly led to the swamp. Waiting for Chloë near the bridge were Mose, played by Gus Smith, and Hill, played by Jess Cavin. They'd been stealing from the turpentine plant.

"All right, fellas," Mickey said. "You've been ogling Chloe from afar, and now's your chance to have your way with her. Leer like you've never leered before. Annnnnd...action!"

As soon as I was over the bridge, Gus and Jess grabbed me and Jess tossed me to the ground. Although he was acting. I landed with a thud, and it really hurt.

"Ow!" I let out, my back screaming as I landed. The impact was hard enough to aggravate my old injury from Rawhide throwing me. Had it really been nine years already?

"Cut!" Mickey yelled.

The set doctor approached, lifting me gently by my arm. I flinched as I rose, holding my hand to my back.

"You all right, Olive?" Mickey asked.

"I'm not sure," I said, dusting myself off and taking stock. I tried to grin and bear it. In addition to hurting my back, I'd scraped up my elbows too. The nurse applied iodine and mercurochrome to them, and Mickey had more moss placed where I'd landed to cushion my fall the next time.

"I'm real sorry, Miss Borden," said Jess as we took our positions to begin again.

"I'll be fine, Jess. But I'm pretty light. Remember you're not throwing Jack Johnson." I smiled at him.

"Yes, ma'am."

We reshot from the toss and finished the scene, and at last I heard those blessed words:

"Cut! Thanks, everybody. That'll be all for tonight. See you all back here bright and early tomorrow. Eight a.m."

We began to cluster in groups to agree on evening plans, and Mickey approached me. "I was thinking of going out for a drink. You up for it?"

"Maybe tomorrow," I said. I was sweaty, my back and my elbows were throbbing, my bites itched, and all I wanted was a lukewarm bath and a drink. I got the hired car back to the hotel, ordered some chicken piccata from room service, and had the concierge find me some Cuban rum and a hot water bottle to dull the pain in my back. With a little of the jasmine-scented oil I found in the bathroom, I ran my bath, soaked my bites, and ended the night passed out after finishing half the bottle of Don José.

The next night, Mickey tried a different tack.

"Say, Aubrey says things are pretty lively over in Ybor City at night. What say we go have a couple drinks and a little fun with everybody?" he said. He wiggled his eyebrows at me. "Come on, we're in Florida, for God's sake. Everybody's on vacation but us."

"All right," I said.

"Good. I'll let him know we're in. Pick you up at six."

I returned to the hotel with the others. I decided on my red frock cut on the bias, with fluttery short sleeves of vivid blue, green, and yellow.

I think Mickey had already had a belt or two when they picked me up. Aubrey smoothly pulled out of the hotel grounds and maneuvered us onto Gandy Boulevard, then Gandy Bridge, which swept in a gently rising curve up over Tampa Bay. Skillfully maneuvering north on West Shore, he threaded through downtown.

We had dinner at the Rex Spanish Cafe, then Mickey gave me a boozy kiss on the cheek afterward. We strolled out to Aubrey's Oldsmobile, with Aubrey and Molly in front, and Mickey, Reed, and me in back.

In Ybor City, Aubrey found a spot around the corner from the El Dorado, at 8th Avenue and 14th Street.

"You can find pretty much whatever you want here," Aubrey said, cocking his head toward the interior balcony, where a big fellow in a double-breasted stood holding a machine gun. "There's even a bordello upstairs."

My Catholic guilt made me blush, which I hoped everyone would put down to the heat. We ordered illicit planter's punch and played roulette, blackjack, and bolita, laying bets on the balls in the bag. We chatted about the possible end of Prohibition, since the fellas said Congress was talking about it. For most people, the nonsense couldn't be over soon enough.

As the piano player banged out something exotic, the guitar players joined in, and Mickey turned to me. *Sotto voce*, so Fred couldn't hear, he asked the important question.

"I know *I* need the coin, but what are *you* doing working for this shithole outfit?" he said.

"Same as you," I said, sipping my punch. "Trying to pay my bills. I really blew it at Fox. Refused to take a pay cut and now look at me."

"Branded as difficult..." he said.

"I see you've been reading my press."

"Have you been working at *all*?" he asked.

"A little in New York. I'll give you some advice, Mick. If you decide to fall madly in love and run away to get married, make sure your *amor brujo* isn't already married."

"Oh, yeah. I read something about that in the paper a while back. The stockbroker?"

"Stockbroker, liar, fraud... yeah, that's him. I don't think there was one thing he ever told me that wasn't a lie." I downed the rest of my punch.

"He ever tell you how god-damned beautiful you are?"

"Once or twice," I said. "Mostly, he told me I had nice tits."

"Well there you go. That wasn't a lie. You *do* got nice tits," he said with a grin. I couldn't help it. I laughed.

"I wanna take you back to the hotel," he said.

"What will we do back at the hotel?" I asked, playing coy.

"I got a little rum. The question isn't what *will* we do. The question is what *won't* we do?"

"Big words, Mr. Neilan." I said. "I'm not stupid, but I can be persuaded."

"By my devastating charm?"

"That and your rum."

Later, Aubrey drove us back to the hotel. Mickey got room service to bring us some glasses, then we worked our way toward the bottom of his bottle.

Although Mickey was balding, paunchy, and five sheets to the wind, the booze made me less choosy. He was kind of cuddly in a crusty sort of way. Like a raggedy old teddy bear come to life, but one with a mouth like a sailor.

"Gimme a lil' kish," he demanded.

I did, and he made a grab for a breast. I didn't stop him.

"Your body makes me crazy," he said, muttering against my ear. "Those pictures you shot with O'Brien for *Fig Leaves* in your little undies? Made my mouth *water.*"

After Teddy's smooth, oily charm, Mickey's bluntness was refreshing. I let his hand continue traveling up my stocking to my garter. He unhooked it, then went further north between my legs. It had been so long since I'd let myself feel anything. After Teddy's treachery, I'd never wanted to look at another man. But deep down, I couldn't deny how good it felt. I did clench up thinking how the last time, this had left me with an unwelcome reminder of Teddy. I never went anywhere without my trusty bottle of Lysol these days, since I never wanted to go through that again.

While Mickey continued his rough caresses, I closed my eyes and once again imagined that I was with George. It wasn't easy. Mickey's breath was boozy and his kisses were sloppy—those of a practiced drunk. I was nervous after the abortion, so Mickey produced a prophylactic to ease my mind. He only took a few minutes, then passed out snoring.

When I awoke, it was morning. We were late to the set. The next day, we had to travel to Tarpon Springs for a scene, and after that, we packed up the crew again for another in Ocala. I wondered where they had come up with the money to put us up in these nice hotels, since everything else was run on such a shoestring. Mickey and I met in secret over the course of the next two weeks.

Unfortunately, the rushes were bad, and the final product was even worse. Despite the local publicity and the proud Tampans who'd come out to watch us and act as extras in the film, I wanted to throw up when I saw it. Aubrey seemed delighted, and he kept calling it his masterpiece.

As long as the checks didn't bounce, I was fine with calling it a mistake, but I couldn't wait to get back to civilization. I was sunburned, I was covered in bug bites from head to toe, my shoulder still hurt from where Jess had wrenched it, and my back was screaming again after years of healing. I needed the Nembutal now to let me sleep due to the pain, but when Aubrey saw me off at the depot on June 12th to head back to New York, he promised me big things.

The company folded by the end of the year.

Hard times had fallen on everyone, not just Sun Haven. Things were tight in Hollywood, and opportunities had dried up in New York too. Producers didn't want to risk money to put on new plays because no one could afford to go to the theater. What little coin people had, they spent on movies—happy, glossy musicals or Shirley Temple films to help them escape.

I got a contract for a couple shorts at Warner's, called *Gobs of Fun* and *The Mild West,* and a few dollars trickled in from *The Inventors* and *Chloë*, but I was starting to worry. That's why I was scanning *Variety* for new opportunities that day at the automat. Sometimes, life takes a detour you're not ready for.

THE HUMBLE SIDE OF TOWN

CHAPTER TWENTY~FOUR

"That's my pie."

"Excuse me?" I asked.

"That lemon pie. It's mine. That was my dessert."
The voice belonged to an older man wearing a raincoat and a battered gray felt hat. I'd left my table to get up and grab some food, and now this joker wanted to start a ruckus over a piece of pie.

"Sorry, pal. I saw it first. I put my coin in the slot and pulled it out." I turned my back on him and moved away.

"You took it when I was gonna grab it," the guy persisted.

"There will be another piece in a minute. Or you can get a piece of apple instead," I said.

"I don't want the apple. I want—"

"Look buddy. Let the lady have her pie. It won't kill you to have apple this once. Leave her alone."

My savior wasn't overly tall, but he was wiry, with sandy hair and piercing gray-blue eyes. His hairline indicated he'd be bald before too long, but he looked intelligent, and his smile was kind, unlike the pie coveter. I caught myself mentally repeating the same refrain. "He's not George, but...' and then I stopped. He wasn't George, but he was also the complete opposite of Teddy. Or Mickey.

The pie man continued to glare at me until Blondie began rolling up his cuffs, spoiling for a fight. "Go on, blow," he told the jerk.

The resentful fellow finally snatched an apple pie from the dispenser and stomped past us, cutting in line to escape the confrontation.

"Thanks," I said. "I should have let him have the pie."

"No, you shouldn't. A lady should be able to pick the kind of pie she wants." He cavalierly paid for both of our meals.

I laughed. "Hey, thanks."

"Share a table with me?" he asked.

I nodded and we found a table near the window, far away from our nemesis, who sat near the cash register, head down, tucking into his meatloaf.

"I'm John," Blondie said. "John Moeller."

"Olive," I said, carefully avoiding my last name for the moment. "I've never had that problem before...somebody wanting my food."

"We're lucky, being able to eat at all right now," he said, nodding at the apple peddler across the street. "We could be like that poor sap."

"There for the grace of God," I said, crossing myself out of habit. "So *you* still have a job?"

"Surprisingly, yes. But I'm one of the few in my family who does. And I've gotta do a lot of sharing." He blew on a spoonful of vegetable soup, then dunked his cloverleaf roll in it and took a bite.

"What do you do?" I asked.

"Electrician," he said over his mouthful. "I work on the Long Island Railroad these days."

"Good job?"

"Usually it is." He shrugged. "I have to help support my father. He's a widower. I brought him into Lenox Hill Hospital today for his diabetes. Plus, I have to help out my sister, her husband, and their kids. What about you?" he asked, taking a gulp of his coffee. "You a secretary?"

I chewed my string beans before offering, "I'm an actress." But I wondered if that was true. Were you still an actress if you weren't doing any acting?

"On Broadway?"

"Off off Broadway. And some revues. And some movies..." My voice faded off at the end.

"Movies? Say, what's your last name?"

"Borden," I said quietly, washing down my last bite of turkey croquette with some tea.

"Olive Bor—? Say, I had the biggest crush on you in *Pajamas* and *Fig Leaves*. What happened to you? You disappeared."

I hoped he didn't mean I was completely unrecognizable.

"I did some really stupid things," I said, sipping my tea. "Imagine ruining the best thing you've ever had because you're too much of an arrogant snob to take a pay cut. Regret isn't an easy thing. I blew it." I put the cup back in its saucer and gazed into its brown depths, then took a bite of the pie I'd worked so hard to get.

"You don't seem arrogant to me," he said, offering a friendly smile.

"Oh, you didn't know me seven years ago. I can look back

now and see how bad I was. But nowadays, everybody's got a sob story." I shrugged, then wiped my lips and set the napkin down. "Anyway, thanks for the lunch and the conversation." I gathered up my things.

"Wait," he said. "Olive..."

I paused as I adjusted my hat.

"I'd like to see you again," he said.

"Me? Why?"

"Do I need a reason? Because I like you? Because defending you and your pie made me feel good? Because we could all use a friend right now?"

I smiled in spite of myself. "All right."

I wrote my address and telephone number on the paper napkin from beneath his coffee cup, then hurried back down Broadway. Lately, attending services at St. Ignatius of Antioch had been comforting me through this whole crummy economy. I went to confession regularly since the abortion, hoping the higher power was a forgiving god, like I'd always been told he was.

Several days later, John called and invited me for breakfast. It wasn't much—a hash house at 10th Avenue and West 57th Street called Sal's. He asked me about my life and Hollywood, then told me about his job and his family. His parents were German, from the old country.

"I call him *Vati. Mutti* died six years ago."

"I'm sorry."

"*Your* parents still around?" he asked, stirring sugar into his coffee.

"My mother is. My father died when I was a baby," I said.

"Is she here in New York?"

"Yes. She lives in Islip."

"Good that she's relatively close then," he said.

"Not really. You don't know my mother."

If that shocked him, he kept it hidden.

"That sounds terrible, I know," I said. "I love my mother, honest I do, but she's very controlling. I've had to lay down the law with her."

He fought the smile playing at the corners of his mouth. "How's that going?"

"The first truly independent thing I did was marry a bigamist. So...not well." I gave a little chuckle.

"Couple of years ago, right? I think I saw some of that in the papers."

"Not *enough* years ago."

He laughed out loud at my joke. "He must have been a piece of work."

"He was a real charmer all right."

"Good looking?" he asked.

"Of course."

"You're probably fed up with men and romance in general."

"I haven't really been looking. You can see why." I conveniently left out the part about Mickey. Since *Chloë* had wrapped, I hadn't heard another word from him. Probably for the best.

John nodded and took a bite of his scrambled eggs. "I realize you're not in the market, but I'd love to keep seeing you. I love your eyes, and I get a little lost when I look in them. I kinda like how it feels."

I smiled and stirred more sugar into my coffee after the waitress topped it up. "You sure you don't already have a wife in Buffalo?"

"Nah, Rochester."

When I recoiled, he patted my hand. "Relax. It was a joke."

I laughed despite myself.

OLIVE'S APARTMENT, 313 W. 91ˢᵀ STREET, NEW YORK, NEW YORK, *August 19, 1934*

The next time I saw John was when he appeared at my door for another date. He had a bouquet of peony blossoms wrapped in some moistened newspaper.

"These are lovely," I said. I took them from him, avoiding the ants crawling between the petals and onto the stems. "Let me go put them in some water."

I escorted him into the living room and looked for a vase. Then I grabbed a shawl and closed the door behind us as we decided on dinner. The diner on the corner of Broadway and West 90th served a good chopped steak for fifteen cents, and even had a decent chop suey. It became our regular haunt.

Most of our dates were very similar. John caught the Long Island Railroad to Manhattan to court me, and he usually brought me flowers, which he eventually admitted he'd filched from his neighbor's small garden patch. We'd take a walk around Central Park and either go to the diner or stay in and I would cook. We chatted, getting to know each other.

The first kiss after one of these evenings out was sweet, yet perfunctory. I wasn't sure how I felt about it, but played along. For everyone else I'd nearly always closed my eyes and pretended I was kissing George. That we were back in the wilds of Wyoming—still in those heady, early days of our romance. I'd done it for years, but this time I thought of John as I was kissing him—of his kindness, soft blonde hair and blue eyes.

130~11 92 AVENUE, RICHMOND HILL, LONG ISLAND, NEW YORK, *October 14, 1934*

"Don't worry, they'll love you," John said, as we stood on the front porch. "Ready?"

I fixed my hat and nodded. "Ready."

He'd brought me home for Sunday dinner to introduce me to the family, and I was nervous as hell. We'd taken the train from Penn Station, and even though John had told me the Long Island Railroad was "close by," I was stunned to realize that the Moeller home was literally across the trestle tracks from the switching yard. It was a constant banging, hissing, clanking presence in their lives, whether John was working there or not, and it was only blocked from view by a tall fence.

The house sat like a red brick cracker box tucked between the LIRR yard and the curving swoop of its route near the St. Albans station. The front yard was a tiny postage stamp sized patch of green. The walk from the station had gone from bad to worse. The houses had gone from charming to less charming, and then from slightly shabby to genuinely rundown, all in a few blocks. No wonder John had never wanted to bring me home. It was hard to hide my disappointment at the house, but I kept a smile plastered to my face, regardless.

John opened the door, and the family descended on us with hugs and alternating cheek kisses like they gave in the old country. He introduced his sisters Martha and Margarethe, and brothers William, Henry, Carl and Adam. Sister Anne waved hello from the dining room, where she was placing a large platter of meat on the table. Then, John approached the sister he'd always told me he was closest to.

"Olive, this is my sister, Marie, my brother-in-law, Norbert Schaeffer, and their boys, Walter, Otto, and Arthur."

Marie had the same gray-blue eyes and sandy hair, but the gray in her hair was much more pronounced, and after three sons, she had the build of a pigeon. Top-heavy and with sturdy German hips. She would not have been out of place on a farm in Westphalia. Her frock and apron had seen better days.

"It's so good to meet you!" said Marie, giving me a big smile.

"Same here," I said.

John had tried to tell me about his big family, but he hadn't been joking one bit. His eight brothers and sisters, their spouses and children were all packed into the space.

The living room contained a small couch and two mismatched chairs with ottomans, a table jammed with old photographs, a tiny bookshelf filled with titles in German, and a cathedral radio set. Every chair was full, as were the sofa and ottomans. The children played with a top on the floor. I didn't think there was any way I'd remember all their names, as they all seemed identical—blonde, blue-eyed and ruddy-cheeked—the complete opposite of me.

"*Vati*," Marie said. "*Kommst du hier. Das ist Olive.*"

"Oh-leev?" said the old man who had come down the stairs. He hobbled toward me slowly and looked to his daughter for more information, his aqua eyes a question.

"*Ja, Olive ist Johanns Schatz, Vati.*"

"Aah! Oh-leev!" He cried in delight. He kissed me on both cheeks and guided me toward the table. I smiled and let him.

The table was loaded down with food, but John had to point and let me know what it all was, because I could barely identify a thing. All I could think about was Murnau eating this stuff, and my stomach churned unpleasantly. Sauerbraten was the main course, along with potato dumplings, sauerkraut, cucumber salad, and spaetzle, all of which Marie said were their mother's recipes.

Vati said the grace in German, then everyone began passing dishes.

"Where in Germany is your family from?" I asked no one in particular.

"From Freiolsheim," said William, Jr. "It's near Baden-Württemberg."

"I don't know much about Germany," I said. "But the cooking is delicious." I still wasn't sure about the last part, but it seemed flattery could help the situation.

Marie beamed. "I'm so glad you like it. We Germans love to cook. And eat."

"And drink!" said Henry with a laugh.

"Funny, so do we Irish," I said.

"Good riddance to Prohibition! Prost!" Norbert lifted his glass, and we all raised ours in a toast.

As I glanced at Carl, I noticed the cross behind him on

the wall, and remembered John mentioning the fact that they were Catholic.

"John tells me you're Catholic. I thought most Germans were Lutheran?"

"Not us," William Jr said. We've been going to St Benedict Joseph Labre for years. As long as I can remember."

Vati nodded. "*Sehr Katholische Gegend.*"

"Where are *you* from, Olive?" Anne asked, delicately spearing a piece of spaetzle.

"Virginia, originally," I said, then mentioned my time at school in Baltimore.

"And is it true? You really lived in Hollywood?" little Arthur asked.

I laughed. "Yes, it's really true," I said.

"Do you have a big fancy house and a butler and a Cadillac?" he continued.

"I *had* a big house, but I had maids. And I had a French car instead of a Cadillac."

"You don't still have them?"

"Arthur! That's enough!" Marie said. "Olive is our guest, and you're being rude. Henry, pass the potatoes, please."

"It's all right," I said. "No, I don't have them anymore. I'm living more frugally these days. So you should be a clever boy and save your money for the future. I wasn't very smart with my money, so don't be like me."

The boys seemed to take this in and absorb it. I hoped that it had an effect.

"What's California like?" Norbert said. "I haven't been anywhere outside New York and New Jersey. Is it like we hear about from the movies? That it's sunny all the time?"

"Most of the time," I said. "But in the mornings, we have fog, and then it burns off. There are beaches and deserts and even snow in the mountains."

"Snow? We have plenty of that," Henry said. "I'd be happy never to shovel another dump of snow as long as I live."

I laughed. "I think it snows in Los Angeles once every fifty years or so. Your would get your wish, and you could have your very own lemon tree."

"And a swimming pool!" Adam said with a chuckle.

"Is it true everyone has a swimming pool?" Carl asked.

"Not everyone," I said, thinking of mine on Hillcrest. "But they're very popular."

"Is George O'Brien as dreamy in person as he is on the screen?" Anne asked with a wistful expression.

All conversation screeched to a halt.

CHAPTER TWENTY~FIVE

"Anne!" Marie said. Her expression said it all. Not an appropriate topic asking about my ex-sweetheart in front of my current one, who happened to be their brother.

I looked up to see every face at the table concentrating on me. Then, I looked down and tried to tamp down the pang of emotion she'd stirred up.

"He's very handsome, but your brother is too," I said, trying to extricate myself from a tight spot.

John came as close to preening as I'd ever seen a man do in my life. The rest of dinner was uneventful, and I helped with the dishes to further ingratiate myself.

"Anne told me she really likes you," John told me as he escorted me home on the train.

"She did? Good," I said, straightening my skirt.

"Marie will be a harder sell, but she's always been a tougher nut. She had to step into *Mutti's* role when she died, so she's much more motherly. Wanting the best for all of us."

"Like my mother," I said. "She's had to be both mother and father to me. I know it can't have been easy."

He took my hand as we sat side-by-side in the car as it rattled along the track.

"*Vati* liked you, and that's most important," he said. "Marry me."

I almost laughed out loud. With my history, it would be a disaster.

He held up the very small, very modest ring he said had been his mother's. "*Vati* gave me this to give to you. We've been out plenty the last few months. I've gotten to know you well, and I love you."

"John, I'm a terrible person. You don't really want to be married to me," I said, thinking of the abortion.

"Funny, but I think I do," he replied.

"You see an actress and the glamour that goes along with it. But that's not me anymore."

"Here's what I know. You're spoiled rotten and beautiful. You've got a temper, but you can be soft and sweet too. That first day I met you, you were ready to fight that guy over a piece of lemon pie, but you're so generous it makes my heart burst. You'd give someone the shirt off your back and that's what I love about you. You're a mess of contradictions."

"I'm not sure I'm supposed to be married. I don't think I'm very good at it."

"You'll do fine," he said.

"I had maids for so long I think I forgot how to cook and clean."

"It's like riding a bicycle."

That made me smile.

"I...I'm getting older. I'm not sure if I can have children." Who knew if the abortion had done any damage.

"We can keep trying," he said. "Please say yes. I love you."

I sighed. These days, times were tough. We'd have two

incomes and one rent. Practicality battled with thoughts of romance and the fact that I might be settling—especially in that neighborhood. I took a couple of days, but finally came back to him with an answer.

"All right, John. I'll marry you."

He slipped the ring onto my finger above my pansy ring and it fit perfectly. I considered that a good sign.

On November 2nd, fighting a fierce wind and a sky that threatened rain, we went to a justice of the peace after getting our license. There was no money for flowers. I wore a tailored navy frock and my navy Drecoll coat. There was no honeymoon either. It was straight home to the crowded house in Queens, where my Catholic guilt made me bite my lip on our wedding night so I wouldn't be too loud. For once, I actually enjoyed it.

Unlike with Teddy, John and I were happy. Even though I was living in far reduced circumstances, I was surrounded by a big family, which I'd never had before. I had sisters-in-law for company, plus young nieces and nephews who liked to play tag and checkers. *Vati* and I surmounted our language barrier with a kind of pidgin German and English mix and lots of hand gestures.

In the morning, I would rise early, make breakfast, help *Vati* get up, and prepare John's lunch—a sandwich of bacon, lettuce and tomato with the crusts cut off, a hard-boiled egg, and a shiny apple. Sometimes, I'd include some boiled beef or potato, or squares of fudge or Granny Shields' meringue that I'd lovingly prepared. I'd enclose a note inside his aluminum lunch pail, something like:

John darling-
This is a little note to tell you that I'm thinking of you. I

hope you have a wonderful day.

Your wife,
Olive

Then I would walk with him to the yard, and his coworkers would snicker at John in his overalls and me in my last remaining fur. We made a strange pair, I'm sure.

Using John's mother's old recipe file, I learned how to cook the family's favorites. My first attempts were sad concoctions, but I got better, learning how to manage a household in the middle of the Depression. It was a challenge, but John told me how proud he was of me.

While he was at work, I took *Vati* to his doctor's appointments, and sometimes watched the kids when Marie had to go to the market or on other errands. I didn't conceive, but I told myself that God was punishing me for my sin. John never asked me about it, but I was sure it bothered him. He had all the nieces and nephews a man could want, but no children of his own.

We settled into a routine, and it worked well. Until I started climbing the walls from boredom.

130-13 92 AVENUE, RICHMOND HILL, LONG ISLAND, NEW YORK, *November 1934*

"Anything interesting today, Charlie?" I asked our postman as he paused on our front step.

"Here you go, Mrs. Moeller," he said, handing over several letters. He touched his cap and went on his way.

The envelope had traveled rough. It had my maiden name and two of my old addresses on it before it had been forwarded to Long Island by the post office. I slit it open and unfolded the letter, curious to see who it was from, since I didn't recognize the handwriting.

Manhattan
April 4, 1933
Dear Miss Borden-
Not sure if you remember me from Gobs of Fun or Mild West when we appeared at Warners Studio together. My name is Earl Faber. I was an extra. Used to be in Faber and Bernet. They called me 'The Paramount Comic.'

I'm trying to throw a touring show together. With the Depression eating everyone's lunch, I wanted to give folks a little glamour and a little oomph without charging them a mint. I want to book people who can bring in crowds, but aren't necessarily A-list these days. I've got some good backing and Helen Kane has already signed on. I'm in talks with others too. I remembered what a trouper you were in those shorts and thought you'd be great to have onboard for some skits and maybe a song or dance or two.

Jimmie Fidler gave me your information, and he said glowing things about you, so I'm hoping you'll contact me at your earliest convenience and let me know if you're interested.
Sincerely yours,
Earl Faber

Good old Jimmie. He'd been my first press agent in Hollywood, back when I'd still been at Sennett.

After weeks of walking John to work and handing him his lunchbox, I had started to wonder if maybe my decision to retire had been too hasty. I missed the spotlights and the excitement of it all. It could be scary and intimidating and nervewracking, but that was the nature of show business. Besides, we needed the money. *Vati's* doctor bills went up a little more every year.

Earl Faber had provided his number, so I rang him, figuring he was already out on the road with his new company and I'd blown it but good.

"Operator, Vanderbilt-4398."

"Hold, please. I'll connect you."

After a series of clicks, there was a hello at the other end, and the operator chimed in. "Long Island calling."

"Thank you, operator."

"Could I speak to Earl Faber please?"

"This is Earl."

"Mr. Faber, this is Olive Borden. Actually, I'm Olive Moeller now."

"Olive Borden! Well, I never! I figured you weren't interested. Wrote you off a long time ago."

"I'm sorry about that. I received your letter today. I've moved several times, and with the name change..."

"Aah...I see."

"I suppose you probably already mounted and produced your show."

"Actually, no. I had to put the idea on hold for a while. I got sick, then Helen got sick, but we're both doing better now, so your call is coming at the perfect time."

"It is? Marvelous! So what are you picturing?"

"I'm thinking a run through the Midwest at some good sized opera houses. We do a little song and dance, some comedy skits, get Babe in there with her boop-boop-a-doop thing...I even have a name picked out! Get this...the Hollywood Revue. Whaddya think?"

I thought it was ridiculous, considering how little any of us had to do with Hollywood these days, but John and I needed a repair to the furnace, so any extra scratch I brought in before winter would help. I still thought I had a tin ear and an even tinnier voice, but maybe Helen could do all the singing.

"Tell you what. I'll start coordinating everything and get back to you in a week, all right? Let me have your number and new address."

I gave it to him, and in a few weeks, we were rehearsing at a tiny warehouse space in the Meatpacking District. John gave me no end of grief about being away from home, but I pointed out how much I'd make and how much the new furnace would cost, and he finally laid off. Rehearsals stretched out until Christmas, meaning we'd be touring the Midwest in the middle of January. I wondered if Earl really thought this through.

"Have you *been* to the Midwest from January through March?" I asked Earl. "It's blizzard season."

"Everybody says that, but it's that attitude that keeps the theaters from being crowded. That's good for us. We can extend our run if the show is as popular as I think it will be."

I shut up and thought of the cozy, warm home we'd have when I got home.

Helen was as bubbly as she seemed on her records, a pixie with a capful of dark curls and cowlicks, and a Bronx-flavored squeak. Also on the bill were Ralph & Teddy and Donell & Bonita, all dancers with goofy routines; and Percy Freed, a comedian who told horrifically hoary jokes. Joe Fasso was an accordionist who dressed like a clown, and there were plenty of pretty, leggy showgirls for added interest, with routines staged to numbers by the Cocoanut Grove Orchestra. Earl billed the revue as 'music, dancing, comedy, merriment, girls, gags, and Hollywood stars.' Usually, we accompanied a lightweight musical or a comedy like *Transatlantic Merry Go-Round* with Jack Benny or *Flirtation Walk* with Dick Powell and Ruby Keeler.

Our schedule took us to Louisville, Kentucky; Hammond, Indiana; Chicago, Sheboygan, and Green Bay. Earl did a comedic rendition of "California Here I Come," and a parody of Al Jolson singing "Avalon," Helen Kane sang her hits, "I Wanna Be Loved by You" and "Button Up Your Overcoat," and I sang "That's My Weakness Now" and appeared in a skit with Earl, where we did a joking routine to "Jeepers Creepers."

Onstage, I pretended I was still the same Joy Girl who'd captivated audiences, but even as I smiled and pretended like I was still as glamorous as I'd been in *Fig Leaves*, I knew I'd hit the bottom of the barrel. I had a few more wrinkles and gray hairs, and I'd put on weight from the starchy German cooking.

Almost as soon as it had started, the tour was over. I nursed my disappointment on the Commodore Vanderbilt train home. I watched the wintry landscape drifting by, and imagined a life back in Hollywood, back on the stage, back anywhere that wasn't Long Island. I'd let it all slip from my grasp.

My whole life, I'd looked at large families with envy, but now that I was living with one, and visiting with one on holidays, and having them interject themselves into everything we did, I'd changed my tune. It was too close for comfort.

Things had steadily gone from happy family dinners to resentment, and now bitterness. Marie felt overwhelmed with her husband and kids and she took it out on me, because we didn't have children. John wanted children, but blamed me for not getting pregnant, especially when he found the bottle of Lysol I'd stashed in the bathroom. He grew angry and short with me. At this point, every month I didn't conceive I considered a blessing.

Momma didn't mind John so much at first, but the minute she heard us sniping at each other, she began to resent him too. In her usual way, she made things worse with her cutting comments to him when she visited. I begged her to stop, but her constant refrain was, "He's hurting you. I can be angry if I like." Dr. Tedford's advice seemed to be fading these days.

Marie took out her frustration by cooking, and the worst thing she could inflict on me was making homemade sauerkraut. The smell drifted in the windows and polluted every nook and every crevice. It lodged itself in my sinuses and made breathing impossible. Despite the heat I kept the windows on that side of the house closed to keep the stench at bay, but it didn't help much. To myself, I even began calling our place Sauerkraut Street. I could never figure out why her food all tasted so similar until I saw the can of grease on the counter next to the stove. She used the same stuff for everything she cooked.

Marie also sniped at *Vati*, so I took on nursing him full-time. Diabetes had taken a great toll on his health, and he wasn't able to get around very well anymore. He had nerve problems and his feet had oozing ulcers, which I disinfected and bandaged. John had bought him a wicker wheelchair, and now *Vati* spent the day with me. Later, I would prepare dinner for us, bathe him, and put him to bed. He was a sweet old man, and lately I was closer to him than I was to John.

Marie and *Vati* would sometimes listen to broadcasts from Germany on Norbert's shortwave radio. Germany had now annexed Austria and Czechoslovakia, and the world was on edge waiting to see what Hitler would do next. Personally, I couldn't stand the man. All his yelling gave me a headache.

RICHMOND HILL, LONG ISLAND, NEW YORK,
November 19, 1938

"I want to get a job," I told John. I was stirring up a batch of sweet potatoes to go with the turkey in the oven, and I'd put him to work cutting bread cubes for the stuffing.

"Doing what?"

"The Macy's at Herald Square is looking for clerks to help for the Christmas rush. I can be a salesgirl."

"But what about dinner? I'll be tired when I get home from work."

"John, we need the money. If I'm working, Marie and Norbert are right next door. Get them to set an extra plate. I'll return the favor when Norbert has the late shift. Let me help."

At last he agreed that because things were so tight with *Vati's* medical bills, I was probably right.

The next morning, I took the Long Island Railroad to Penn Station, then hurried down 33rd Street to 6th Avenue to reach the store, where I interviewed with a Mrs. Rossmore.

"It's not unheard of for us to hire married women, Mrs. Moeller, but it is unusual. Fortunately, your lovely smile will go a long way at attracting male *and* female customers. Can you be here tomorrow at nine a.m.? We need help in the shoe section."

"Of course."

"Wear something fashionable, if you have it. Employees do receive a slight discount, so you are encouraged to wear our clothing, and especially our shoes."

The money got us through the holidays. I liked my job, and I also grew close to my coworkers, Belle Gordon in millinery, Thelma Barr, who worked in lingerie, and Gerda Pechstein, who worked with me in shoes. Gerda had left Germany because of the rising tide of anti-Semitism, but she had wonderful style, and looked very good in Macy's clothes. I was convinced they hired her because her accent made her sound like Marlene Dietrich.

Going into the city was my escape from the rundown house on Long Island. I boarded the LIRR every day, and at night, I trudged the route home from the depot on feet that felt like they were on fire. I was tired, but there was no way I'd give up this job. I'd lose my mind merely being a housewife again.

For fun, I caught myself staring at handsome male customers—even those who came in with their wives. They'd catch my eye, and I'd return the glance, maybe with a side eye or a wink when the wife wasn't looking. Then, feeling guilty,

I'd go to confession at St. Malachy's and tell Father Gallagher all my sins. They called St. Malachy's the "theater church," so I began attending with the hope of seeing some of the friends I'd once known.

When I returned home, a conflict with Marie would inevitably flare up over how I'd cooked dinner or how I hadn't cleaned something properly. She and John argued in German about me, and I could tell John and *Vati* were doing their best to defend me (or at least it seemed like they were), but because I was unable to pick out more than "Nein," I couldn't defend myself.

One word I did come to recognize because it was used over and over—*die Schlämpe*. I asked Gerda about it.

"She's calling you a bitch, Olive. And this is your sister-in-law? I'm relieved not to be living in your house. It must not be very pleasant."

You don't know the half of it.

I grew to hate the sound of German, and whenever the arguing started, I'd find an excuse to leave the house.

"I'm going for a walk," I'd say.

"Honey, it's after eight. It's dark outside."

"I don't care. I need some air." I'd grab my coat and slam the door behind me. There was a liquor store at the corner of Jamaica Avenue and 130th Street that had been doing very well since Prohibition had ended. With a bottle of Muscatel tucked in its brown paper bag, I could forget every remarkably bad decision I'd made for the last six years, and it helped dull the pain in my back too.

When I felt especially maudlin, I'd use some of my work money at the Keith's theater on Hillside, then maybe get an ice cream at Jahn's next door. I'd watch a musical or a comedy, but if I was feeling extra sad, there would sometimes be a western playing, and George might be starring in it. Seeing him kiss his female co-star would break my heart all over again. I'd been such a stupid, selfish brat. No matter what I picked though, I'd still see the newsreels, reporting every new outrage from the Nazis and the Fascists.

The first day of September arrived with its usual heat, but the leaves were beginning to turn a burnished shade. I worked my usual afternoon shift, but decided to take myself to the Dyker to see *Bachelor Mother* with Ginger Rogers. Newsboys for the *Times* and the *World* were outdoing themselves, dueling from opposite corners.

"Extry! Extry! War in Europe! Poland invaded!" they shouted.

People clustered around their purchased copies, making predictions about what would happen next.

"Think Roosevelt will pull us in?"

"He wouldn't dare. Nobody wants a new war."

"Those poor Polack bastards, getting it from both sides. The Krauts *and* the Reds."

The scene repeated itself over the next six months—first in Holland, then in Norway, Belgium, France, and Luxembourg. England was being bombed nightly. The world seemed to have lost its mind. Still, in the U.S., life went on as normal. For me, that meant long, lonely walks to and from the train station and the liquor store.

At least, Norbert, Marie, and the boys moved to Brooklyn for Norbert's new job. Marie wasn't in my business every day, and I no longer had to deal with the stench of sauerkraut or the Nazi broadcasts. Now, I hid the rest of the bottle in a niche between the bricks on the side of the house. Then, I'd use some sen-sen to disguise my breath before going inside. Every day, I dreamed of escape. I wasn't sure how, but I was determined to save for a divorce and get the hell out of Long Island.

CHAPTER TWENTY~SIX

MACY'S DEPARTMENT STORE, NEW YORK CITY,
April 25, 1940

"**O**live, is that you?"

"Artie?"

"It *is* you! Olive Borden! Well, I'll be gosh-darned!"

The last person on earth I expected to see at my shoe counter was Arthur Benline. Artie had been the chief construction engineer at Fox when I was there. He'd generally worked out of the New York office, but Winnie had introduced us at Munchers once when Artie had been out west for a project.

Artie was kind of a nebbish, with a thick head of dark hair and full, pneumatic lips that looked like they'd been inflated with a bicycle pump. But he was sweet, and that counted for a lot these days. With things as awful as they were at home, I was happy to see someone smiling at me. From the high shine on his shoes to his starched shirt and silver cufflinks, Artie appeared to be doing all right for himself.

We did some catching up, and I conveniently omitted the fact that I was married and that John was currently talking about having a baby, which I was uninterested in.

When I saw Mrs. Rossmore giving me the eagle-eye across the shop floor, I transitioned into my perky salesgirl voice and slipped my wedding ring into my pocket.

"And how may I help you, sir?" I asked, making pointed eye contact with him, then glancing at her so he'd get it. "A pair of spectator pumps for your wife? A pair of sock garters, perhaps?"

"Why, yes," he said. "I do need some sock garters, miss." Sotto voce to me, he added, "I don't have a wife though."

I noted this with satisfaction.

"The sock garters are on a rack over here, sir. Please follow me." I turned away and he followed. We reached for a pair at the same time and our hands touched.

He mumbled an apology as I pulled my hand away. "May I ring up a pair for you?" I asked.

"Two pairs. Thank you." He followed me back to the cash register, handed me $1.50 and told me to keep the change. "Olive, I know it's awfully forward of me, but I'm going to ask anyway. Would you have dinner with me?"

I was miserable, I hated my life, and I was only thirty-three—too young to feel like such a hausfrau. "I'd love to," popped out.

"Tonight?"

"Fine. I get off at six. Meet me outside near the cabstand at seven," I said, placing the garters in a paper sack.

"All right. I'll see you then." He flashed me a winning smile, then retreated with his small sack of sock garters.

When my shift ended, I used some of my salary savings to purchase a black crepe de chine frock I'd had my eye on, then telephoned John and told him that I had to stay late due to a store inventory that had been called. I felt no guilt as I did a quick change in the ladies fitting room.

A little before seven, I strolled out the revolving door and then to the cabstand at the corner of Broadway and 34th. Artie waited, smoking a Chesterfield, and he eagerly stepped forward.

"You made it," he said happily.

"Where are we going?" I asked.

"I thought Luchow's might be nice," he said.

I made a face. "German? Could we pick someplace else?"

"I...I'm sorry," he said, looking flustered. "How about L'Aiglon?"

"French? That will do," I said. *How long had it been since I'd had a meal like L'Aiglon? Too long.*

"You look very nice," he said. "You changed your clothes."

"I didn't want to wear a work frock out somewhere nice."

We didn't have a reservation, but Artie slipped the maitre d' a bill from a thick money clip, and the man led us to a corner table. He held my chair out before Artie could consider it.

The white damask tablecloths, fresh flowers in crystal vases, and tinkling piano in the corner made me so happy I wanted to cry. I hadn't thought I'd ever be able to experience luxury like this again. We ordered wine, and Artie leaned back in his chair.

"You must tell me everything you've been doing the last few years," he said.

I sighed and fiddled with the stem of my wineglass. "Well, when my Fox contract ended, I moved to New York to do stage work. I wasn't very successful. A play, a couple of shorts, a couple of low budgeters, and a revue or two, but that's it. I've been working at Macy's for two years. "

"I guess everybody assumed that you and George would…"

"So did I," I said. "But sometimes things don't work out like you plan. What have *you* been up to?"

"I'm working as an architectural engineer," he said.

"So you build buildings and things?"

"I *design* buildings and things," he said, chuckling at my phraseology. "Mostly bridges."

"That must be interesting," I said.

"Not as interesting as Hollywood, but I never really felt at home there. I'm not one of the beautiful people, like you."

I smiled.

"I always thought you were the biggest knockout in Hollywood," he said, nervously meeting my eyes. "George was a lucky guy."

"Thank you," I said, eyes cast down daintily. He used the past tense. I wondered if he still felt that way. I'd packed on thirty pounds from bratwurst and booze.

We had a pleasant supper, and he didn't blink an eye when I ordered the lobster. When he suggested dessert, I agreed, and we split a peach melba.

When dinner was over, he insisted on driving me home, but I told him that wasn't a very good idea.

"Then come back to my place for a nightcap," he said, pausing in front of his shiny, chocolate brown Buick Roadmaster. "It wouldn't be right for me to drop you at a subway stop."

I thought a moment. I could tell John I'd gone to a diner after the inventory with Gerda, Belle, and Thelma. Then I could tell him that it got late and Gerda insisted that I stay over.

"All right."

Eventually, he pulled up in front of a beige stone building on W. 59th Street across from Central Park. It even had an awning and a doorman—something I thought I'd never experience again. He escorted me inside, and with his hand at the small of my back, he led me to the elevator. When the doorman greeted him, he cheerily returned the hello.

The elevator operator smiled at us. "Evenin.'"

"Evening, John Henry," Artie replied.

At the seventh floor, we exited onto a corridor, and Artie unlocked the door to his apartment. The first thing I noticed was the incredible view out the picture windows. It drew me across the room and I stood there admiring the park. Up here, the noise of the traffic and the city was not as noticeable, and neither was the filth and the stink and the clamor. I heaved a sigh of relief.

"Can I fix you that drink?" he asked.

"Of course," I said. I tore myself away from the view to amble around his apartment, learning about the man by inspecting where he lived.

The living room included two tasteful small couches facing each other over a dark wood coffee table and an expensive-looking Middle Eastern loomed rug. They were all in shades of beige and crimson. There were several framed photographs of an older couple in front of a house. Artie had the woman's eyes and chin, and the man's inflatable lips.

"Your parents?" I asked.

"Yes. That's in front of our house in Mount Pleasant."

He also had photos and paintings of bridges of various styles. A large watercolor of the Brooklyn Bridge dominated one wall, and one of a smaller less elaborate bridge hung next to it. He saw me looking and moved closer.

"That's one I designed in Santo Domingo. I was down there a few years ago for the dedication ceremony. One of the locals painted that view and gave it to me."

"Your apartment is lovely," I said.

"It serves my needs." He handed me a drink and took a sip of his own. "Little lonely though."

He looked down at me a moment, and I knew what he wanted. I thought of the crackerbox that stank of cabbage and the nice dinner he'd bought for me. I thought of the steak and lobster and compared it to potato pancakes and knockwurst (when we could afford it). There was no denying it. If Artie wanted me to be his mistress, I'd do it.

I let him kiss me. And when he led me to the bedroom, I let him do that too.

130-13 92 AVENUE, RICHMOND HILL, LONG ISLAND, NEW YORK, *April 26, 1940, 9:00 a. m. the next day*

"Where the hell have you been?" John said.

"Gerda, Belle, Thelma and I went out for a bite after the inventory. It was so late, Gerda let me stay over," I said, closing the door behind myself. I'd left the fancy dress at Artie's place and changed back into my work frock, which I'd folded neatly in my bag.

"Went out for a bite? With your household allowance, I suppose?"

"What household allowance?" I muttered.

"What did you say?"

"Nothing. Gerda treated."

"Could you have telephoned me to let me know you were all right?"

"Why? God forbid your eggs might not make themselves this morning?" I snapped.

He looked at me suspiciously and narrowed his eyes. "Be careful, Olive. The sen-sen's not working and neither are the flimsy excuses."

"You're being ridiculous," I said. I refused to even look at him, and instead collected the dirty dishes to begin washing them. They clanked loudly as I stacked them.

"We'll see about that."

"Will we?" When I thought of an evening eating lobster and drinking something besides cheap Muscatel, I'd do it again.

From then on, our relationship consisted of venom and recrimination, and I didn't care. If he'd left me alone that day in Horn & Hardart, I would have been fine. I would gladly sacrifice that piece of pie for my old life back. I'd been doing all right on Broadway. No blockbusters, but I'd still been acting. Most importantly, I'd still had my looks. John and his family had driven me to drink, and now I looked like a matron—someone ten to fifteen years older than I was.

After that morning, I took no pains to hide what I was doing, and John took no pains to disguise his anger at it.

Artie took me to fancy dinners at Longchamps and Beefsteak Charlie's, we went dancing at the Carousel Club, and I saw my first Broadway shows in years—*Louisiana Purchase* at The Imperial and *DuBarry Was a Lady* at the 46th Street. I hadn't had this much fun in a long time. His lovemaking was nothing spectacular, but I didn't even care. It wasn't the reason I was with him. I kept a bottle of Lysol at his place, just in case.

Artie and I spent more and more time together, and I cared for him, but I didn't know if I'd ever be able to call it love. He was like the favorite older brother that I never had. He pampered me and bought me nice things, and even told me he loved me. I responded with the same, but I wasn't sure if I was serious.

I knew I had to tell him about being married. If I didn't, I was no better than Teddy. Surprisingly, he took it well. By then, we were too far involved for him to break it off. He knew I'd been unhappy, but he hadn't known why. Now, he had the whole story. He was sad and disappointed that I hadn't told him sooner, but he told me he still loved me. He kept hinting at marriage, but I wasn't ready to make the final break with John. I didn't want to be in Richmond Hill with him, but I was terrified of what people would say if I left.

Artie was a fun conversationalist, and he made me laugh again. Even more important than being witty and interesting, he made me think important thoughts.

"What? You don't vote?" he asked me one evening over glasses of Chianti at Barbetto's. "Olive, you can't mean that."

"I never know who to vote for," I said. "I don't know anything about the issues, or how one candidate's better than another. I leave the voting to people who know what they're doing."

"But you're a citizen. This is how laws are decided. It's *important*. Women worked hard to get you that right."

I shrugged. "I know, but I have so many other things to do."

He took my hand across the table. "You know what's going on in Germany right now, don't you? You've seen the newsreels,

Olive. Think about the poor people in England being bombed."

"I know. It's awful. That Hitler fellow is terrible. John's father and sister listen to the broadcasts from Germany," I said, twisting my spaghetti around my fork.

"Do you know how Hitler came to power?"

I shrugged again.

"Because some of the people in Germany didn't think it was important enough to go vote. Like you."

His words hit me like a ball peen hammer.

"Hitler was legally elected. And after everything he did and said—his book laying out everything he planned to do— the people who *could* have stopped him *didn't*. They didn't feel like their vote made a difference either. What if everyone in America felt the way you do? What could we end up with if that happened?"

"I never thought of it that way before," I said.

"Voting is important. People in dictatorships don't have that right. Look at the Soviets. Make no mistake, we will be drawn into this war sooner or later. England needs our help, and if they don't get it, the Germans may bomb them into submission, despite what Churchill says. You have to pick a side. Do you want to help to defeat the fascists? Or will you sit back and assume everyone else will do the hard work?"

I was quiet a moment, feeling suddenly very small and self-involved. I'd felt like that after Fox called my bluff, and I didn't like it. "Thank you, Artie."

"For what?"

"For making me think about something besides myself. I've never had to do it before. I've always wanted to grow up and be an adult, but Momma shielded me from so much. I

haven't known how to do any of these things. This really matters. Will you help me register to vote?"

"Of course I will. You know that. Anything you need, you
ask." He patted my hand reassuringly. "Now, would you like to
try that *zabaglione*, honey?"

Once he'd convinced me to become a good citizen, Artie
pushed me to take notice of other matters as well. I began to
feel a deep sense of civic responsibility. We didn't have much
space, but I started a tiny garden in the front yard. It was
merely a few carrots and zucchini, but I took pride in them.
I told myself if things got worse, it could eventually become a
victory garden like Mrs. Turpin had had back when we lived
in Norfolk during the Great War.

I finally got up the gumption to begin apartment hunting
and found one in Brentwood. Still on Long Island, but away
from John and his entire family. *Vati* was really the only one I
spoke to anymore anyway. I broke the news to John one night
when I got home from work.

"Here's the thing, John. I don't love you, and you don't love
me anymore. We've been miserable for a long time, and I don't
want to live like this. All I've been for you lately is a nurse and a
purse. I take care of *Vati*, but this entire family still resents me."

"They resent you because they know you're having an
affair."

"I'm having an affair because he can give me a life, which
you can't. Honestly, you're like old, lukewarm coffee I don't
want to drink anymore." I began pulling my clothes out of the
bureau in our bedroom.

"You can't go. You have responsibilities here," he said.

"What? Taking care of your father because everyone else is

tired of doing it?" I shook my head. "I'm leaving."

"That's desertion," he said.

"And anyone who could see exactly why I'm going wouldn't blame me a damned bit," I snapped. To celebrate my impending liberation, I'd even bought a new carpetbag with my employee discount. I packed it with jubilation.

As I strolled to the front door on my way out, I saw the sorrowful look on *Vati's* face, and leaned down to give him a kiss.

"Bitte verzeihen sie mir," I said, asking his forgiveness. I'd asked Gerda to tell me how to say it. His lip trembled as he took my hand and squeezed it.

John stood glaring at me. Marie had come over for coffee and *kuchen*, and had to dig the knife in a little before I left.

"I knew she was trouble. Good riddance."

"Marie, I've always wanted to tell you this, and I've never been able to," I said.

"Yeah? What's that?" Marie said.

I smiled, remembering the lessons Gerda had given me in the stockroom prior to my departure.

"Du bist arschlock."

I slammed the door behind myself and marched out for the very last time. I marched straight to my new place from the train and tried to start saving for a lawyer.

Everyone watched Europe, nervous but still relieved that we could go on about our lives, finally seeing a light at the end of the tunnel after over ten years of scrimping and struggling as the Depression loosened its grip on the country. Even though I was separated, I was happier.

All of that changed on December 7, 1941. It was a Sunday, and like everyone else, I learned about the attack on Hawaii from the radio. I was at a diner on Suffolk Avenue and they had WEAF on behind the counter. It brought us the frantic reports from Hickam Field and from the harbor.

Overnight, the nation began mobilizing, and that included Artie, who'd been commissioned as a Lieutenant Commander in the Civil Engineering Corps of the Naval Reserve. He'd been in the Eighth Coast Artillery Corps in the Great War, so it was logical he'd be called up again. In mid-May, he told me he was shipping out, so we met at the Hotel Commodore, since he'd sublet his place.

"I wish you didn't have to go," I said. "I'll miss you."

"I'll miss you too, little girl."

"Artie, you know how I feel about you calling me that."

"Sorry, baby."

I glared at him.

"I'm sorry, Olive. I'm sorry. I'd hoped we could have a nice romantic goodbye. God knows when we'll see each other again."

"You're right. I'm sorry. Let's go out. Wherever you want. Dinner, dancing, the works."

"Or we could stay in. Did you bring the picture like I asked?"

"Yes. Here it is." I handed him a candid portrait I'd had done, flush off the success of *Fig Leaves*—a garden shot of me wearing a big white picture hat and holding a tulip.

"This is beautiful," he said. "It'll be something to keep me company on those long nights at sea." He kissed me, and we decided on dinner at L'Aiglon, to celebrate where he'd taken me for our first date.

The next day, I accompanied him to Penn station, where he was catching a train to Norfolk to be assigned to a ship.

"My old stomping grounds," I said, straightening his tie as we waited for them to call his train.

"Got any tips?" he asked, arching an eyebrow.

"Never mention you're from New York," I teased him.

"I think they'll be able to tell I'm a Yankee the minute I open my mouth."

"Say 'y'all' and 'fixin to'. You'll fit right in."

"The Alexandria to Washington D.C. now boarding on Track 10," came the announcement.

"That's me," Artie said. "I gotta go. I love you."

"I love you too. Don't die, OK?"

"I'll do my best."

He kissed me again, then hurried off toward his platform. When he turned back for a moment, I waved. Then from the train station, I went straight to the Jamaica Red Cross on Parsons Boulevard and volunteered to help. I didn't know much about nursing, but I wanted to do my part somehow. I helped pack and ship medical supplies, prepared non-perishable care packages for POWs, and got certified as a nurse's aid. All this while still holding down the department store job. Momma said she was very proud of me. I had to admit I was too.

When their husbands were both called up for Basic Training, Belle and Thelma and I got an apartment together in the city on 45th Street in Hell's Kitchen and began settling down to life as single women in the big city without our men around.

At the end of September, I began seeing recruiting posters for the Women's Army Auxiliary Corps appearing around town. One of them hung outside the Morosco Theatre, and I stopped and read it. I must have stood there at least ten minutes, reading the whole thing several times.

WAAC Women's Army Auxiliary Corps
This Is My War Too!

Maybe I could make a fresh start. I could learn some discipline, and even more than the Red Cross, I could feel like I was making a difference to the war effort. What better way to clean up my act? I'd been trying to stay sober since Artie left. What better way than being forced to do it? Below the poster was an urging to sign up at the nearest army recruiting center, which was at the Grand Central Palace on Lexington Avenue.

I could hear Artie in my head: *"Do you want to help defeat the fascists? Or will you sit back and assume everyone else will do the work?"*

When I wrote him to tell him I was considering it, he was ecstatic.

Finally, I picked my day off, October 4th, and showed up at the recruiting station. The man at the counter handed me a pink sheet of paper, and I filled it in with all my particulars—*my* vitals, Momma and Daddy's vitals, the fact that I didn't have any serious illnesses, and a statement that I'd never tried to overthrow the U.S. government.

"What do I do now?" I asked the man behind the counter when I handed him the form.

"Wait," he replied. "We'll be in touch with a yea or a nay."

Yea it was. I received a telegram two days later to report for a written test called an AGCT, or Army General Classification Test. I received an 89, and then was told that I'd progressed to the personal interview. They would also need testimonies from Momma and several other people who knew me, to vouch for my character and loyalty to my country. Artie said yes immediately. I also asked Father Gallagher at St. Malachy's, figuring I couldn't go wrong with a nod from the church.

My knees were knocking on my third visit to the recruiting station. Behind the desk sat a gruff older man, around mid-50s, who made me think of the heads on Mount Rushmore—a great stone face, no reactions, and impossible to read. His desk nameplate said Lieutenant Fowler.

"Please, take a seat," he said, barely looking up from my file.

He asked me questions about my life, my family, and why I wanted to become a WAAC. I answered as truthfully as I could, but I omitted the part about Hollywood until I could no longer avoid it.

"How have you supported yourself in the past?" he asked. He pushed his glasses up his nose and peered more closely at my form. "You say you're divorced."

"I...I was a motion picture actress," I confessed.

At last I got a reaction. His eyebrows lifted and he registered shock.

"Of course!" he said. "I recognize your maiden name now. And I recognize you too. Mrs. Fowler loved *Fig Leaves*. Especially Dobbin the Dinosaur." He chuckled.

"It's my favorite of all my films," I said with a smile. My favorite was actually *3 Bad Men* but he didn't need to know that.

"Where have you been?" he asked. "You got married, obviously. And divorced. I'm sorry to hear that. Perhaps his loss is the WAAC's gain. I have one last question for you. When we've won this war, if it were up to you personally, how would you dispense justice to the Nazis?"

I thought a moment and tried to put my loathing of John

and Marie and Murnau aside. I was sure not every German was awful. But how could we know the good ones from the bad ones?

"I know the Nazis have done some horrible things, but what if there are any who didn't? Perhaps they were ordered to shoot someone and might have been shot themselves if they hadn't? I would find it unbearable punishing anyone. I don't think I'm qualified to judge. I suppose they'd have to have some sort of trial first, wouldn't they?"

"That's a very astute answer for someone without a diploma. You'd be amazed at how many recruits have told me to hang them all and let the devil sort them out." He smiled at me, and I knew I'd scored a point.

The next hurdle was the physical exam. If I'd been able to take it eight years before when I'd been slim and fit, it would have been easier. I'd swum nearly every day, I'd ridden horses, golfed, and played tennis, and then there was all the dancing George and I did. Thanks to eight years of life in Long Island, I was overweight.

When I arrived at the recruitment center this time, I was directed upstairs. A few other women were already waiting on two benches in the hallway. They gave me the eagle eye, and I did the same.

"Cute shoes," I told one. "Macy's, right?"

"How'd you know?" the girl said.

"I sold about ten pairs last month."

At that moment, an older woman wearing all white with her hair in a graying brown pompadour stepped from one of the rooms.

"Attention, ladies. Please listen carefully to my instructions and follow them. First, answer 'present' when I call your name."

She ran through the list, and we answered, then she told us to get undressed, leaving our brassieres and underwear on.

We stared goggle-eyed at each other, seemingly unable to move. One girl even got up to leave.

"Sit down, recruit," she was told. "I'm not done yet. Fold your clothes into a tidy pile so you can take them with you, and wait on those benches until I get back."

I did as I was told. I wasn't in my best physical shape anymore, but considering all the racy promotional photographs I'd taken for my films, I'd be a hypocrite now if I didn't do this to help my country. It seemed like such a small thing.

I tried to be an example for the others, stripping, folding up my blouse, skirt, and stockings, setting my shoes on top, and sitting down calmly next to the pile, where I awaited further orders.

One of the girls complained and looked at me. "Why are you so calm about this?"

I shrugged. "They're trying to get us used to seeing other women undressed. Either you want to do your part to fight the Japs and the Nazis or you don't."

The girl deflated like a balloon with a slow leak, eventually sinking onto the bench and removing one item at a time, slowly. She had removed her stockings, and was holding her clothes in front of her when the supervisor returned.

"Hope this bench doesn't have splinters," the girl grumbled.

The woman in white now told us to form a single line, carrying our things.

We were each, one at a time, called into an examination room. I sat on the cold metal table, and a distinguished-looking doctor with salt and pepper hair and thick, dark brows entered. He thumped my chest, he poked and prodded, he checked my spine and my feet, and then he directed me down the hall for a chest x-ray. He offered me a cloth hospital gown.

"You can put this on now," he said.

After the x-ray, it was onto an ear, nose, and throat check, blood typing, and the eye exam, where I read the chart across the room. I pegged each letter perfectly, but there was still one last challenge: color blindness. An orderly toted a box into the exam room, and in it were small clusters of wool in lots of bright colors.

First I had to pick all the red clusters, then all the green ones, which I did.

"Perfect. Thank you, Recruit Moeller. You will be notified if you've been selected. You may get dressed now."

The telegram arrived two weeks later.

"What's this?" Belle said, holding up the telegram when I arrived home from an especially brutal day on the sales floor. She didn't look happy.

WESTERN UNION TELEGRAM

REPORT TUESDAY JANUARY 5, 1943 08:00 a.m. PROMPTLY AT PENNSYLVANIA STATION NEW YORK CITY FOR TRANSPORT TO FORT DES MOINES IOWA FOR BASIC TRAINING STOP. LIEUTENANT LEANDER J. FOWLER

"You joined the WAACs?" she said.

"I meant to tell you about that," I said. "I honestly wasn't sure if they'd take me. I wanted to feel like I was doing something for the war effort. The lease is up next month anyway.

You and Thelma can still get a place together. It should be easy to find someone to replace me."

"You can't know that. We'll have to find a complete stranger to move in."

"Belle, I'm sorry. I really am, but I need to do this. Everybody has to do their bit, like they've been telling us. You understand, don't you?"

"I suppose so," she said grudgingly. "I was considering it myself, but I'm a bigger coward than you. I can't believe you did it! Anyway, you better send us some postcards when you get where you're going. I'm trying to imagine you in combat boots."

Before I left for Iowa, I needed to pay Momma a visit. I took the train out to Islip to the address she'd given me. I hadn't visited her since the break with John, and she'd moved in the meantime.

I arrived at her door on a frigid Saturday mid-morning. The house was a cottage on a corner lot, covered with grayish wooden siding with crisp white trim. An American flag hung in the window. The man who answered the door was swarthy, wearing an undershirt and brown trousers with his suspenders dangling past his waistline. He looked at me suspiciously.

"Yeah?"

"Hello, I'm Sibbie Borden's daughter, Olive. This is the address from her letters."

Suddenly, his demeanor changed. "You're Olive Borden, the actress! She told us about you!" He became more welcoming and took my coat. I stamped my boots to get the snow off.

"Hello," I repeated.

"Ernie Zitella," he said. He shook my hand, then yelled

over his shoulder. "Sibbie! Your daughter is here!"

"Oh!" Momma squealed in surprise from upstairs. "I won't be a minute!"

Ernie changed into a different person, introducing himself, and telling me he worked at the Long Island Sea Clam Company, the picture on the wall was his late wife, Irene, and that their son, Ernie, Jr. was overseas fighting.

Momma swept down the stairs and into my arms, proudly showing me off to Ernie, then took me back upstairs where she showed me her room.

"Ernie's very sweet. He needed someone to cook and clean after his wife died, so it's been a good arrangement for us," she said. "It's so good to see you, Olive."

"You too, Momma."

"How are you doing, since the...separation?"

"Well, that's why I'm here. I'm leaving for Basic Training the day after tomorrow."

"I wrote your recommendation, but I really hope you won't be branded an old maid for the rest of your life."

"I had to get out of that house. I was miserable."

"I'm not surprised. The man was insufferable. But you were married. That was the important thing."

"Why would you want me to stay with someone who made me miserable?"

"Divorce is so messy. Remember everything you went through with Teddy."

"Teddy was a *bigamist*, Momma."

She sighed and changed the subject. "What does this require, this WAAC business? Is this Basic Training like a soldier, with combat boots?"

"I don't know yet. I'll find out when I get there."

"Olive, I wish you'd talked to me about it first."

"So you could try to talk me out of it? No, Momma. I'm thirty-six. I'll make my own decisions about my life, and this is something I want to do. I didn't want you to convince me not to."

Despite the tearful goodbye scene (Momma's tears and goodbyes), I felt elated when I left.

When I got back to the city, Belle and Thelma had come around to see my patriotism, and to show there were no hard feelings, they saw me off at Penn Station to catch the Broadway Limited. I promised to write as often as I could. My big adventure was about to begin.

BUGLE CALL RAG

CHAPTER TWENTY~SEVEN

C, B & Q BURLINGTON ROUTE TRAIN
AROUND KNOXVILLE, IOWA, *January 11, 1943*

"*D*es Moines, next stop! Next stop, Des Moines, Iowa!" the conductor called as he filed through the lounge car.

A number of the girls with whom I'd traveled west stubbed their cigarettes into ashtrays and stood up. We all shared a look—a little excited, a little apprehensive. After all, our mothers and grandmothers could never have dreamed of becoming soldiers. It was a thrilling yet terrifying prospect.

The train chuff-chuffed into the depot, and we stepped out onto the platform. The weather wasn't half as cold as I'd expected it to be. Still, the depot was warm and welcoming, and women in uniform shepherded us through it pretty quickly. After summoning a porter for my trunk, I followed a large group of girls outside.

Three large, canvas-covered trucks sat parked at the curb, and two women in moss-colored great coats, kepi-style hats, and winter boots stood near it.

"Inductees into the Women's Army Auxiliary Corps, step

this way, please! These trucks will take you to the fort! Line up here!" one shouted.

We lined up at the open back of the vehicle and were helped up by the other WAACs. Our trunks and hand luggage were hefted into the last truck. When we were all seated on the bench seats inside, a deep rumble signaled the engine being started up.

It was above freezing, but the wind whistled around us as the truck sped up. I tugged on my gloves and nestled my face and neck more deeply into the collar of my coat. We bounced along the street that led south out of Des Moines. The anemic setting sun was no match for the open vehicle. The roads were a mess of muddy slush like home. There was very little conversation during the trip, as everyone concentrated on staying warm. The further we got from town, the more the view became ragged remnants of cornstalks surrounded by snow. At last we made a turn into a driveway, and as we drove past the entrance, I glimpsed stone walls with the name:

FORT DES MOINES

I craned my neck, the better to see the neat rows of red brick buildings, the directional signs to places within the fort grounds, the review stand, cannons, and the muddy parade ground. We passed a sign that said Chaffee Road, and a flagpole with Old Glory waving, then the truck hung a right onto Thayer Street. We pulled to a stop in front of a group of brick and wood buildings, and our trunks and bags were set onto the sidewalk, which had been cleared of snow.

Two WAACs stood at the back of each truck to help us out,

and although we'd been warned to wear sensible shoes, some of the women had dressed in the height of fashion. Their tight skirts and slips and spectator pumps made it harder to get out of the truck beds.

"Where to now?" I asked one of them.

She pointed to a pair of tables set up between two of the barracks. "Linens," she said. "Over there."

I nodded and moved closer to the tables. An officer with carrot-colored hair, a pug nose, and a face full of freckles spoke up to make herself heard.

"Ladies, line up single file here," she said, gesturing to one of the tables. "When it's your turn, provide your name and the army serial number that was assigned to you. You will then take two sheets, three towels, and a pillowcase."

We began lining up like she asked, then filing one-by-one to the front of the table.

"When you've gotten your linens, immediately go to the barracks and the bunk that I will assign you to," the woman continued. "We call it Stable Row. The building directly behind me is Building One. It will house First Platoon. The middle one there is for Second Platoon and that building..." she pointed at another. "...will house the Third Platoon. You'll find blankets and pillows on your beds. Get them made up immediately. I know you're all tired from your long journey. We'll call lights out when I've checked the last recruit in. Reveille will be at oh-six-hundred."

"Moeller, A-201285," I said when I reached the front of the line, grabbing the armful of linens I was handed. I received my assignment to the Third Platoon, and followed a group of recruits into that building.

The long room smelled faintly of hay. It housed a series of metal beds, with upright lockers between them, and at the foot of each bed was a metal footlocker. I looked around, then found my bunk number and began to unpack. Some of the girls who'd arrived earlier were already in pajamas, and were writing letters, filing their nails, or chatting.

Compared to Long Island, it wasn't bad. Sure, it had a strange musty odor, and there were still wagon wheels hanging from the ceiling, but even though I'd be sleeping in a barracks with twenty strangers, I still felt freer than I had with John.

"Esther Holloway," said the girl on the bed next to me, holding out her hand. She was a petite little sparrow with chestnut curls and dimples. She paused from scrawling on her pink note paper.

"Olive Moeller," I said. We shook. "Been here long?"

"Group of us got in yesterday afternoon," Esther said. "Where ya from? Me, I'm from Philly."

"Virginia. But I've lived a few other places." It seemed simplest for the moment not to offer too much.

"Where in Virginia?"

"Richmond and Norfolk."

"We'll have to gab about that some time. I've got family in Richmond. Why'd *you* join up?"

"Wanted to serve my country. You?"

"Same as you. But I needed to keep from going crazy while my fiancé is overseas. This seemed like a good way to do that."

"Where is he?"

"The Pacific somewhere. Uncle Sam censors everything he tells me, so I'm not sure where exactly."

I nodded. "I should get ready for bed while I still can," I said, hoisting my suitcase onto the bed.

"Oh, don't put your suitcase on the bed. If the Lieutenant sees it, she'll pitch a fit. Put it under there, and put everything in your locker." She pointed to the locker next to hers. I unpacked and stowed everything, then realized how long a trip it had been.

"Say, where's the bathroom in this joint?" I asked.

She laughed. "Make sure to call it a latrine. It's that way, then down the stairs."

As soon as I'd changed, I made up my bed. It wasn't long until a whistle blew and a voice loudly called "Lights out!"

I lay on my bed in my new home, exhausted but satisfied. Eventually, I drifted off, but it seemed like only minutes before the cacophony started at six a.m. First, the bugler tooted Reveille, then one of the higher-ups strode through the barracks, banging a garbage can lid with a wooden spoon.

"Everybody up!" the woman yelled. "Up! Up! Up! Out on the company street!"

I glanced at the window over the opposite row of beds. Still dark outside. I groaned and crawled out of bed. Women were rushing to and fro, dressed and undressed. Some women headed to the latrine for a quick makeup job, while others went au naturel. It was nearly impossible to find a spot at the mirrors, so I gave up and hurried downstairs.

In front of the barracks, our three platoons stood in awkward formations, not even in uniform yet, and freezing in our street clothes. The ones in heels could barely navigate the sodden ground.

"Atten-hut!"

We all stood up straighter and thrust out our chests at attention.

"Ladies, welcome to Fort Des Moines. I am Lieutenant Marjorie Robertson. You obviously heard the call that your country needs you, and Uncle Sam is pleased to see you here. WAAC training is not easy, but it can be damned rewarding knowing you're doing your part to stamp out fascism and tyranny.

"We're going to be organizing you into squads. You will assume this formation for roll call, announcements, ceremonies, and instruction for military practice. Your first week here, you will be in a Receiving and Staging Battalion. Then we'll move you into a Basic Training Company."

We were formed into five squads, from tallest to shortest. Each squad had ten women abreast. On this morning, they taught us to march, then we were ordered to go a hundred yards away to the mess hall. Outside the mess hall, we were allowed to break ranks.

"At ease," announced the lieutenant. "Have some chow. You're going to need every scrap of energy for today."

The mess hall was big enough to feed a huge chunk of the base—I estimated around two companies' worth, at least.

At the back of the room was the service counter, which ran its entire width. Further behind that were the giant stoves, pots and pans (literally, big enough for an army), and cooks in fatigue green ladling scrambled eggs, bacon, pancakes, stewed peaches, toast and vats of oatmeal. Others poured coffee by the gallon.

There were four massive washtubs and three huge garbage cans in a row down the center of the room. On either side of them were three rows of five wooden tables with attached benches, arranged in perfectly parallel rows. With ten to a table, that was a lot of women eating, chattering and laughing. Boy was it loud!

After we'd eaten, we were directed to the Quartermaster's warehouse to be issued our uniforms. Holloway and I followed the others, and we were given a rucksack. As we moved down the line, we provided our sizes to the clerks and stuffed the sacks with what we were given. Into the bag went two skirts, five "waists" (the required blouse), two brassieres, one girdle, two sets of pajamas, four pairs of panties, three slips, multiple sets of different types of stockings, one summer hat, one pair of galoshes, one pair of athletic shoes, one summer-weight bathrobe, one toothbrush, one pair of cotton dress gloves, one comb, one green and white striped seersucker exercise suit, two barracks bags, and three insignias to be placed on either my collar or my cap. Also, two neckties (fashioned by El Ricos-Log Wigwam Weavers of Denver, Colorado, according to the label).

After being a small for so many years, I was sad to admit that I was now a large. I returned to the barracks and laid everything on the bed to prepare it for hanging, feeling very glum. If Adrian could see this muddy, monochromatic nightmare I'd volunteered for, he'd wring his hands in despair. When I thought of the stunning silks, chiffons, satins, and laces he'd designed for me, I moaned. From the skimpy little French underthings I'd bought at Mademoiselle Ghislaine's on Wilshire, I'd gone to off-the-rack at Macy's, and now to these hideous drawers in the same putty shade as our uniforms. They hung low, and although they did cling somewhat, they stretched to the knee. Most bagged in all the wrong places. The government-issue bras were no better. It took some doing to figure out the neckties, but after Private Dodds, two bunks down, figured it out, she gave us pointers in how to do ours.

Every matron in America had a pair of these awful shoes. Forget sandals and smart spectator pumps. These hideous black lace-up oxfords were now the required footwear. The girls christened them gruesome twosomes.

Hard to believe, but by the time we'd all gone through the line for clothing, returned to the barracks, stowed away our items and dressed in our regulation skirts, waists, neckties, stockings and galoshes, with our kepi caps on and insignias all in place, it was already time for lunch.

At the signal, we all filed downstairs and across the muddy grounds again, back to the mess hall. I loaded my tray with beef stew, bread and butter, fruit salad, a piece of apple pie, and coffee.

After lunch, there was more drilling, to teach us the proper positions, facing right, then left, then about, then oblique (which they pronounced o-BLIKE). We marched in formation, and it didn't matter if my nose twitched or the girl to my right passed out. There I stood, and there I would stand until given the command, "fall out!" We also learned proper saluting and how to address an officer.

Later that afternoon, we were sent back to the barracks and told to wait there. I had begun a letter to Momma when the "Atten-HUT!" summoned us to the feet of our bunks.

"As you were, ladies. I'm Lieutenant Bolton," the woman said. She was extremely pretty, with a shy smile, and reddish-blonde hair swept back over her ears into a bun. She had delicate features, perfect teeth, and her voice was pleasant. I wondered why she had joined up. She probably had her pick of every fellow in her hometown. "I'm here to give you a primer on army life. You may sit if you like, as long as you can hear."

The bunks near me filled with two and three girls apiece.

"Are you settling in all right, and do you have all your government issue?"

At the community of nods, she continued. "Good. Now, you may have noticed that reveille is at oh-six-hundred." She went on to explain how military time worked, along the twelve-hour system. "Retreat is at the end of the day, and it's at five p.m. military time. Can anyone tell me what that is in military time?"

"Seventeen hundred?" One of the other girls said.

"Very good," Lieutenant Bolton said. "Lights out is nine p.m. Which is..."

"Twenty-one hundred!" piped up another.

"Correct. Bed check is eleven o'clock." She paused.

"Twenty-three hundred," drawled the redhead from Atlanta who had the bunk opposite from me.

"Excellent. And ladies, when bunk check comes, I recommend that you *be* here. Understood?"

"Yes, lieutenant," we echoed.

The lieutenant held up the booklet we'd been issued. "I *also* recommend that you memorize the WAAC handbook. Of course, you may ask questions if you're unsure, but chances are, the answers can be found in here.

"The first person to see an officer approaching calls 'Attention.' From noon on Saturday until reveille Monday morning, your time is your own. There is a lot to do in Des

Moines. For theaters, there's the Des Moines, the Paramount, and the Orpheum. The Younker's store carries ladies' fashions and gifts for the folks back home. The Cardamon Drug or the Butterfly Coffee Shop have soda fountains, and so does the PX here on base. They also serve donuts, hamburgers, and that sort of thing. I can personally recommend their hot dogs with chili. But don't eat *too* many or your uniforms won't fit anymore." She gave a short chuckle, and we tittered.

"While you are at liberty, you must eat indoors, not on the street. You will not put your hands in your pockets. At cocktail lounges, you sit at a table, not the bar, and you do not dance with other WAACs. Also, there is to be *no* fraternizing with the commissioned officers. I don't care how much the fellow looks like Clark Gable. Don't risk both of your careers.

"For the faithful, we have a post chapel, and you're allowed to attend services. Now...onto the lockers. Private Neary, I'm going to use yours as an example."

Neary beamed. Having your locker professionally arranged by the lieutenant? Who wouldn't jump at that chance?

The lieutenant explained the proper placement of pajamas, underwear, and stockings on the bottom shelf. In the front went toiletries, cosmetics bag, and washcloth, and in the back of it went the sewing kit, bath powder, foot powder, and other assorted sundries. There would be no deviation from this arrangement.

Lieutenant Bolton then showed us the proper way to make a bed by stripping the existing sheets and blanket from Neary's bed, and remaking it, performing an intricate lifting and tucking maneuver with each corner. When she was done, the bedclothes were pulled perfectly taut. She pulled the sheet back down over the top of the blanket, and tugged a small ruler out of her breast pocket.

"This measurement—from the top edge of this sheet to the top edge of the blanket? *Six inches*, ladies. Six inches exactly. No more, no less."

Lieutenant Bolton chose Private Ericsson, a farm girl from Minnesota, to demonstrate her technique, and everyone watched closely. Ericsson got very close. The lieutenant showed her where her technique was lacking. After that, she explained inspection, and how each recruit should keep her area clean and tidy.

"That includes your bed, your footlocker, your wall locker, and half the floor area on either side of your bed. You will also have a task assigned to you on the weekly duty roster. That could be the latrines, the hallway outside the latrines, the inside stairway, or the outside stairway and its landing. Any questions?"

"Excuse me, lieutenant?" one girl asked. She was named Viaggio and hailed from Brooklyn. "Is that the *entire* latrine?"

"Affirmative, Viaggio. The sinks, the toilets, the bowls, the shower stalls, the tile, all of it. I want you to make me proud, but I also want you to be proud of yourselves," she continued. "I want you to develop a deep, satisfying commitment to Uncle Sam, but also to your own future and a career, if you so choose. If you're not a good typist, and your cakes always fall, you do not have to join the administrative group *nor* do you have to go into the cooks and bakers. As I said, it's all important.

If you're cool as a cucumber in a crisis, you could assist with landing disabled aircraft. You could be an x-ray technician working at one of the hospitals. Or you might make antitoxins or vaccines. You could work in a printing office operating a multilith. If you enjoy photography, you might become a photo lab technician or make identification cards. Maybe you'd like to do weather observations, compiling charts and graphs. As I said, *every* job is important."

After our informal chat, blankets were pulled tighter on the beds, lockers were neater and arranged just so, and even KP didn't evoke as many groans. It was all seen as a stepping stone to bigger and better things.

After a few weeks, we moved out of Stable Row and into real basic training, in an area called Boomtown. We soon learned there would be inspections Monday through Friday while we were drilling or otherwise engaged. Saturday morning's inspection was the real killer. The company commander conducted it, accompanied by three platoon commanders. Any infraction could mean the loss of liberty—shoes not adequately shined, a spot of dust, red nail polish in a locker, sheets not tight enough on the bed—anything. Infractions resulted in demerits that were called gigs. A daily summary of gigs was posted on a board downstairs. Too many meant punishment for the entire company.

Our classes included map reading, how to fly and fold the flag, current events, close order drill, safeguarding military information, airplane identification, and military hygiene and sanitation.

We performed calisthenics in our green and white seersucker playsuits, and we attended retreat at the end of the day with the firing of the cannon and lowering of the flag. After supper, we had study hall.

Learning how the military worked was a little like learning the ins and outs of Hollywood. The other WAACs were the co-stars and crew. Instead of studio heads, there were COs, and it reminded me of acting classes, having to hit my mark or hold my chin at the correct angle for the cameraman to get a shot.

Several weeks into our training, we had gas mask drill. We had to learn how to pull the mask from its case, secure it with the strap, then enter a latrine building we'd been told held a concentration of poisonous gas. It was terrifying counting to ten and praying. I'd never counted so fast in my life.

I thrived in the regulated environment. Without the booze, I felt better. I got really good at making my bed—even in the dark, by flashlight. I still loathed drilling because I had a problem no one else did. My feet had always been tiny, but I had to get permission from the lieutenant to get extra socks to wear. Otherwise, even the small boots flopped around on my feet and caused blisters during drilling. Unfortunately, my feet still hurt, so I finally went to the infirmary to see what was wrong.

The doctor who examined me checked my feet over thoroughly.

"What is it?" I asked.

"Worst case of tinea pedis I've ever seen," he said, rolling his stool back from the examination table.

"Oh no."

"This week." He chuckled. "It's athlete's foot. A fungal infection that gets between the toes. It can be very painful, I'll admit, but it's not serious. Barracks bathroom floors are breeding grounds for it. If your feet stay wet, it can get worse."

I explained about my tiny feet and my special dispensation for extra socks.

"There you go. Your feet are staying hot and sweaty, but they need to breathe. Try to change your socks a few times a day if you can. Clean the area well and frequently, at least twice a day. I recommend soaking them in epsom salts. Don't wear socks to bed so your feet can get some air, and use foot powder to help keep them dry. I'll prescribe a boric acid salve and I'll also give you some cream. You can get a pass from drilling for a couple days while it clears up. Nurse, let's get Auxiliary Borden a bed and get her admitted so she can stay off her feet."

"Yes, doctor."

"Auxiliary, is there anything else?" he asked, making notes in my chart.

"Doctor, I've had some problems sleeping on base, with all the noise and all. I was an only child, so it's been difficult to adapt to the change."

"I can prescribe some Nembutal for you to take occasionally so you can get some rest, but don't take it every night. It can become habit-forming."

"I've taken it before. Thank you, doctor."

The fourth week would be our last at the fort. From there, we'd be assigned to staging, trained in our specialty field, then sent to far-flung locations and training to replace male soldiers.

Of the four assignments for which we could be selected, cooks and bakers school, cadre (teaching other WACs how to drill), administration school, or the motor pool, I thought the motor pool sounded the most exciting. It would at least allow me to get up and around. But if it got out that I'd once had a chauffeur, I figured I'd have zero chance of being selected.

On our last day before reassignment, we sat on our stripped beds and waited for our orders to arrive.

"What are you hoping for?" I asked Holloway.

"The adventurous part of me thinks landing planes would be a real thrill, but the homebody part of me thinks baking bread and cakes all day would be right up my alley. You?"

"I think driving important people around would be a wonderful experience," I said, picturing a four-star general in the back of my vehicle.

"Atten-HUT!" yelled Ripley, who was closest to the door. We leapt to our feet.

Lieutenant Bolton entered at gazed at us fondly. "At ease," she said. "I'm going to be calling you in groups, so you can stay seated until I call your name. Anderson, Burmeister, Dumont, Ericsson, Krebs, McDonough, Orloff, Palmer, Tadinsky, Viaggio. Follow me, please."

The number of girls dwindled. Holloway was assigned to Cooks and Bakers Training, so she was hustled off to join them with a smile on her face. We'd already exchanged addresses for our families so we could stay in touch. We hugged and said goodbye.

To my delight, I discovered that my group was headed for motor pool training, but we were merely told to be at the depot on a certain date. Our destination was to be Bolling Field in Washington, DC. We hopped a transport train and arrived at Union Station on February 12th, emerging from the depot onto Massachusetts Avenue in blowing snow, and a truck took us to the base at Anacostia, where a staff member described a little of its history for us.

We were taken to our barracks and settled in, preparing for our first classes in motor pool training, which would start in two days. During that time, I scribbled a couple quick letters to Artie, Belle, Thelma, and Momma. I also met my new bunkmates.

Lillian Rison was a dark-haired Kentuckian with a drawl and a friendly demeanor. Merle Lundquist, a North Dakotan, was friendly enough, but would doubtless be an old maid. Pretty black-haired Theresa Nucifer loved talking about her hometown of Altoona, Pennsylvania. There were several third officers, Betty Terrell, Lois Wilen, and June Keisler. Our CO was Ida Coates.

The first morning of training, February 14th, I was raring to go. A swarthy fellow in fatigues stood in front of the blackboard, and next to him was a military vehicle of some sort.

"Recruits, I'm Sergeant Figlio. This little fella is a Willys-Overland quarter-ton truck. Affectionately referred to as a jeep." He slapped the hood of the car beside him.

"We're going to begin with the basics," he continued. "Then we'll move you onto some of the larger vehicles—command cars, trucks, and so forth. Very soon, you should be able to take one of these engines apart and rebuild it with your bare hands. I'm happy to see so many of you here, because rest assured, your manicures will suffer in this unit, and I know you gals won't like that. I recommend keeping your nails short, with a coat of clear polish to hide the damage. You'll thank me later."

We started with classroom lessons, where Figlio went over the material in our technical manual documents put out by the Quartermaster Corps. I learned how to recognize an intake manifold and a bevel gear drive, and the differences between straight-cut, angle-joint, and step joint piston-ring joints.

He quizzed us on the parts of the four-stroke otto cycle and compression ratios, among other things. Finally we moved into the practical hands-on work. We began with easy procedures like oil changes and timing belt repair, then learned to fix flats, siphon gas from one vehicle to another, and adjust timing.

"If you'll refer to page sixty-nine, you'll see this all explained. Your timing is crucial," Figlio said. "The valves have to stay in step with the cylinder piston movement. Your stroke should start at the top or bottom center of the movement of that piston, and go through a crankshaft rotation of one-hundred eighty degrees. Your valves should open or close when the piston is at the top or bottom of its stroke, depending on when that happens. But you got other stuff affecting that. You got pressure from the gases, momentum, and such. Look at page seventy-one and you'll see a diagram of the opening and closing points of your valves during the four cycle events."

I dived in, enjoying learning about all the vehicles, but I wasn't as close to the new squad. I missed Holloway already. And Belle and Thelma and Gerda. Heck, I even missed Momma. And then there was Artie. I had a letter from him on the eighteenth.

Hi Baby-
February 15, 1943
Hope you are learning lots and can singlehandedly take out a Nazi corps by now. Ha ha.

We just got the word. I'm shipping out, day after tomorrow. Now, try not to worry. I'm sure I'll be fine. Even if we get torpedoed, I'm a good swimmer. We'll show those Germans what for.

I'll send you another letter as soon as I get settled on the ship. Love you, honey. You're a brave girl and I'm so proud of you!

Love, Artie

PRAISE THE LORD AND PASS THE AMMUNITION

CHAPTER TWENTY~EIGHT

WALTER REED HOSPITAL, BETHESDA, MARYLAND,
February 24, 1943

N ot long after we arrived at Bolling Field, my feet started hurting again with the same stabbing pains that had kept me from marching in Iowa. Finally, it got so bad that I had to go to the infirmary at Walter Reed, because I was limping during drills. My athlete's foot was back.

The main building at Walter Reed stood on Wisconsin Avenue. It was stately and respectable looking, constructed of red brick, with columns flanking the front entrance. Wings branched off in multiple directions from it. I was directed to a wing for minor complaints, and saw a doctor there. He decided to keep me for twelve days, so my feet could heal. Who was I to argue? I think it made me soft. Otherwise, I can't explain what happened when I got back to the barracks.

First, I ran into Auxiliary Nucifer outside the post exchange on my way back.

"Borden! Good to see you! How's that foot?"

"Better," I said. "Lots of vinegar foot baths and some salve."

"Heads up. The new CO, Fodness, has a real pole up her... well, you know."

"Yeah? How so?"

Nucifer lapsed into a strong Midwest nasal accent, talking out of the back of her throat to imitate the most upcountry Minnesotan, like Ericsson back at Fort Des Moines.

"'Nucifer, this locker is shameful. Clear it all out and start from scratch.' 'Baker, that's a gig for the Tangerine Temptation nail lacquer. That's not regulation and you know it.' 'Hennessey, that's KP for a week for those shoe scuffs. Starting now.'"

At my shocked expression, she continued. "I'm not sure what happened to Coates, but she's been replaced with this Viking Hard-Ass from North Dakota." She stressed the Midwestern accent on North Dakota. "She's ready to put Eisenhower out of a job. Oh, and heads up. Nicks told her you used to be a movie star, and she looked none-too-pleased."

Great. Frosting on the cake. I was already in a bad mood. I'd liked Lieutenant Coates. Thanks, Nicks, I thought.

"See you later, Borden. I need to get these letters mailed before I have to start jumping through hoops again."

I first met Lieutenant Fodness the next morning when we lined up for inspection.

"Auxiliary Borden, so glad you could join us," she said, her voice dripping with sarcasm.

"Permission to speak, ma'am," I said. She granted it. "I was in the infirmary."

"For a case of athlete's foot?" she said with a laugh. "Must have been a very bad case to be out of commission for twelve days!"

"I was following doctor's orders, ma'am." I bit back my anger and continued to stand at attention.

From then on, I was fair game. She considered me weak,

and because her outfit had the 'gutsiest gals in the W.A.A.C.', Fodness rode me hard and she gigged me for everything. My locker wasn't neat enough, there was a speck of dust on my trunk, I'd missed a spot polishing my shoes. When I got KP, she purposely walked through the floor I'd just mopped with her muddy galoshes. My back began to ache from the stress, and that made the craving for booze more acute. I couldn't take the Nembutal because I'd oversleep. Still, I finally had to go to the dispensary for a refill because I couldn't get any sleep without it. Then, I'd drag the next day and the cycle repeated. It didn't help that I'd taken a position at the PX as a sales-clerk, so I was run off my feet most days. I missed my friends from basic training, and I sent Holloway long letters telling her she didn't know how good she had it. When I thought of her baking bread and pies all day, I wanted to cry. This was the outfit I thought I'd wanted—driving around captains and generals, and saving the day when a truck or a command car broke down.

Figlio had moved onto more challenging tasks like fixing oil oxidation, engine carbon, and water sludge. He tested us on every aspect of multiple vehicles. Each make and model had its quirks, from the General Ops command car to the 2 ½ ton CCKW-353. We learned about 1/4–ton trailers and Harley-Davidson 50 WLAs. Then, we examined ever-more challeng-ing vehicles like semi-trailers, crane trucks, and tanks. Figlio also taught us defensive driving techniques like being obser-vant to all surrounding movement, serpentining, and know-ing when to slow down or when to speed up to avoid hazards like strafers, tanks, and snipers. It was almost like being one of the stunt drivers we had back in Hollywood.

However, Lieutenant Murl Fodness brought my dreams of military glory to a screeching halt.

"What's the matter, Borden?" she said one day as I mopped. "You couldn't hack it in talkies and you can't hack it as a WAAC."

When I wasn't on duty, I discovered the Fort Stevens bar in Anacostia. The drinking that I'd kept under control all during basic became my escape.

When I next wrote Momma, I told her that things in DC weren't as good as they had been in Iowa, and I got a reply a few weeks later.

Baby- You know you are absolutely welcome to visit any time. I'm so proud of my girl for being so brave! From your loving mother

It seemed like a good idea. Anywhere was better than here. The next time I got leave, I was determined to head for New York. Artie wasn't able to get leave, and for the first time in years, I needed my mother.

WAAC BARRACKS, BOLLING FIELD, *April 6, 1943*

When I'd enlisted and mentioned my entertainment background, I'd been told that it could come in handy for helping with morale. They picked the absolute worst time to take me up on my gifts.

They'd persuaded me to appear in a USO production with Bob Hope while he was in town. He'd be performing with Jerry Colonna and Tony Romano, and a young actress named Frances Langford. Soldiers and sailors from all over D.C.—Anacostia, Bolling, the Washington Barracks, and the Navy Yard—would be able to attend, and that included WAACs. It would be one night, but I felt so out of practice and dowdy now. I hadn't been on a stage since I'd gone out on the road with Earl Faber. Hard to believe that had been eight years ago.

On the sixth, First Officer Hilliard, Third Officer Kiesler, and I hitched a ride with Ted James, an airman second class from Foggy Bottom who had a second-hand Oldsmobile.

Considering the name a service joke, we chose Gung Ho Chinese Restaurant on G Street for dinner and feasted on chow mein and chop suey before the show.

Keisler and Hilliard thought I looked nervous and said a drink or two might make me a little less stiff on-stage.

"Come on, Moeller, live a little. You've been really keyed up since you got back from the infirmary. You'll be great. Relax!" said Keisler, gesturing with her chopsticks.

I didn't want to tell them that it wasn't the best idea, but they ordered me a whiskey and water, and then another. It did relax me, but then I was nearly giddy by the time we got to the show, at Memorial Continental Hall.

A pretty pompadoured redhead named Gloria Dooley started things by cartwheeling onto the stage in her red, white, and blue costume and red ankle-strap shoes, and she did a dance routine to "Beat Me Daddy, Eight to the Bar" that really got the crowd going.

Then, Bob Hope stepped to the stage and waved at everyone. He waited for the applause to die down before launching into his schtick. "Thank you! Thank you, ladies and gentlemen. I'd like to thank you all for coming out tonight. I know you all must think I entertained at Valley Forge, but that's not true." Then, it was rapid-fire jokes for two hours, with breaks for more talent.

"I've got the scores for the week!" he continued. "Let's see here." He consulted his notes. "The Pirates over the Indians, the Yankees over the Newark Bears, and the Yanks over the Krauts in Tunisia!"

The audience exploded in cheers.

Frances Langford and I were up after intermission with our comic rendition of "Der Fuehrer's Face," and we were funny enough to get some applause. That was all that mattered to me.

When Ted dropped us back at our barracks, I discovered that someone had placed Artie's latest letter propped against my pillow, so I ripped it open.

Hi Baby-
March 18, 1943
I have a few minutes to scribble some news to you. We had a pretty crazy storm here the other night. Scary when you're sailing through it! It's really hot here, but I can't say more where I am. The censors would go to town with black pens if I told you. How is it, being a Lady GI? You know I love you in any color, but seeing you in your uniform sure was a thrill. Thanks for the snap! I hope you're enjoying learning everything about cars. After the war, you can open your own

garage! Nyuk-nyuk. Anyway, must close now, they need me on the bridge. Love you and miss you.

Your Artie

The letter sent me into a funk. With the constant bullying from Fodness, the pressure of the performance, and the relief of having it over, everything suddenly overwhelmed me. I sat down on my bunk and started to cry.

Keisler saw me and approached quietly.

"Borden, anything I can do?"

I thought fast. If I told her the real reason, she'd think I was being ridiculous. That Fodness was running me ragged, and I couldn't hack the service.

She sat down next to me on my bunk. "What is it? Are you all right?"

"No," I said.

"What's wrong?"

"It's...my husband. He's an officer in the navy. He's been reported missing."

Even as I said it, I couldn't believe what was coming out of my mouth. Why did I say it? For sympathy? To get them to go a little easier on me? Probably both. Too late to take it back now.

"I'm so sorry," she said. "What's his name and rank? We can check on him through our connections here in DC. We may be able to find information on him a little more quickly for you."

I knew it would come back to bite me, but if it kept Fodness at bay for even a moment, I'd take the risk. I'd always been more of a live-for-the-moment kind of girl anyway.

"It's probably nothing," she said when I told her. "We'll do some checking. Meanwhile, why don't you get some shut-eye. By the way, you were great tonight."

"Thank you, ma'am," I said. When she was gone, I washed my sadness down with a couple of furtive sips from the small bottle of Four Roses that I'd kept hidden, moving it between my locker, trunk, and sheets, and sometimes under my mattress to avoid detection.

The next day, I went to the dispensary to get some more Nembutal, but for three days I was sleepless and tense. The pills barely touched it. I decided to go home to see Momma for my weekend leave. She would know what to do.

I began packing a bag to head north to New York, but I was so keyed up that it was hard to concentrate on what I needed to pack. After a Nembutal, I sipped from the bottle as I folded stockings, blouses, and underwear.

When lights out came, I tried falling asleep, but my thoughts raced. What would Momma say about my misgivings? What would happen to Artie? What if his ship *was* torpedoed? What if he ended up in the water? He said he was a good swimmer, but what if there were sharks?

"Sharks..." I whispered. "Torpedoes..."

It became a refrain in my head, louder and louder like a tom-tom. Artie was the first man since George to really love me (even if he did sometimes treat me like a child. What would I do without him?

"No!" I shouted, heedless of lights out. I couldn't help it. "No!" What the hell was wrong with me? I seemed to have no control over my own voice.

A few of the girls stirred in the dark. Some sat up.

"Shhhhhhhhhh!" one hissed. "You want to get us all gigged?!"

I got up and began pacing, and when George appeared at the doorway that led to the latrine, I decided the time had come to kiss and make up. I'd been an idiot. But when I got there, he faded to nothing. I'd imagined him. I began to cry, then laugh hysterically. Rison crept over in the dark. Nucifer and Lundquist approached me too.

"Moeller, are you all right?" Nucifer asked, lightly touching my arm.

"Don't touch me!"

"I want to make sure you're all right. Relax, everything will be fine."

Lundquist and Nucifer shared a back and forth glance, then crept into the latrine, where I heard them muttering.

"Why don't we get you back to bed, Moeller. You'll be fine once you drop off," Rison said.

I allowed her to lead me back to my bunk and I got in bed, but she joined Nucifer and Lundquist in the latrine.

"Go get Terrell and Fodness," someone said. "I think she's cracking up."

One of the girls threw on a robe and rushed from the room. Closing my eyes, I lay back on my bunk, wiggling my toes. I guess it would have been better if I'd just stayed here and shut up, but it was too late now.

Soon, Rison was back, and behind her, looking furious, was Fodness. Lieutenant Terrell brought up the rear, surveying the room as she followed Fodness down the aisle between the rows of beds.

"On your feet, Moeller," Fodness demanded.

I looked over at her but my head lolled to one side. It was hard to hold it up. "Why?" I asked.

"I am your superior officer, and I issued a direct order, that's why. On the double."

"I don't feel like it. I'm tired." My eyes were starting to feel heavy.

"I said *up*, Moeller. You'll be gigged you so hard you'll see KP for the rest of your natural life!"

"Yay, gigs. My favorite!" I replied sarcastically. I felt drunk, but I hadn't had that much.

"Get up, *now*. Terrell, help me get her up."

Fodness took one arm, and Terrell took the other, and they hoisted me to a sitting position, then yanked me out of bed.

"Ow!" I said. "That hurt!"

"Tough," Fodness said. "Put on some shoes. You're coming with us."

"I have rights," I slurred. "It's in the consti... the constitution."

Fodness nodded at Rison, who was standing next to my footlocker. "Get a robe and a pair of shoes for her. And clean up her area. Report back to me with anything you find." They nodded.

Fodness and Terrell hustled me into the latrine, which was brightly lit compared to the rest of the barracks. They strong-armed me into a shower stall and turned the jet on full blast. It hit me in the face, and I choked out water. When they were done, they dried me off and bundled me into a robe over my sopping wet clothes. I nearly tripped going down the stairs, but Fodness almost wrenched my arm from the socket pulling me up to right me. It hurt.

"Let go of me, you raving bitch!" I spit out.

Her eyes blazed, and Terrell's mouth nearly dropped open in shock. Fodness continued to prod me forward down the company street. We stopped in front of the officers' quarters and Terrell pulled open the door. Fodness pushed me inside. I aimed toward a chair so I could sit down. I could barely keep my eyes open now.

They found a small dark room with a single bunk in it and pushed me in. Terrell and Fodness conferred, and the last thing I remember was lying on the bunk and their faces looking down at me. Then I passed out.

CHAPTER TWENTY~NINE

WALTER REED HOSPITAL, WASHINGTON, DC,
April 10, 1943, 10 a.m.

My mouth tasted like a Mongol horde had ridden through it, and I was so thirsty. I looked everywhere for a glass and water and couldn't find one.

I couldn't figure out where the hell I was, other than the fact that it looked like a hospital. Everything was white and chrome, shined to a high, very sterile state. I was wearing a white hospital gown that felt two sizes too large because it hung on me. Another person lay in the bed next to mine, but a screen was stretched around them, so there was no help to be had there.

I tried the door to my room and found it locked so I wandered to the window. A glance outside revealed a lawn and benches, and I was finally able to recognize the front lawn of Walter Reed. My memory of the previous night was fuzzy, but I didn't appear to be injured. Why was I back here? I wasn't complaining if it kept Fodness away from me, but I still wanted to know.

As I stood at the window, there was a short knock at the door and a dark-haired man with a thin moustache poked his head in.

"Oh, good. You're awake."

"Where am I? Who are you? Why am I here? And why is my room locked?" I asked.

He wore an amused expression that I wanted to smack off his face.

"Full of questions," he said. "You're at Walter Reed Hospital, and I'm Doctor Donald Willson. I'm on the medical staff here at the hospital. As to the other two questions, I'm assuming that you don't remember much of last night."

"Should I?"

"Frankly, yes, but I wouldn't call it one of the best additions to your service record."

I crossed my arms. "Why's that?"

He pulled a pipe and a pouch of tobacco out of his pocket, filled the pipe and lit it. Then he turned the chair next to my bed towards me and took a seat. "Are you familiar with the term 'drunk as a skunk?'"

I let out a bark of a laugh. "Me? Don't be silly."

"Do you drink?"

"Well, of course. But I barely had any last night." I looked at my fingernails, in truly sad shape from the engine work. I nodded at the person in the next bed. "Should we be discussing this in here?"

"Auxiliary Schroeder is catatonic. She won't even know you were here."

"Oh. Well, maybe I was too last night," I said, attempting a little levity.

"Auxiliary Moeller, this is serious. You are in very hot water right now."

"For what?"

"You don't remember *anything* that happened at the barracks?"

I thought a moment. "No. I don't."

"You created a huge stir. You even called Lieutenant Fodness a..." he consulted his notes. "...a raving bitch."

"I did?" *Good. Somebody had needed to do it.* Still, the fact that I didn't remember doing it was worrisome. "How did I get here?"

"Wait. We're not done with the drunkenness. You said you barely had anything to drink. How much?"

"A nip or two of whiskey," I said with a shrug.

"Anything else? I want to know what caused your behavior."

"I took a Nembutal. The doctor prescribed them for my sleeplessness."

"Which doctor?"

"Dr. Donnelly at the Bolling Field dispensary," I said.

He noted this in my file, then took a puff of his pipe and peered over his glasses at me. "You should never mix alcohol with any kind of prescription drug," he said. "It can cause all kinds of adverse reactions. Like what happened last night."

He read from his notes.

"You were kicking, screaming, and cursing out your superior officers. It says that Third Officer Keisler and Auxiliary Perri were instructed to inspect your belongings and they found multiple bottles of alcohol in your bed, your locker and your suitcase. Lieutenant Fodness and Lieutenant Terrell called an ambulance and had you brought here. Lieutenant Terrell insisted that you had to be having a medical emergency."

"Maybe I was," I said absentmindedly.

"How do you mean?"

"I got back from here a month ago, and Lieutenant Fodness has been riding me like a work horse, ever since she found out I used to be a movie star. I don't know why she hates me so much. I used to love being a WAAC. I signed up to make a difference. I liked Fort Des Moines and meeting all the other girls. I like learning about cars and trucks and how to repair them, but I really hate Lieutenant Fodness because she hated me first."

"Hate's a very strong word."

"Tell *her* that. I get that officers need to be strong and not take guff from anybody, but she's awful, doctor. I don't know why she won't let up. I work as hard as anyone else."

"Regardless, we need to keep you for observation. Some other doctors are also going to be speaking to you to see if this is an isolated incident or if this is something the service needs to worry about."

"Worry, how?"

Dr. Willson took his pipe out of his mouth and gestured with it. "Auxiliary Moeller, your record must be exemplary before you can be fully placed into a unit and deployed. If any of you ladies has a psychological problem, it could put your entire company in danger. It's a short hop from drinking to excess in your off hours to drinking on duty. What if you were to be chauffeuring a general around once you get to Europe? You could drive the staff car into a tree. We must ascertain if you pose a hazard before you can be allowed back to duty."

"Oh," I said, the wind sagging out of my sails.

"We'll also be interviewing your mother and some of your original references about your past experiences. We may not have vetted you as thoroughly as we should have. I'm going to note in your file that we spoke today, and Dr. Lemkau will be by to speak to you as well. Until we talk again, I'll say good-bye." He stood and made a final remark on the papers clipped on his clipboard.

Dr. Willson left the room, and I didn't see anyone else until dinner time, when I was fed a plate of rubbery chicken, a roll, some overcooked green beans, and a piece of apple cake. Of course, I didn't sleep. It was even worse here than it had been in the barracks. Down the hall was someone I assumed was a recent returnee from the Pacific, moaning and ranting about Japs. I covered my ears, tossing and turning for hours before dropping off around 2:00 a.m.

Breakfast was runny powdered eggs, a sad piece of bacon, toast with jam, a cup of fruit cocktail, and a small orange juice.

A day or two went by. I was allowed to walk in the garden, spend time in the library, nap, and play checkers with some of the other patients. After breakfast one morning, as I sat in the chair next to the window of my room, a fellow in white scrubs walked in. He had black curly hair trimmed short, a prominent nose, and dreamy dark brown eyes. I assumed he was another doctor.

"Auxiliary Moeller," he said with a nod.

"Hello." I did the same, but did not stand or salute. I wasn't sure if you saluted a military doctor or not. He didn't comment on it.

"I'm Doctor Lemkau. I've come to speak to you about your life and your time in the service," he said.

"Dr. Willson said there would be more of you."

"I'll be consulting on your case. We need to find out if this was an isolated incident or if you regularly get this inebriated and why."

"All right," I said, relaxing a little. Thanks to the brown eyes and cute dimples, he seemed harmless. He asked me questions about my youth and how I was raised. I told him about Daddy dying when I was a baby and about Momma raising me alone.

"You say you stayed with your Aunt Bessie and your cousin Natalie for a few years off and on. This is your mother's sister?"

"Yes."

"What was that like?"

"It was hard. Momma was busy working a lot, but Aunt Bessie and Natalie were nice to me. Auntie took me to the Columbia Theater in Norfolk when she could afford it. Momma took me back from them when I was about six, but she was a maid at the Monticello Hotel, so she worked a lot. The other hotel maids took me under their wing and watched me for her when she was on her rounds cleaning rooms."

"How long did that last?" he said, pencil at the ready.

"Until I was seven."

"And what about your schooling?"

"Momma sent me to St. Michael's for school and she still worked at the hotel and as a caterer. Later, we moved to Baltimore and she sent me to Mount St. Agnes."

"Private schools? How was your mother able to afford that on her maid's salary?" he asked, nibbling on the pencil eraser.

"She had a little stashed from an insurance policy daddy had. That, and Momma can be very self-sacrificing when she wants to be."

"That's very noble of your mother, worrying about your education."

"Don't fool yourself, doctor. There's always a reward for

Momma down the road."

"What do you mean?" he asked, pushing his glasses further up his nose.

"Momma's payoff is that she gets to *be* self-sacrificing, then use it as leverage to get me to do what she wants. All I ever wanted was to become independent and successful and confident."

"You were a successful Hollywood actress. You haven't done that?" he asked.

"Not really."

"Tell me more about that."

"I wanted to move to Hollywood and become a famous actress. We had some hard times, but with a lot of hard work, I finally did it. When sound came, and Fox asked me to take a pay cut, I was stupid enough to listen to Momma. Fox fired me, and I've been paying for it ever since. I've also had two unsuccessful marriages that she loves reminding me about."

"Tell me about those marriages."

I babbled on about Teddy and the bigamy and John and Sauerkraut Street and what an idiot I'd been both times. He nodded and took more notes.

"There is a notation in your file that you were very upset a few days ago. You were saying your husband, a naval commander, was reported missing. But when Lieutenant Terrell tried finding out more about this man, she found out he was perfectly fine, and that you're not married to this person. Mr... Benline. Why would you make up something like that?"

I thought a moment. Other than trying to stop Fodness from riding me like a Preakness winner, I had no excuse.

"All right, so I lied," I said. "You got me."

"But why did you lie?"

I sighed. "Lieutenant Fodness was at me constantly. I wanted a little sympathy. I wasn't getting any sleep, my feet hurt from my athlete's foot, and I wanted to be back at Fort Des Moines with my friends, doing good work and trying to win the war. I hate it here. *Hate it*!"

"When you say *here*, you mean the hospital? Or Washington? Or Bolling Field?" he said.

"Bolling," I spat out. "I loved basic training, Dr. Lemkau, with the marching and drilling and the camaraderie. I felt like I was doing something important for the country. I'd never felt so patriotic in my life. But here? I feel like a failure even though I'm not. The lieutenant hates me."

He looked thoughtful and steepled his fingers under his chin.

"Why does she hate you? Why do you think that?"

"How should I know?" I said. "One of the girls told her I was Olive Borden from the movies and ever since then, she's had it in for me."

"Did the rest of the auxiliaries in your unit have it in for you as well? I have statements here from several of them that multiple bottles of alcohol were found in your bed, your trunk, and your footlocker."

I swallowed hard. *The bitch had them go through my stuff.* "I don't know," I said quietly.

He jotted a note and read over the rest again. "So Mr. Benline...*are* you involved with him?"

"Yes," I admitted.

"Is it serious? I don't see a divorce from your second husband listed here anywhere. Merely a separation."

At my nod, he continued. "Talk to me a little about this relationship with Mr. Benline."

I sighed. "I like Artie a lot. He's not very handsome, but he treats me well, and he has money to take me out to nice places and buy me things."

"Is money important to you?"

"Put it this way," I said, fiddling with a loose thread on my hospital gown. "I'd rather marry someone rich than someone poor. I tried the poor thing when I was young and with my second husband. I didn't like it."

"Have you and Mr. Benline discussed marriage?"

"Yes, but I haven't given him an answer."

"Because you're not yet divorced."

I nodded. "Well, there's that. Also, Artie's a lot like my mother. He wants to treat me like a little girl and do everything for me. He drives me crazy doing that sometimes."

"Doing what?"

"Always calling me things like 'Baby' or 'Little Girl.' I can't be *Olive*. Like, when I sign my letters to him, I have to sign them 'Baby,' or he wonders what's wrong."

"You're saying he won't let you act your age?"

"Yes, like my mother."

"Tell me more about your relationship with your mother. We touched on it earlier, but let's go back to that for a minute."

"She's been an anvil around my neck for as long as I can remember. Sure, the movie magazines made us look like best friends, and sometimes, we can be, but I want to be an adult so badly, and I can never seem to do it. I'm nearly thirty-seven years old, but I'm still acting like a child because I don't know how to do anything else."

I told him about Momma's overprotectiveness, her crowding George out of my life, and then her hospitalization. His eyebrows lifted and he scribbled for quite a long time. I moved to the window and gazed out at the groundskeeper caring for the lawn. In the tree right outside my window, a robin twittered around her nest. Two small pale blue eggs sat inside. I gazed at it in fascination. That little bird had mated, and was making a home and a family better than I ever could.

"What else do we need to talk about?" Dr. Lemkau said, seemingly out loud to himself. "So no children with either husband? That's unusual."

"I douched," I said.

His eyebrow rose.

"A lot."

"You must have been very thorough. Are you sure that's the only reason?"

I glared at him. "That depends if I can be sent to the brig for my answer."

"This file is purely for diagnostic purposes, not legal ones."

I sighed. "I found out I was pregnant right as everyone discovered Teddy was a bigamist." Then I told him about the abortion, praying he wouldn't ask me for more details. Thankfully, he didn't. To distract him, I told him more about my marriage to John. It seemed to work.

"All right, Auxiliary Moeller, I think that's all for now," he said. "I'm going to go have my secretary type up this report."

"Doc, will they kick me out?" I said. "Of the WAACs, I mean."

"I don't know yet. The inquiry board will be meeting on April 27th to make a decision."

Then he was gone.

CHAPTER THIRTY

N~P CONFERENCE ROOM I, WALTER REED GENERAL HOSPITAL,
April 27, 1943

"So, gentlemen, to reiterate, I recommend a diagnosis of psychoneurosis and a stay at Forest Glen for Auxiliary Moeller," said Doctor Lemkau.

"You said you've received certificates from Lieutenant Fodness and the rest of the witnesses to the incident?" asked Major Janjigian.

"Yes, Major. They indicated what happened the night of April 9th and 10th, but as we've previously noted, there has been friction with Lieutenant Fodness since the beginning of her time as Moeller's CO. In addition, Auxiliary Moeller took a Nembutal pill the night of the incident, which exacerbated the alcohol she'd previously consumed."

"'Friction' with Lieutenant Fodness sounds like another way of shirking, Lieutenant."

"Permission to speak, sir," I said.

"Granted," said the major.

"Sir, that simply isn't true. I'm one of the hardest working girls out there. I love being a WAAC. I loved Fort Des Moines and basic training. But ever since I arrived here at Bolling

Field, Lieutenant Fodness has shown herself to be petty and mean. I've had problems sleeping for several years now, and although it improved during basic training, it's been worse since I got here because of her. If I could possibly be moved to another unit, I know that..."

Major Janjigian let out a deep guffaw that seemed to go on and on.

"Are you drunk *again*, Auxiliary Moeller? You took an oath to the United States when you joined up. That means you go where the U.S. government most needs you to go. How would it look if every soldier with a personal beef with their CO wanted to transfer? During the last war, General Pershing would have had no one to go over the top with. The Kaiser would be relaxing in Buckingham Palace right now. I'm sorry, but that's not how things work."

Lieutenant Colonel Hamlin shook his head at my impertinence, and Lieutenant Feinberg finally spoke up. He'd been quiet the whole meeting, listening and absorbing.

"I'm with Doctor Lemkau. I think a stay at Forest Glen with proper care and observation could be good for Auxiliary Moeller. We can judge how badly she wants to remain a WAAC and see how she does with treatment."

"Major?" Doctor Lemkau said, looking over at Janjigian.

"All right, Moeller. We'll give you another chance, thanks to Lieutenant Feinberg. I hope our trust is not misplaced."

"Thank you, sir. I'm looking forward to getting back to work," I said, trying to sound peppy and gung ho. I was an actress, after all. I had to play this convincingly.

They all stood up and saluted, as did I, and I went back to my room, as I'd been told to do. Eventually, an orderly arrived.

He told me he was there to transfer me, so I gathered up the few things that Rison, Nucifer, and Lundquist had packed of mine that had arrived at my room.

Forest Glen had previously been the National Park College, a women's private school a mile or two from the main hospital. The buildings were a mishmash of Greco-Roman, rural farmhouse, and thrown-together barracks styles. They'd kept the original beds and other furniture in the dormitories, so it was almost like being back at Mount St. Agnes again.

This was where they sent soldiers who were shell-shocked or had 'psychiatric problems.' I didn't, even though *they* thought I did. But if it kept Fodness off my back for a while longer, I was all for it.

The food wasn't as good as the main hospital, but one of the nurses made me think of Aunt Bessie. She was always so cheerful—asking me how I was, and really caring if I answered with anything less than a hundred percent. If I mentioned that my cough had come back, she gave me a dose of brewer's yeast and said that would clear it right up. If she saw me writing letters, she'd ask me who to and engage me in lively conversations about my family and friends.

At Forest Glen, I rested and did my best to get better. It was like Hollywood, with every need taken care of. No one expected anything of me except to be well enough to go back. No Momma, no John and his family, and best of all, no Fodness. Actually, it was *better* than Hollywood.

For the first time in my life, I was a real lady of leisure. I could sleep late or I could stroll the grounds. I could sit by the window and enjoy a book that I'd found in the patient library down the hall. I'd chosen *A Tree Grows in Brooklyn* and was already four chapters in. I could also play dominoes with Butch Myer in the patients' lounge. Butch had been at Kasserine Pass and had been peeing himself so he wouldn't have to go back. He was in for observation. I liked Butch well enough, but I had to remember to watch where I sat.

Eventually, it came time to go back, but Doctor Willson was stymied by the upper brass. He came to my room and told me that there would be a seven-day delay before I had to report back to Bolling Field. I mouthed a silent thank you to God for protecting me for one more week.

"Doctor?" I asked, as he headed for the door. "Do I have to stay here on campus or is this week something I can negotiate?"

"Why?" he asked.

"Well, I was packing to visit my mother the night I had my...episode." I stumbled over what to call it. "It would be nice if I could make the trip before I have to report back."

"Until you have to report, your time is your own, Moeller."

"Thank you. I know I told you all those awful things about Momma, but she is my mother. It's been a year since I've seen her."

"You don't owe me any explanation, Moeller. Have a good trip. But be back here by the fourteenth, or you'll be considered AWOL."

"Yes, sir."

I put on my WAAC dress uniform, which the gals had been kind enough to pack. Then I had one of the ambulance drivers drop me off at the depot on his way to pick up a new group of patients back from overseas.

I caught the National Limited north, and the Maryland countryside comforted me, reminding me of my years at

Mount St. Agnes. The B & O depot was actually in Jersey City, so I had to catch a bus into New York. One of them went all the way to Brooklyn, so I took that, then grabbed the LIRR to Long Island.

The house on Chestnut looked the same except for the victory garden carved into the front yard. Mr. Zitella answered the door and gave me an enthusiastic handshake.

"Let me salute you, Olive. It's so wonderful what you're doing. You're brave like my Junior."

"Thank you, Mr. Zitella. Is Momma here?"

"Oh, yes," he said stumbling over his words. "Sibbie! You have a visitor!"

There was a sudden pounding of footfalls on the stairs, and Momma threw herself into my arms in that overly melodramatic way she had. The emotion was almost as overdone as the cheap American Beauty perfume she'd recently discovered. I pulled back before I choked.

"Hi Momma," I said.

"What are you doing here?" she said, her eyes narrowing.

"I've got a week of leave before I have to go back," I said.

Seeing the question mark on Ernie's face, Momma's lie came out like spit on a shoeshine. So smooth, she impressed even me.

"Olive was injured in a training exercise," she drawled. "Her foot. Come on, pardner, you can tell me all about everything!" She took my arm and led me upstairs to her room. Same crocheted spread with sadly dingy crewelwork throw pillows and grungy rag rug on the floor. Momma sat down on her bed and patted the spot next to her. I sat.

"Tell me what's going on," she said, putting an arm around

me. "I've missed you so. You still owe me an explanation for why you didn't make it last month. What happened?"

"I started a letter, but I couldn't tell you. It's too embarrassing," I said.

"What is?"

I told her about the sleeplessness and the episode and the going to Walter Reed, then Forest Glen.

"They think I'm a drunk, Momma. That I'm... psy-cho-nu-raw-tik," I said, sounding out every syllable so I didn't trip over them. "Forest Glen is where they send the head cases. They think I'm a *head case*, Momma."

"*No one* calls my daughter crazy," she said, getting her back up.

"They haven't used that word..." I began.

"Of course they haven't. They're doctors, Olive. Doctors have all those code words they use instead. Code words for everything from 'mildly disturbed' to 'loony as a cuckoo clock.'"

"But I'm not. I'm not crazy. It's that Fodness bitch. She hates me."

"Then you must be twice as strong. You can't let her have this effect on you. You can't let her *make* you crazy." She paused a moment. "But if you *are* crazy, it definitely came from your father's side. That family of his was..."

"Momma, that's not important!" I said, already out of patience. "All that's important is whether I'm going to stay or not."

"Well, are you?"

"I don't know yet."

"What do you mean, 'I don't know yet'? Of course you are. You are a patriotic American. You signed up to do your duty, and you are not a shirker. I did not give birth to a shirker."

"Momma, you don't understand. I'm scared that if I go back, it will be as bad as before with Lieutenant Fodness. Worse."

"Fiddlesticks. You are a strong woman. Strong and brave. I did not raise you to be a coward, do you hear?"

"If this was a matter of being in combat and driving a general around, I could prove that I'm brave. Dodging bombs or repairing a command car in the nick of time. But it's the constant harassment, Momma. She's at me constantly. She picks at every little thing until I want to scream. That's why I drank, and why I took the Nembutal. I needed to relax. Now she has something to hang over my head. 'Moeller's a screw-up.' 'Moeller's a washout.'"

"I hate that you're still using that awful name, Moeller. *Bank* on your name. You're Olive Borden and always will be."

"It's ridiculous to argue about that now," I said, disgusted. Everything I was telling her, and that's what she chose to focus on. Besides, Fodness hated that I was Olive Borden. In the WAACs, it was a liability.

"You will go back with a stiff upper lip and you will show this Lieutenant Fosdick..."

"*Fodness...*" I said impatiently.

"Whatever. You will show this woman your mettle and when this war is over, you will have a nice handsome pension. We'll be on easy street again. Not as wealthy as your movie star salary, but we can buy a cute little cottage—maybe in Santa Monica again. You liked living at the beach, Baby." She watched me for a reaction after her slipup in calling me Baby. "Olive, look at me. Look at this sad, pathetic little room I have to live in."

I hoped Mr. Zitella wasn't eavesdropping at the door, or

Momma might not have even this before too long.

"Losing your Fox contract was bad, but you were still working, for goodness sakes. You've made mistakes, Lord knows. Marrying that bigamist Jew, and then that...penniless Hun! If you don't fix this, you're damning the both of us to a life of squalor. Is that what you want? That life we left behind? That sad existence of cheap apartments and dinge?"

"Of course not, Momma."

She clutched my shoulders and gazed directly into my eyes. "Then straighten up and fly right, my girl. This is our *future* you're gambling with. Get your head in a good place. When they call you back, you put a smile on your face and a spring in your step. When they tell you to march, you march. When they make you clean up something, you scrub it until it glows. Do I make myself clear?"

"Yes, Momma."

"Now I'm going down to the kitchen to make us some tea. Then we can chat about more pleasant things."

B & O DIPLOMAT TRAIN BETWEEN NEW YORK AND WASHINGTON, D. C., *May 14, 1943*

Get your head in a good place. Get your head in a good place. It ran through my head over and over, like the rhythm of the tracks beneath us.

I gazed out the window at the fields of New Jersey. The dogwoods were in bloom, so I leaned my head back against the linen headrest and tried to concentrate on them so I wouldn't slip into the lavatory and have a nip.

The more I thought about Momma's 'pep talk,' the angrier I got. Getting me fired up to go back to Bolling Field was all about Sibbie Borden and how my getting drummed out would make *her* feel. How me looking unpatriotic would reflect on *her*. Most of all, how the lack of salary and pension would hit *her* pocketbook.

I thought about what going back would mean—knuckling under to Fodness, having to deal with the now-constant pain in my back with no booze to help me sleep, and being under extra scrutiny upon my return. I was so tired. If I had to be completely honest, service life was not for me either. At least in Hollywood, there were obscene amounts of money, beautiful clothes, and wonderful parties. If the service wouldn't move me out from under Fodness, there was nothing for me there anymore. I'd have to figure out a way to get a transfer myself.

The Washington B & O depot was in Takoma Park, and I grabbed a bottle of Old Granddad at a liquor store nearby before catching a cab to Bolling with a bunch of other WAACs on their way back from a weekend pass. Banners proclaiming the one-year anniversary of the WAACs greeted me.

Walking up to the barracks door, I felt my stomach roll over with a thud. Going in was even worse. Women I'd considered bunkmates and friends eagle-eyed me, and all chat ceased. I held my head high as I made my way to my bunk.

"Welcome back, Moeller," Perri finally offered.

"Thanks," I said. I set down my bag without unpacking it. Then, pulling a *Photoplay* out of my trunk, I stretched out on my bunk and pretended to be engrossed in it.

"How are you feeling?" Perri asked.

"Fine. I feel fine." *Thanks for going through my stuff and informing on me, you Judas.*

Like clockwork, here came Lieutenant Terrell, striding toward my bunk.

"I hope you're feeling better, Moeller. The captain would like to see you in her office. I'm supposed to escort you there."

I followed her past the other women, out the door, and the others began gossiping as soon as I was out of earshot.

The captain's office was across the green, and up a flight of stairs in another building. There was a photograph of President Roosevelt on the wall, and an American flag in the corner. I stood at attention and stared at the fringe on it instead of making eye contact.

"Thank you, Lieutenant Terrell. Dismissed," said the captain.

Lieutenant Terrell nodded and shut the door behind herself as she departed.

"At ease, Moeller."

I relaxed a little and looked at the sign on her desk. Captain Fisher.

"I hope you're feeling better. Well-rested. Doctor Willson told me he thought you would do well with a second chance. I hope his confidence is not misplaced."

"Permission to speak, ma'am."

She looked up at me and nodded.

"Before we go any further, ma'am I'd like to request a transfer. To *any* unit that is not under the supervision of Lieutenant Fodness. I want to do well here, but she's made that impossible."

Her eyebrows shot up, but she retained her cool demeanor.

"I'm sorry, Moeller, but the service doesn't work that way. While you were at the hospital, they finished the new mess hall. We're putting you to work there on KP for a little change of scenery. Speak to your CO. She'll give you all the details. Dismissed."

I stood there a moment, still in shock. They were really going to send me back into hell, working under that woman again. No explanations, no qualifications, just do it or else.

The captain looked up at me, her eyebrows raised. "Is there a problem, Moeller?"

"No ma'am," I said with a sigh. I saluted and left her office, dragging myself back to the barracks, trying not to cry. Why had I ever done this? I wasn't army material. Who was I kidding?

I'd finished putting my clothes and toiletries back in their places when the shrill whistle and "Atten-hut!" sounded, alerting us that Fodness had arrived. We all hurried to stand attention at the feet of our bunks, and I wanted to throw up. Of course, she made a beeline to me. I stood at attention, and she moved in a few inches from my face and stared at me, doing her best to intimidate. I tried not to react.

"Auxiliary Moeller. I'm surprised to see you back here, after your little stunt. Back for more? We'll see about that. Personally, I don't think you can hack it. You couldn't make it in talkies, and you can't make it here."

I didn't flinch.

"You've put away your things already. Impressive." She raised an eyebrow and moved to my locker, surveying everything in it.

"Washcloth on the wrong shelf, one gig. Shoes are scuffed, one gig. These blouses are wrinkled. One gig. EACH."

Never mind that I hadn't been able to do laundry or shine my shoes since I returned. I seethed.

"Thanks to you, Moeller, I'm canceling leave for this entire outfit. You'll all clean this place until it sparkles. Fall out and get to it!"

She retreated, and as she left, the glares from the other girls were murderous. When we were done with cleaning, I went back to Captain Fisher again and begged her to send me back to the hospital for my nerves.

"Denied," she said, looking me up and down. "You look fine to me, Moeller. Toughen up and go back to your unit. You joined up to make a difference, so go make one."

"Permission to speak, ma'am," I said.

She looked up from her papers with a cynical expression. "Granted."

"I joined up to make a difference, that's true. But Lieutenant Fodness has had a problem with me since I arrived, and I'm still in her unit, even though I've asked to be reassigned. You may think I look fine, but I'm not. If you won't allow me to be sent back to the hospital, then you leave me no choice, and I'll purposely do something to be sent back there." I raised my chin so I could look down my nose at her.

She glared at me. "You'll return to your unit or you'll be headed for the brig. Dismissed."

Furious, I stalked back to the barracks and pulled my new bottle of Old Granddad out of my footlocker, then I sat down on my bunk, put my feet up, and proceeded to take a couple long draws on the thing.

"Moeller!" Perri cried. "What are you doing?! They'll gig all of us along with you!"

"I. don't. care," I said, narrowing my eyes. "I've had it with this place."

"I'll go get Lieutenant Fodness," Hilliard said.

Fodness arrived in minutes, and she was boiling mad. "Moeller, give me that bottle," she said with gritted teeth.

I took another huge swallow. "Come and take it."

"You're in big trouble. This is *it* for you here."

"Good!" I said. I was past caring. "I'm sick, remember? I'm a neurotic alcoholic. *You've* driven me to drink more than I ever did. Send me back to the hospital right now." I took another long swig, emptying the bottle. She snatched it away from me, then grabbed my arm and hustled me toward the door.

"Hilliard, pack up her stuff again. Pack it *all*. She's not coming back this time."

"Promise?" I said with a laugh.

"*March.* To my office. *Now.*" I did, and she aimed me toward a chair. "Sit down before I really lose my temper," she said. Then she called Walter Reed and had them dispatch another ambulance to pick me up.

I felt lighter than air when it arrived at the hospital. They put me in a room down the hall from my previous one on Ward 19. Doctor Lemkau was *not* happy to see me.

"What are you doing back here, Moeller?" he said. "When we sent you back to Bolling, you said you were excited to return to duty. You were going to keep your nose clean and try to be a good soldier. What happened?"

"I tried, Doctor Lemkau. But I had those seven days before I went back, so I traveled home to New York to see my mother."

"And? I seem to recall your relationship with your mother as being very fraught," he said. "So again, I ask, what happened?"

"My mother happened. She gave me a pep talk to send me back, but I realized something."

"What's that?" he said.

"I'm not here because of me. I'm not sure I ever was. I don't want to be a soldier any more than I want to be an actress. I'm here because my mother wanted me to come back."

"I was under the impression that you'd had another breakdown."

"Oh no," I said with a laugh. "I made it up. When they sent me back under Fodness, even though I asked for a transfer, they wouldn't do it. I pulled out my bottle of whiskey and told old Fussypants Fodness to come and take it. The old bag did it. So here I am."

"Let me get this straight. You *purposely* committed a disciplinary infraction to get sent back here?" He shook his head and let out a deep sigh.

"You said yourself that I'm sick, that I'm neurotic," I said. "The truth is that I can't sleep and I'm miserable."

"Lieutenant Feinberg and I vouched for you in that hearing. We thought if we sent you back that you would remember why you joined up in the first place."

"You did, and I'm sorry, but Lieutenant Fodness killed that feeling all over again."

"Lieutenant Fodness is not the problem here, Moeller. She has a job to do, like you, but you're not doing yours."

"Look, doc. We both know what's happening here. You want to drum me out. I *want* you to drum me out. I absolutely can't go back and serve under that woman. I don't want to be court martialed, but the government won't reassign me. I'm not sure where that leaves us. All right?"

He continued scratching away at his notes, and it was some time before he said anything. He finally looked up at me, but I couldn't read his expression. "Dismissed, Moeller. We'll talk again tomorrow."

I nodded and gave him a cocky, half-hearted salute before heading back to my room. The next day he gave a quick rap on the door and took a seat beside my bed, as I was reading an article about PT skippers in *Life* magazine. As he spoke, I continued to casually flip past ads for Nescafé and Heublein's Club Cocktails, determined to show him I was done with the service. All I wanted was my freedom.

He asked me a few half-hearted questions, then rose and departed abruptly. I shrugged and kept reading. I was determined to enjoy this break while I had it. I had no idea what to expect after this.

Until they decided what they were going to do with me, I took long walks on the grounds—the garden path, the formal garden, and around the Memorial Chapel. I also read, wrote letters to Artie and Holloway, or did my laundry. I still wasn't sleeping well, but at least my days were a little less stressful.

Four days after I arrived, I was called into another conference with Colonel Hamlin, Doctor Lemkau, and Lieutenant Feinberg. When I entered the room, all three were glowering at me.

"Auxiliary Moeller, have a seat."

I did.

"Captain Lemkau has told us about his interviews with you this week. Why don't you tell us in your own words what happened upon your return to Bolling Field?"

I told them about Fodness once again harassing me and wrapped up by saying I'd loved much of my time in the

WAACs, but that I wouldn't go back to Bolling Field, and that she didn't want me back.

"All I wanted was a different superior officer. That could have solved all this," I finished.

"You seem inordinately proud of drinking contraband liquor in the barracks to get you sent back here," Colonel Hamlin said.

"I did what I had to do, sir. No one would listen to me."

"That is the most selfish, self-serving thing I have ever heard in all my years of service," Lieutenant Feinberg said. "Entirely egocentric. Gentlemen?"

"Agreed," said Hamlin.

"Permission to speak," I said.

"Denied," said Colonel Hamlin. "I've heard quite enough."

"So, Forest Glen until we make it official?" said Feinberg.

"Let no one say we didn't do this by the book," Lemkau said.

"Dismissed, Moeller."

"But sir, I..."

"Dismissed. You're being ordered back to Forest Glen until a Section VIII can be arranged. You're lucky we're not court martialing you. The less you say now, the better."

The brass left the room, so I took a walk to clear my head. I'd gotten what I wanted. Now what?

They moved me to Forest Glen, and once again, I was a lady of leisure for a few weeks until I figured out what to do with the rest of my life. I wrote a long letter to Momma, telling her about being sent back here and how going back was something I'd done for her and not for me. I had no idea what her reaction would be, but I knew it wouldn't be good. When I received her reply a week later, it was as bad as I expected.

Olive—

Your selfishness dictated your behavior, and it has turned out badly for you. I can't say I'm surprised. Even after my begging you not to do this, it had no effect. You're leaving us both in dire straits,

I have decided to move back to Los Angeles because I miss the warmth and friendliness of the people. I moved to New York because you were here. I've written to my friend Sister Essie, and she has offered me a place at the mission, helping unfortunates.

When I think about everything you've thrown away—the career, the marriages, the service pension—it makes me sad. I'll most likely have to fall back on my cooking and cleaning skills, but I'd rather be a maid in California than here.

Your Loving Mother

Typical Momma. Pointing the finger at me, while refusing to admit any responsibility for her part in my leaving Hollywood.

On the 25th, the official news finally came. The papers were filed, I was escorted to the front gate of the facility, and they handed me my discharge. That day, I left Forest Glen, the WAACs, and the service behind for good.

I GOTTA RIGHT TO SING THE BLUES

CHAPTER THIRTY~ONE

3428 13TH STREET S.E., WASHINGTON, D.C.,
May 27, 1943

When Artie had written the previous month, he hadn't been able to tell me much, other than that he was alive and well. He'd been commissioned as a SEABEE, one of the construction battalion engineers who built spur-of-the moment bridges, repaired them, or dynamited them so the enemy couldn't use them.

Artie was the soul of discretion, and absolutely wouldn't tell me where he was going, no matter how much I begged, so his letter wasn't as censored as some of the girls' sweethearts' letters were.

"I know you wouldn't do it knowingly, honey, but you have to assume the walls have ears now. It's better that you don't know," he'd told me during our last phone call.

"I know. You're right. But it's so hard not knowing where you are."

I'd really grown to care for that receding hairline and paunch, even if I still wasn't sure about marriage. This had all started as a lark to get me away from John, but with the whole world on fire, I clung to Artie as the only bit of normalcy I had left. When he told me he had gotten a week's liberty in DC, I was ecstatic.

I wrote him back, but knew he'd wonder why my address was a room in a house in Congress Heights that I'd had to fight tooth and nail for. Washington was packed to the gills with service people and government employees. Before he arrived on the 27th, I had several nips out of the flask in my purse, covering up the smell with Doublemint gum.

At National Field, they pushed the stairs up to the door of the Clipper, and Artie caught my eye and waved. He strode across the tarmac with a new confidence in his step. I thought how handsome he looked in his dress blues with their white trim and polished brass buttons. By contrast, I was wearing a maroon dress with a peplum and black spectators. I knew he'd wonder why I wasn't in uniform.

Artie carried a military duffel in his right hand, and as he approached me, he dropped the bag and scooped me up in a big hug.

"How was the trip?" I asked as he loosened his hold.

"Bit rough," he said. "But the stewardesses were real pros. They sat me next to a Norwegian diplomat, and we had an interesting chat about Narvik. I left Bizerte four days ago. Bizerte to Lisbon, then Lisbon to New York, then here. I'd kill for a shower. Whaddya say I get a room at the Willard?"

"We can see if there's any space," I said.

He frowned. "That bad, huh? I haven't been to DC since the war started."

"If there's no room, you can stay with me," I said.

"Not sure your CO would like that idea," he said. "And I meant to ask...why wasn't there an APO on your last envelope?"

"We have lots to talk about," I said brightly. "Let's get a cab."

His eyebrow arched, but he nodded. Once outside the terminal, we stood at the curb and Artie raised his arm. A taxi pulled up and we crawled in.

"Where'll it be, mac?" the driver asked.

"The Willard," Artie said.

"Yeah? Hope you got a reservation. They're packin' 'em in there."

Artie sighed. "Guess that was a daydream. Know any smaller, out-of-the-way hotels where I might be able to find a spot?"

"Let's try the Mount Vernon near the Lincoln Memorial," the driver said. "You might get lucky there."

"Thanks," Artie said, finally relaxing against the seat back. We were in the middle of sharing a reunion kiss when the driver decided to get chatty.

"Seen much action?" he asked.

"Just got back from North Africa," Artie said. "SEABEES."

"Glad you beat those Frog bastards. What a buncha traitors to their own country. Especially that Darlan. Glad somebody fixed *his* little red wagon."

Artie smiled.

"Me, I couldn't join up. Four F cause of my flat feet."

"Sorry to hear that," Artie said.

"Whaddya gonna do?" the driver shrugged. "Still, there's plenty of pretty girls around here who want dates when the weekend comes around. I'm doing important work stateside." He chuckled at his own joke.

It wasn't on a par with the Willard, but the Mount Vernon had one precious room still available. Artie checked us in as

Mr. and Mrs. Arthur Benline, and we followed the bellhop up to the fourth floor.

Artie thanked him with a tip, then we went inside and put the Do Not Disturb sign on the door. Artie placed his hat on the chest of drawers, then unbuttoned his coat and loosened his tie. I flicked on the table lamp and we embraced next to the bed.

"I missed you so much," I said, laying my head on his shoulder.

"I missed you too. Are you going to tell me what's going on now?"

"Not yet. Can't we relax for a little while?"

"Let me take a shower first. He grabbed his shaving kit, a towel, and a robe and headed down the hall to the bathroom. When he returned, he smelled of bergamot aftershave. "Now, where were we?"

I cuddled up close. "Here. I want you to hold me. Kiss me, Artie."

He did.

"Harder. So I know you mean it."

"Olive, I—"

"Shhhhhhhh...."

I lifted my face to his and kissed his cheek, his lips, his eyes, his forehead...as if I could somehow shift all the pain I'd been carrying onto him and it would go away.

He stroked my hair soothingly, as he'd always done, and I closed my eyes and led him to the bed. It wasn't what I wanted, but he'd expect it, and considering what I had to tell him, it was the least I could do.

When I came to the next morning, the sun was beginning to filter through the drapes. Artie still lay on his back with his right arm flung out, me nestled against his side.

I checked my little Timex and it was eight a.m. I suppose he felt me moving.

"What time is it, Baby?" he asked, rubbing the stubble on his chin.

"About six," I said. "Should I order us some breakfast?"

"Sure," he said. "Whatever you get is fine with me, as long as there's coffee."

I nodded and dialed room service, able to get us eggs, fruit, and farina, along with a pot of coffee. But we'd be drinking it without sugar, thanks to rationing. When it was delivered, we spread everything out on the lowboy cabinet, and I poured the coffee. I sipped it and spooned up some eggs as Artie broached the subject again.

"If that was buttering me up for bad news, I can take it, you know."

"Bad news? Meaning what?"

"I'm not stupid, Ollie. You're not in your dress uniform. You're not mailing from the APO. What happened?"

"Oh, that."

"Yes, oh that."

I took a drink of coffee to wet my whistle but my mouth stayed dry, so I took a deep breath before beginning.

"I got drummed out."

"You what?"

"You heard me."

"Is this because of that Lieutenant Foster you told me about in your last couple of letters?" he asked, his face full of concern.

"Liertenant Fodness. Yes. I... I've been in and out of Walter Reed for almost two months."

"Oh, baby."

"*Please* stop calling me baby. I've told you."

"It's a pet name."

"I'm not a *pet*, Artie. I'm a grown woman!"

"Then maybe you should act that way. What did you do to get drummed out of the WAACs?"

I lowered my head, unable to meet his eyes. I outlined the USO show, the drinks, the Nembutal, and the incident on base that got me sent to the hospital. He ran his hand through what was left of his hair so that it stuck up in little points and cow-licks from his pomade.

"For God's sake, Olive, you're smarter than that. Washing sleeping pills down with booze? Are you completely crackers? You had to know the result wouldn't be good."

"I wanted to escape," I said hoarsely.

"You could have escaped permanently. Is that what you want?"

"I don't know what I want."

"Ever since I first met you, it seems like you've been trying to escape from something. First it was your mother, then lingerie movies, then John, now the WAACs?" he said.

I sat quietly chewing, but my eggs now felt like rubber in my mouth.

"Do you want to escape from *me*?" he asked. The quaver in his voice cut me to the core.

"No. You're all I have left."

He stood up and crossed to his jacket, which was hanging on the bedpost. He pulled something out of the pocket.

"I was going to give you this."

He set a velvet box down next to my plate. When I opened it, a square-cut diamond ring lay inside against the white satin.

"You *were*?" The past tense was scary.

"Let's get one thing straight, Olive. I love what I do. I'm a navy man through and through. I love my men, and I'm proud as hell of them. Defending America is important to me."

"What does that have to do with a proposal?"

"The navy expects a certain kind of wife for its officers. Beautiful, elegant, dignified, and someone who will support her husband. She'll manage the household efficiently, raise the kids well, and move anywhere without complaining."

"And?"

"And I'm not sure how I propose to someone who has such different goals than me. Do you know how selfish you look right now? I vouched for you, for Christ's sake! I can't marry a woman who would have so little regard for herself, for me, or for her country." He grabbed the ring box back and put it back in his pocket.

I nodded, tears clogging my vision.

"I still love you," he said. "I've loved you since I first met you. I'm still your friend, but I can never be your husband. That hurts me more than you will ever know."

"I understand," I said hoarsely.

"What will you do now?" he asked, not unkindly.

"I'm still trying to figure that part out," I said.

"Do you need any money?"

"I don't want your money, Artie."

"Please let me help. I don't want you to have to go crawling back to Sibbie."

Against my protests, he handed me forty dollars and told me to send him updates so he'd know how I was doing. He wanted me to stay at the Mount Vernon, but I wanted to get back to my place.

When I left the hotel, a light drizzle had started. I wasn't sure where I was going, but I kept walking. As I trudged onto the Arlington Memorial Bridge and watched the raindrops pelt the surface of the Potomac, I considered jumping, but my Catholic nature screamed in protest. I twisted Daddy's pansy ring back and forth on my finger, imagining all the good luck I'd thought it would bring me. If anything, it had done the exact opposite, my entire life. Or maybe it was simply me, making bad decision after bad decision.

I finally slipped it off, and with a sob, I hurled it into the river, then stalked away.

CHAPTER THIRTY~TWO

or over a year, I took a series of jobs, trying to make a new life for myself, first in Washington, then elsewhere. DC was still bursting at the seams from all the service people, and rents were high. Somehow, the topic of work always came up, and things turned awkward with whomever I met. The seat of government was nowhere to admit I'd been kicked out of the WACs, which the service had now become, dropping the second A. It was too embarrassing. After a few months, I decided to head further west.

I wrote to Artie a few times, and he continued to write back, but it was merely cordial. I was now a liability for him, and my conversations with the doctors at Walter Reed had shown me that I'd been using him as a crutch. I didn't really love him, and if I *had* married him, it would merely have been for money and comfort. Another mistake.

I ended up in Chicago for a few months, but my first winter there was miserable, so after hoarding all my tips and quitting my job waiting tables at the Triangle Restaurant on South Wabash, I booked a ticket to Reno just before Christmas and stayed there for the first few months of '44. It took me a while, but I finally made the divorce from John official.

I wrote Holloway to see how things were going. Her unit

had been sent in after D-Day and now she was stationed in Reims, along with British Women's Services, Auxiliary Territorial Services, Women's Royal Navy Services, and the WAAFs. I got a reply a few weeks later.

Hi Moeller—

Wow. Nevada, huh? How'd you end up there? I'm baking my little heart out here in Joan of Arc's old digs. Lots of bread and pies for hungry soldiers. I love it. Who knew my hands could get so flour-y? Your mother mentioned you were out and moving around. Sorry it didn't work out. You were gung ho back in old FDM. What happened?

Evidently, your mother has gone through quite the conversion. She mentioned Jesus about ten times in her letter. Said you might be wanting her address, so here it is:

Sibbie Borden
Sunshine Mission
558 Wall Street
Los Angeles, California

It's getting to be about chow time, so I'm going to wrap this up.

Write soon,
Holloway

Jesus? Well, at least now that Momma had found *him*, she might let up on me for a change.

UNION STATION, LOS ANGELES, CALIFORNIA,
November 15, 1944

The new depot was a cut above the old La Grande Station. The whitewashed stucco stood out against the vivid blue sky. It looked like an old Spanish mission.

Delighted squeals echoed around me as servicemen on leave from all branches were reunited with their sweethearts, and there were tears on the platforms as others departed, possibly for the last time. The war was still ongoing, but since D-Day there was a new optimism. At last, Hitler's Master Race was on the run. The Royal Navy had just sunk ten ships in a convoy, and the Soviets had crossed the Danube. In the east, Midway had turned the tide and we had island hopped closer to Japan.

My navy skirt and basic white blouse with navy sweater had seemed comfortable enough when I left Reno, but were now oppressively hot, even in fall. I hated the thought of having to stay with Momma, but I was on my last few bucks, and I was too proud to ask Artie for more money. I was completely out of options, short of prostitution.

On the platform, Momma stood craning her neck to search for me. I'd caught sight of her first thing from the train but kept away from the window as much as possible. After we'd pulled to a stop, I filed through the car to the exit. I'd dreamed of returning to Hollywood in triumph after a smash on the east coast, but that hadn't happened. Now I'd be spending the rest of my days in hell.

"Yoohoo!" Momma shouted, waving her arm like her life depended on it. She enveloped me in a hug and chattered as if the last year and her last letter was water under the bridge.

"I've missed you so, pardner. You and all the adventures we used to have. I can't *wait* for you to meet Sister Essie. You'll simply *adore* her. Everyone does. And they can't wait to meet you at the mission. I've been talking about you forever.

"Are you tired? You must be after that trip. Do you remember Beauregard Lee? His family lived down the street from us in Norfolk? His mother wrote me that he was badly wounded at Monte Cassino. He's doing better now, but he was at Walter Reed too. Same time as you. It's such a small world."

We retrieved my trunk, full of not very much, then caught a cab to 6th and Wall. The Sunshine Mission was a three-story, yellow brick apartment building behind the Nazarene Church. The cab driver helped us with the trunk, and I stood for a moment taking in my new home.

A sign above the door read:

SUNSHINE•MISSION
There's•Always•Room•for•One•More.

We entered the front vestibule, and once again, Momma let out a cheerful "Yoohoo!"

Down the stairs swept a chestnut-haired woman in a loose white blouse and white skirt, wearing a short black silk cape. Around her neck hung a large gold crucifix.

"Sister Sibbie!" she said. "I thought that was you! And this must be your lovely daughter, returned from the war. Thank you for your service, dear. I hope you'll be very happy here with us. Sister Sibbie, would you like to take Olive to your room? Sister Beatrice put fresh linens on the bed. Olive might like a nap before helping us with the dinner service. I expect you must be quite tired. Our little G.I. Jane! So *brave*, turning over that enemy truck!"

I looked sideways at Momma, at a loss. Only God knew what she'd been telling them.

"I'll have Brother Ike come get her trunk," Sister Essie continued. "Sister Sibbie, you can help her get settled in, can't you? I need to get back to the lunch flock."

"Of course. We're bunking together, pardner," Momma said, turning to me. "This way."

At intervals along the wall as we climbed the stairs were a series of badly painted biblical pictures—Daniel in the lion's den, Joseph's coat of many colors, Judith with the head of Holofernes, and Moses with the tablets.

"Enemy truck?" I said.

"Well, I had to tell them something. I couldn't very well tell them you'd gotten yourself drummed out of the service, now could I?"

We entered a small room next to a storage closet. Inside were two twin-size beds with utilitarian spreads of navy cotton. A small cheap nightstand fit between them, and on it, a lamp with a cracked ceramic base and dusty pleated shade provided low light. A portrait of a beaming Jesus hung on the wall next to a primitively carved wooden cross. The venetian blinds were angled to block the glaring western sun, and the room was like a hotbox.

"I'll open the window when the sun goes down," Momma said. "No point now." She moved to the corner and switched on an electric fan. It only circulated the hot air.

Plenty of silent stars had fallen by the wayside, but I could have risen along with Joan Crawford and the rest of them—kept my beautiful home, saved my money, and been living it up, but for my spendthrift ways and my pride. If I'd married George, I would have kept it too. If if if. Regret was the most important word in my life.

Momma continued to chatter about the mission, about Sister Essie, and about the people they helped until I wanted to scream.

"...and of course, Inez wouldn't sit next to Maria because she didn't like Mexicans, but then Sister explained that we help everyone, regardless of where they're from, and Inez—"

"Momma, hush!" I said, placing my hands over my ears.

"Oh, silly me," Momma said. "Here I am gabbing away. Of course, you're tired and want to rest. I'm sorry, honey."

"Yes," I said in relief. "Please leave me be for a while."

"Here you go," Momma said, plumping up the pillow on the bed. "This one's yours. Do you need anything else? Another pillow? A sheet to put on top of you? It's awfully hot, but—"

Momma's love also meant Momma's smothering. There could never be one without the other.

"I'll be fine, Momma," I snapped.

Momma sighed. "I'm trying here, honey. I missed you so. You have no idea how much."

"Just leave me alone, please," I said. I kicked off my oxfords then pulled off the sweater, unbuttoned my skirt and blouse and lay down in my slip. Momma moved closer and touched my face tenderly.

"I'll be downstairs helping get lunch ready," she said. "When you wake up, we'll give you the tour. I'm glad you're here."

She retreated downstairs and I curled up in a ball, eventually falling into an exhausted sleep.

When I woke, my trunk had been moved to the foot of my bed. My hairbrush and toothbrush were packed inside, along with some Ipana, and I discovered a powder room down the hall where I freshened up a little. Lots of clanking and the smell of cooking led me downstairs, then through a set of double doors that stood open to receive the needy.

A sign printed in big block letters said:

GIVE US THIS DAY OUR DAILY BREAD

A stack of plates and tubs of forks, knives, and spoons stood ready. Next to them, Momma wore a hair net and dished up vegetables. She greeted everyone with a smile, and after every three or four, she'd call regulars by their names, or say, "Blessed are the hungry, for they shall have spuds!" or something equally pithy to keep the line moving.

"How are you, Lorraine?" she asked an older woman with graying hair, an old brown dress with cabbage roses, and shabby shoes. "How's that cough? Any better?"

Lorraine nodded as Momma put mounds of mashed potatoes and string beans on her plate. The others shuffled through the line, generally quiet, but occasionally brightening at Momma's remarks. She looked up from her pots to see me.

"Margie, this is my daughter Olive. She's going to be joining us here at the mission. She's a war heroine!"

Margie filed past, giving me a nod, and I did the same.

Another woman serving cloverleaf rolls joked, "Sister Sibbie, we should be serving fish today with all these loaves I'm handing out!"

"Hallelujah!" Momma cried. To a blowsy blonde in a baggy

dress, Momma spooned up an extra large helping. "Here, Doris. You need a few more potatoes, honey. You take care now, all right?"

What was it the chaplain in B Company had told me over mess one night? There was no zeal quite as intense as the newly converted? Momma was now among those. I appreciated Sister Essie for caring for us when I no longer could, but now, in addition to smothering me, Momma would smother me with Jesus. For all his faults, Teddy and his lackadaisical Judaism had suited me fine.

"Grab a tray, honey," Momma said, drawing me out of my reverie. "I'm sure you're hungry after your long trip."

I did, and the lady next to Momma plopped a thin chicken cutlet on my plate with a smile. "I'm Sister Edith," she said. "It's nice to meet you at last. Sister Sibbie's told us so much about you. I feel like I already know you."

"Hello," I said, moving down the line. It was strange feeling like everyone knew you, when you didn't know them at all. Like a horrible parody of Hollywood.

I took my tray and sat in a corner away from the crowd, reminded of the mess hall at Fort Des Moines. The difference was that my fellow diners weren't pretty, smart-aleck recruits, but the unfortunate, down-on-their-luck women of Los Angeles and their children—hookers, panhandlers, alcoholics, drug addicts, and other lost souls.

A towheaded kid in a sailor suit made a beeline to my side and stared at me, so I scowled at him. He paled and moved away to another table. Afterward, I slipped back upstairs, trying to avoid Momma. Despite the heat, I pulled the sheet over my head. According to the little alarm clock next to the bed, it was close to two p.m. when she returned to the room.

"All right, pardner, up and at 'em," she said, tossing the sheet aside.

I groaned. "No, Momma."

She frowned. "Do you know how unusual this is? Sister Essie letting a grown mother and daughter stay here together to *work?* It's unheard of. She's doing this because she has a good heart, but you *are* going to help. Without us, without the meals we make and the hope we give these people, they would have nothing. *You and I* would have nothing! Do you understand?"

I sighed. "Can I start tomorrow? Please?"

Momma gazed down at me. "All right. But tomorrow morning, you wake up ready to work. Got it?"

"Got it," I said. I pulled the sheet back over my head and tried to blot it all out as long as I could.

The next day and every day afterward became a blur of changing sheets and pillowcases, scrubbing toilets, peeling potatoes, and chopping carrots. Although I'd never been an exceptional cook, strangely enough it was easier for me to follow the recipes for a hundred people rather than cooking for two. The steps were all spelled out for me. Best of all, sauerkraut was never on the menu.

I also fed and diapered the babies, cooing to and cuddling them. It hurt to hand them back to their mothers, but I did it. As for the orphans, I was sad that there were abandoned babies in the world, but happy that I was the one who got to care for them, rocking them until they fell asleep. I made believe they were mine and George's and I'd snuggle them close and think about how I'd ended up here. George had married back in 1933, to an actress named Marguerite Churchill, and they had two kids. I couldn't help but wonder what their lives were like—if he ever thought about me...if he ever wondered about me.

Life at the mission was a lot like the military. I rose at five to make my own breakfast, take a bath, and dress. At 5:30, I fed and diapered the babies, then helped cook for the whole mission. We opened the doors promptly at 6:30 and did the dishes afterward.

Around 7:30, I changed the beds and got the sheets ready to launder. At ten, I began cleaning, which included dusting, sweeping, mopping, polishing, and washing windows.

"Cleanliness is next to Godliness!" Momma would chirp, using newspaper and ammonia to polish the windows until they shone. All the better to view the spectacle that was Skid Row.

Since lunch service was at 11:30, those of us on kitchen duty started cooking around 10:30. After we washed dishes, we went back to cleaning. If I was lucky, I'd be able to squeeze in a short nap before I had to cook dinner. Those of us who worked the lunch service line were given a reprieve for dinner, then the next week our shifts would change. Because of rationing, we observed meatless Tuesdays, and tried interesting things with organ meats, disguising them in casseroles and stews.

We fed the babies around six, and I ate my own quick dinner before 7:00 prayers, then bed. The next day, I got up and did it all over again.

I knew what was expected of me, but Momma had been there a year longer, so she felt that gave her the authority to critique my mopping, bedmaking, and everything else. She'd casually toss off things like, "Honey, rags leave streaks on glass. Use some ammonia and a newspaper," or "Pardner, I know they taught you how to make a bed in the service, but you don't have to bounce quarters on them here. We have a lot of beds to make. Time is of the essence," or "Olive, let me show you a faster way to chop an onion. Then you can work on the celery."

Roosevelt declared Thanksgiving for a week after my arrival, and I helped with the big meal service. Americans had been lucky that our Thanksgiving turkeys hadn't been on the rationing list for most of the war, but this year, shortages had finally hit home, and we were making do with a few scraggly-looking birds. However, Sister Essie had begun a Victory Garden, with carrots, potatoes, beans, and herbs, so we were still able to provide a decent meal. I'd only been prepping for half an hour when Momma started harping on me again.

"Out!" I announced, shooing her from the kitchen. "This meal won't cook itself and you're making things worse!"

I salted and peppered, trussed and basted the birds and made a giant pot of gravy with the giblets. It felt good to see the women laughing over a meal, but that night, I returned to our room even lower than ever. Momma joined me after ten.

"What a day the Lord hath made!" Momma crowed. "I am chock full of the Holy Spirit!"

She droned on about the food the Lord had blessed us with, and about the hymns we'd sung after dinner, and how I had missed the best part.

"Night, Momma," I said. Then I turned over and faced the wall, trying not to scream. If I did, I might not stop.

BABY WONT YOU PLEASE COME HOME?

CHAPTER THIRTY~THREE

SUNSHINE MISSION, 55 WALL STREET, LOS ANGELES, CALIFORNIA, *December 1946*

I came to dread holidays at the mission. They were usually an occasion for some overwrought special production that involved colored tissue paper, hand-made decorations, and off-key musical numbers provided by the mission's "band." This was Brother Ike on ukulele, Brother Wilfred on banjo, Sister Edna on piano, and Sister Essie on her trumpet. They were accompanied by Momma singing carols in her off-key warble.

Worst of all, Momma continually pressured me to help them with their program. It was an overly generous term. None of the unfortunates looked especially overjoyed to be watching, but I think they felt obliged to look enthusiastic to get the holiday meal that accompanied the show.

By the time 1945 arrived, I was exhausted by Momma and Sister Essie, and the grinding poverty and sadness that I saw every day. At least Easter of that year saw the invasion of Okinawa. We were at the Japs' back door, about to kick it in, and in Europe, our boys had crossed the Rhine and were making tracks toward Berlin. It was only a matter of time. VE

Day arrived May the eighth, when we were already celebrating the news that Hitler had shot himself. It took until August for the Japs to finally surrender, but the news was like a nice, cool breeze in the middle of our sweltering temperatures.

It was hard to believe that the country could finally get back to normal again, but it was true. The Christmas pageant that year actually inspired me to get involved, because there really was "joy to the world" for the first time in a long time. I left the sewing of the costumes to Momma and Sister Edna. Instead, I baked trays and trays of Christmas cookies and helped Sister Dorothy make papier maché stars, which we wrapped with aluminum foil, now that it was easier to find again.

By the time 1946 arrived, America was filled with new optimism. However, on The Nickel, things were still bleak for the women at the mission.

"Are you going to help us with the Christmas pageant this year, pardner?" Momma asked.

"I'm not sure, Momma. That's a lot of work."

"We need someone creative to decorate and paint sets. You're good at that type of thing. Your stars last year were wonderful."

"Maybe."

"You saw all those sets at Roach and Fox. It might give you some ideas!" she pushed.

"I said 'Maybe.'"

"Well, I need an answer. I'm making a duty roster for everyone."

It had been the same with the Easter pageant, May Day, Fourth of July, and Thanksgiving.

"I told you how important it is that—"

"Yes, Momma, I know, it's important that we give back to Sister Essie since she's been so generous to us. But *stop* volunteering me for everything. I want to do my chores and be left alone. Have you *thought* how hard it is for me to be here? *Have you*? If I'd been smarter and taken a pay cut at Fox, I might have kept that job. But no. I was so terrified of being poor again that I told them to take a hike instead. Do you have any idea how humiliating this is? I've been paying for that stupid mistake ever since! And now I'm stuck here with you, for the rest of my life, beholden to Sister Essie for every bite I put in my mouth and every wink of sleep that's not on the street!"

Momma's mouth dropped open.

"So stop! I mean it! I don't want to work on the Christmas pageant! And stop calling me pardner. It was cute when I was little. But I'm *forty* for Christ's sake! Now leave me *be*!"

Momma deflated like a circus balloon, and her mouth settled into a flat, stubborn line. I knew that look well—resentment at having her authority (such as it was) questioned. It had terrified me when I was young because there would be punishment coming when I least expected it. But I no longer cared. There was very little she could threaten me with any longer. We were in the same boat.

I turned back to the toilet I was scrubbing, officially ending the conversation. Momma turned on her heel, footsteps clicking on the bathroom linoleum as she retreated to the cafeteria.

Panhandling often looked better than this. The sheer independence of it. But there was still the matter of no dependable square meals in a day or sleeping rough. It was an expensive price to pay for a little freedom.

I'd inadvertently gone out on my own the previous year. To celebrate the Allies taking Hürtgen Forest, I'd snuck in a bottle of gin, and Momma found it. She gave me hell for it, and our argument spilled out of our room. Terrified of losing her place there, Momma told me to make my choice—the mission or the booze. I hit the pavement looking for jobs, and found a gig at a hash house on Hill Street, close to the courthouse. I stayed at a fleabag, and when I'd saved enough for a place, I found an apartment at the Alhambra Arms on Grand Avenue. It wasn't much, but it was mine. Any night I could come home and pour myself a glass of cheer and listen to KFWB through the paper-thin walls I shared with my next door neighbor, old Mr. Schatz. I didn't have to hear Sister Essie rail about the evils of John Barleycorn, and I didn't have to listen to Momma berate me for my mopping technique. I began to dream about getting my act together and trying to make a comeback. The weight was coming off after being on my feet all day every day. But then, I had a little nip on my lunchbreak, and a customer caught a whiff. That was the end of the restaurant job and the end of the dream.

I had to drag myself back to the mission with my tail between my legs. Fortunately, Sister let me come back, but after that, her tone around me was much cooler. Despite my best efforts, I could not get back into her good graces. I doubted I ever would, and once again, it was my own damned fault.

Not long after I returned, Momma had approached me as I was mopping the floors in the front hallway.

"Olive, I want to tell you about an article I read. It was in the *Scribner's Commentator*. A man who had problems with liquor founded a group that helps other people in the same situation. You give your life to Christ at the meeting and every-one shares stories about their struggles with drinking."

The minute I heard Christ, I tuned her out.

"I don't want it," I said, "I want to be left alone."

Every few months, the harping from either Momma or Sister Essie got to be too much, and I'd take off in the middle of the day. I'd walk down The Nickel—for blocks and blocks until I reached Spring Street and its respectable stores and banks and cafes. I'd watch through the front window of the Tiffany Tea Room at the ladies laughing and gossiping over consommé and shrimp Louis, and I'd imagine the good old days, shopping at Bullock's Wilshire.

"Are you all right, dear?" an older woman in a puce suit with a red fox stole asked me, touching my arm.

"I'm sorry?" I asked, emerging from my daydream.

"Are you hungry? You look like you could use a good meal."

My clothes and grubby oxfords gave me away. The shabby skirt and blouse hung on me these days since I'd lost so much weight.

"Here. My husband gave me a little for my shopping trip, but you look like you could use it more." She slipped a five-dol-lar bill into my hand.

"That's so generous. I couldn't possibly..."

"Piffle. Please take it. Get yourself lunch somewhere."

"Thank you," I said.

"Take care of yourself, dear," she said. Then she was gone in the crowd.

OFF FIFTH STREET, DOWNTOWN LOS ANGELES, CALIFORNIA,
June 1947

The rain sluiced through pipes and gutters, off the sides of buildings and between arcades. It didn't matter how I tried to get away from it. I was soaked and would stay that way. The only thing filling my panhandling cup today would be rain. No one gave when it was like this. They were too busy running from place to place to get out of the downpour.

A man in a houndstooth jacket and a brown fedora rushed past me on his way toward the State Theatre, and surprisingly, tossed fifty cents at my cup. Right then, it looked like a fortune.

"Thank you," I said, but he was already two storefronts away.

With my new windfall, I sprang for coffee and a Danish at the Monterey Café. Adding plenty of cream and sugar, I picked a table toward the back, where I knew the draft from the front door wasn't as bad.

A woman at the next table scooted her chair further away from me. I scowled at her and cupped my fingers more tightly around my cup. Eventually, the coffee would be gone, and I'd be forced to move on. Clifton's would be an obvious choice. Big-hearted Clifford Clinton had an open, friendly face, with slicked back hair and wire-frame glasses. He charged what you could afford, and he never turned away anyone who was hungry. If I was lucky, it would be roast beef day, and I could get the lime Jell-O salad.

I arrived at Clifton's, soaked and bedraggled, hoping Clifford would take pity on me once again. He did. It wasn't roast beef, it was chicken and dumplings, but they were hot and delicious. Especially when you were wet and cold.

I tried to ignore the squelching from my shoes and set to figuring out my next move. Standing on Broadway with a tin cup looked completely unattractive at the moment.

Clifford strolled by my table.

"Here," he said, spooning more onto my plate. "You're skin and bones, Olive. And you're worrying me."

"Thanks, Clif," I said, tucking in gratefully.

"You left the mission again?"

"Do I look that bad?"

"No, your mom came in yesterday looking for you."

I grimaced. "What'd you tell her?"

"I told her the truth. That I hadn't seen you in over a week."

"Good. Keep telling her that."

"What happened between the two of you?" he asked. "I know it's none of my business, but... she loves you, you know. She's worried."

I sighed. "I know you must think I'm a monster."

"I think no such thing. Mothers love their children. Yours is no different."

"Love to her is smothering. I couldn't stand it anymore. I had to get out of there."

He shrugged. "I worry about you. The Nickel is a hard place, Ollie. It's no place for a woman on her own."

"I can take care of myself," I said.

"You're hardly over five feet tall and I doubt you hit a hundred and five pounds. This town will make a meal outta you. You need to be back at the mission with people who care about you."

"Maybe someday, but not yet," I said over the dumplings in my mouth.

"Can I at least tell her where you're staying?" he asked.

I shook my head.

"Take care of yourself, kid," he said, retreating to the front counter.

When I left, I went to the library for a while to let my shoes dry out while I escaped with a good book. One that Sister Essie wouldn't approve of.

As I was passing the check-out desk, a man was pulling out his library card, and as he did, a bill slipped out of the pocket where he'd removed his wallet. It landed on the floor nearby, unnoticed by librarians or patrons. I watched carefully, torn between self-preservation and wanting to do the right thing. This time, my mercenary side won. When the patron retreated toward the door on the Flower Street side, I pounced on the bill like a squirrel with a fat acorn and winter two weeks away. I'd be able to get a room for the night. Not a good one, but considering the uncomfortable bench in Pershing Square I'd used the previous night, and the one in Westlake Park the night before that, anything cushioned would be a luxury.

At the Barclay, I paid upfront for the room, hoping there weren't too many bedbugs. The Barclay was a comforting space to me. We'd both been beautiful once and had fallen on hard times. We'd both changed names too. The Barclay had been the Van Nuys once. Staying here now felt like being with an old friend. A friend who knew what it was like, its stained glass clerestory windows and elegant stairway providing a glimpse back into its glorious history. I crawled into the bed and fell fast asleep with the rain beating against the window.

They took me back a few weeks later, when I looked like the wrath of God and smelled even worse. Momma sweet talked Sister Essie, but she herself gave me a tongue lashing about abusing Sister Essie's goodwill. I hadn't had much of a choice. I'd developed a hacking cough from standing in the rain. I hated returning with regrets, but I knew the mission had cough syrup and Vaporub.

I got the cough cleared up before spring and knuckled down again, but I was only going through the motions. The mission was merely a rotten purgatory before I died. There was no coming back from here, ever. This was it. Every time someone told me to do something, I snapped at them. When Momma talked to me, I snapped at her too.

It got to the point where the smell of diapers made me gag, and the babies crying set my teeth on edge. I simply couldn't take it another day. I knew if I left this time, that would be it. No going back.

The summer saw me pounding the pavement between Fifth and Seventh. When I needed a change of scenery, I'd divert a few blocks to view the fashions in the displays change at The May Company or see the puppies in the window at Newbaum's Pet Store. I slept rough most nights, usually in Pershing Square, where I had a couple close calls. I'd filched a steak knife, along with ten dollars from Momma's pocketbook when I'd taken off. But my panhandling sometimes paid off, and I could spring for a couple nights at the Barclay or the Cecil. That's where I started feeling sick.

The cough became a harsh bark, and my forehead felt like fire. I had to be delirious because there was a dog in the corner wearing a snap brim and singing Al Jolson songs.

The springs on the torture rack that substituted for a mattress were poking my back, but moving hotels or even rooms was out of the question. I could barely stand up. I reached for the gin bottle next to the bed, disappointed it had a few precious drops left in it. Not for the first time, I missed the days of staying in hotels with concierges who could bring me whatever I wanted, like a good bottle of Gordon's.

A loud knock sounded at the door, and I figured it was the front desk clerk, who was already threatening me with eviction.

"Olive! Olive, it's me!"

Momma. For the first time in years, it was actually a relief to hear her voice.

"Momma?" I cried. My voice was so weak it came out as more of a strangled squeak.

"Open the door this instant," Momma said, trying the knob, and rattling the door in its frame.

"I can't," I said. "I'm too weak."

"I'll be right back," Momma said. She returned a few minutes later, accompanied by the desk clerk. He unlocked the door and stood behind her.

"She owes me two weeks' rent. Who's going to take care of that?"

"I will. Hush your mouth. Can't you see she's sick? How much is her bill?"

"Fifteen dollars."

"Here." She shoved a wad of bills at the clerk. "I'm taking her back where she belongs."

She rushed to my side, stroking my hair. "Oh, my Baby.

My beautiful girl. I've been so worried. I've been to every hotel downtown looking for you."

"I'm sorry," I said. "I'm so sorry I worried you. I can't move." A paroxysm overcame me and I pulled myself up so I wouldn't choke to death.

"You there!" Momma called to the desk clerk. She pulled a dime out of her bag, along with a business card. "I saw a phone in the lobby. This is the number for the Sunshine Mission. I want you to call and summon Brother Wilfred and Brother Ike to this hotel. Tell them to bring the mission's wagon. Can you remember that?"

"Brother Wilfred and Brother Ike," he said with a nod.

"Don't forget the wagon!" Momma called behind him. Then to me, "We'll soon have you out of here and back home," Momma said. "I'll nurse you myself."

It wasn't long before Brother Wilfred and Brother Ike arrived. The desk clerk directed them up the stairs, and Momma called them to my room. She'd left the door open for them.

"In here, boys. You must take Olive very gently down the stairs."

I smelled awful. Perspiration had soaked through my rumpled blouse and skirt, but between the two of them, they got underneath my arms and hiked me up so they could half walk me and half carry me downstairs.

The mission's wagon, a bedraggled-looking 1930 Chevrolet Six that had seen better days, was parked at the curb. They helped me into it, then Brother Ike covered me with a blanket while Momma crawled in back with me. Brother Wilfred got behind the wheel and made a right turn on 6th, then a left to

Wall to return to the mission.

We pulled up and they moved me again, into the room I'd shared with Momma. She covered me with the sheet, then sat down next to me on the mattress and felt my forehead with the back of her hand, like she'd done when I was little.

"Good Lord, you're burning up. Brother Wilfred, please tell Sister Essie I won't be down for the lunch service. I'll be right back, honey."

She returned with a thermometer and some washcloths soaked in cold water. When I coughed again, she handed me a handkerchief edged in blue lace. The stuff that came out of me was green.

"Pneumonia," Momma pronounced. "We'll have to call the doctor."

The doctor later appeared, but I had no conception of time. He used his stethoscope to listen to my breathing, but every time he asked me to take a deep breath, it sent me into another paroxysm.

"Definitely pneumonia," he said, "Sounds like both lungs. I'll write a prescription for penicillin."

"Will it work?" Momma asked.

"It performed miracles on the battlefield. Let's hope it works as well here."

Someone else must have filled the prescription, because Momma never left my side. When the small bottle arrived, she lovingly helped me take it, then held my hand as the drug went to work. As to what would happen to me when the pneumonia was licked, I had no idea. I'd exhausted Sister Essie's good graces.

At some point, I looked up and saw the pain in Momma's

eyes. She looked so worried.

"Momma, am I going to die?" I whispered.

"Of course not. Don't be silly," she said, patting my hand. "You just concentrate on getting well."

"Sister won't let me back after this," I said, my head lolling to one side. I was so dizzy, and my diaphragm ached from all the coughing.

"We'll worry about that when you're well, all right? I could clean houses again. You could help me. We could live at the beach again. You'd like that, wouldn't you, pardner?"

"The beach..." I said. "Yes...the beach. You didn't call me Baby, Momma."

"I haven't called you Baby in years, Olive, remember?"

"Oh, yes," I whispered. I needed to sleep. I was so tired...

When I awoke, it was to a flashbulb cracking in my face. I held my hand up because of the bright light.

"You get out of here!" Momma said. "If you want an interview, that's one thing, but my daughter is very ill. Show some couth!"

She spoke to the reporter for a few minutes, then made him leave.

"Sister says any publicity we give the mission is good, to bring attention to the plight of the indigent," she said. "But that is taking things too far!" She took her place back by my side.

"I'm sorry, Momma," I said.

"Sorry for what, honey?"

"That I wasn't stronger, that I didn't make better choices, that I wasn't smart enough to do things differently." My voice broke as another cough overtook me.

"I wasn't exactly the best manager you could have had

either, pardner. I just wanted to help you...and protect you, the way I couldn't protect your father or little Frankie. You were always my Baby..." She dropped her head over my tummy and began to cry. "You have to get better, Olive. You *must*."

"Trying..." I said, my voice fading. I could feel my energy fading, my eyes becoming too tired to remain open. "Sorry, Momma..."

And then Momma, the mission, Skid Row, all of it...slipped away. All I felt was peace at last.

THE END

THANKS

- Michelle Vogel for her book on Olive and her life, which became my bible while working.

- Thank you to the very amiable and informative Lee Holland of Enon, Virginia, for generously giving me a tour of his motor pool garage, offering to answer any other questions I had after the fact, and even giving me some military equipment magazines, gratis!

- Also, thank you to all the other nice folks I met in Richmond and at the museums at Fort Lee and Fort Eustis for making my 2019 trip to Virginia so special!

- Elizabeth Evans at *oliveborden1947.blogspot.com*. Elizabeth provided several new avenues for me to pursue that I hadn't previously known about. Thanks to her generosity, I was able to continue researching Olive's connection to Arthur Benline, whom I knew nothing about.

- Thank you especially to those of you who supported me during what had to be the worst two years of my life—the pandemic, my husband's illness and death, the grieving, fixing up and selling my house, getting moved into my new one, *then* dealing with my own cancer diagnosis. Eternal gratitude to Shawnna Pracejus, Kristin and Mark Kalmbach, Paula Christensen, Emily Dirk Johnston, Brandi Morpurgo, Joe Moore, Jeff Stolson, Lora and Shane and Gord and Angela in the old neighborhood, Mark Dumont, Kathleen Myers, Sheldon Vivier, Shauna Allan, and Dwight Kroenig.

* Big kudos to the fellas at Riteway Moving and Storage (Gurnoor, Satinder, Summy, and BK), who had the unenviable job of moving all my stuff, including my research library and the rest of my books up multiple flights of stairs—all 40 boxes or so. Thanks, guys!

AUTHOR'S NOTE

Not much is known about Olive's marriage to John Moeller because of New York's law of not releasing divorce information until 100 years after it has occurred. I did the best I could with what was available to me as far as existing records and news stories. Her father-in-law's diabetes and some discussion of the marriage appeared in Olive's military file. Sibbie did NOT like John, saying he was "morose, sullen, bad-tempered, and stingy," and that he "got along beautifully with her while she was supporting him."

Unfortunately, the Moellers kept a very low profile. I found one or two items for them on Family Search, only one memorial on findagrave.com, and no mentions in any of the New York papers I could access.

Sadly, the tales of Olive's exploits in the service as I've written them are true, taken directly from the information in her military file. It was a gold mine of information about all the portions of her life because of the psychiatrists' interviews with Olive, Sibbie, Arthur Benline, Father Gallagher, and fellow WAACs at Bolling Field.

Olive's "foot injury" that appears in many non-fiction accounts of her life appears to have been a story fed to the media, most likely by Sibbie. The worst foot injury Olive experienced in the service was her athlete's foot infection, which was mentioned in her file.

Olive's abortion was discussed in her military file, as psychiatrists tried to understand why she had acted the way she had while stationed at Bolling Field. She did fine during basic training, but she started having problems when Lieutenant Fodness took over as her commanding officer. The doctors who were consulted diagnosed her with antisocial personality disorder.

Of course we can't know for certain who Olive saw for her abortion, but I found a newspaper story about Dr. Gilbert Ashman, who fit the bill. He operated in Brooklyn during this time period, 1932-1936. He worked out of a house at 2746 Ocean Avenue, and had two accomplices in his "business," Mrs. Amanda Groat and her husband Warren, who evidently owned or rented the house. Dr. Ashman provided services to well-to-do women from New York, New Jersey, and Connecticut.

All of the fellow auxiliaries and supervisors at Bolling Field and the doctors at Walter Reed are factual (except Sergeant Figlio). The ones at Fort Des Moines are made up, because no record of them appeared in Olive's military file.

As of January of 1943, testimonials of friends and acquaintances still referred to Olive as separated and not divorced. A very small mention was made of Olive getting a Reno "unhooking" in a December 1943 newspaper, which would negate the previous reports of her divorce occurring in March 1941. I think March 1941 was probably when Olive and John separated.

Despite her use of Mary as an alias in one of her marriage certificates, her military file states NMI (no middle initial).

Sibbie's other child (Olive's deceased sibling) is stated to be a boy in her military file, although he was not named. I took liberty here to provide one.

The two aviators who worked on *Pajamas* were Bigelow, as written, but the other was Bill Williams. Since the real cameraman was Glen *Mac*Williams, Mr. Williams became Wilson to avoid confusion.

Marie's fondness for re-using the same grease when cooking literally everything was a nod to my German great grandmother, who preferred this method. Her daughter (my great aunt) once told my grandmother, who had married into the family, that everything she cooked tasted SO DELICIOUS. Amazing how good everything tastes when you don't recycle your grease!

BIBLIOGRAPHY

BOOKS

Ankerich, Michael. *Dangerous Curves Atop Hollywood Heels*. Albany, Georgia: BearManor Media, 2010.

Arsenault, Raymond. *St. Petersburg and the Florida Dream, 1888-1950*. Gainesville, Florida: UniversityPress@UF, 2017.

Ayers, R. Wayne. *Images of America – St. Petersburg The Sunshine City*. Charleston, SC: Arcadia Publishing, 2001.

Ballenas, Carl and Nancy Cataldi. *Images of America: Richmond Hill*. Charleston, SC: Arcadia Publishing, 2002.

Blake, Penelope A. *My Mother's Fort. A Photographic Tribute to Fort Des Moines, First Home of the Woman's Army Corps*. Charleston, SC: BookSurge Publishing, 2005.

Eyman, Scott. *Print the Legend. The Life and Times of John Ford*. New York: Simon & Schuster, 1999.

First Women's Army Corps Training Center. *WAC Handbook*. Fort Des Moines, Iowa: no date.

Fleming, E. J. *The Movieland Directory*. Jefferson, NC: McFarland Publishing, 2009.

Helm, Charles and Mike Murtha, ed. *The Forgotten Explorer- Samuel Prescott Fay's 1914 Expedition to the Northern Rockies*. Surrey, BC: Rocky Mountain Books, 2009.

Huyler, Jack. *and That's the Way It Was in Jackson's Hole*. Jackson, Wyoming: Jackson Hole Historical Society and Museum, 2000.

Jasper Park Lodge brochure: Canadian National Railways, 1928.

Marconi, Richard and the Historical Society of Palm Beach County. *Palm Beach*. Charleston, SC: Arcadia Publishing, 2013.

Menefee, David W. *George O'Brien. A Man's Man in Hollywood*. Albany, Georgia: BearManor Media, 2009.

Pfeiffer, C. Boyd. *The Big Book of Fly Fishing Tips and Tricks*. Minneapolis, MN: MVP Books, 2013.

Rode, Alan K. *Michael Curtiz: A Life in Film*. Lexington, Kentucky: University Press of Kentucky, 2017.

Rosenthal, Rose. *Not All Soldiers Wore Pants. A Witty World War II WAC Tells All*. Rochelle Park, N.J.: Ryzell Books, 1993.

Schaffer, Mollie Weinstein and Cyndee Schaffer. *Mollie's War: The Letters of a World War II WAC in Europe*. Jefferson, NC: McFarland Publishing, 2010.

Troyan, Michael Troyan, Jeffrey Paul Thompson, and Stephen X. Sylvester. *Twentieth Century Fox: A Century of Entertainment*. Guilford, Connecticut: Lyons Press, 2017.

U.S. War Department. *Technical Manual TM 10-570 The Internal Combustion Engine*. Washington, DC: US Department of the Army, 1941.

Vogel, Michelle. *Olive Borden: The Life and Films of Hollywood's "Joy Girl."* Jefferson, NC: McFarland Publishing, 2010.

Wallach, Ruth, Linda McCann, Dace Taube, Claude Zachary and Curtis C. Roseman. *Historic Hotels of Los Angeles and Hollywood (Images of America: California)*. Charleston, SC: Arcadia Publishing, 2008.

Williams, Vera S. *WACs Women's Army Corps*. Osceola, WI: Motorbooks International, 1997.

FILMS

- *3 Bad Men* - https://www.youtube.com/watch?v=c8CUDB3RDmE
- *Chloe Love is Calling You* – https://www.youtube.com/watch?v=5B5O-Cfsj4o
- *Dance Hall* – https://www.youtube.com/watch?v=OZNba6fPj8M
- *Fig Leaves clip* - https://www.youtube.com/watch?v=oLKpPS5d-MA
- *Gobs of Fun* - https://www.youtube.com/watch?v=_luF7lXrYNM
- *Half Marriage* - https://www.youtube.com/watch?v=bXx4farq4rw
- *Noah's Ark* – Personal DVD copy
- *Sunrise A Tale of Two Humans* – Recorded from Turner Classic Movies
- *The Monkey Talks* - https://www.youtube.com/watch?v=cP7E4UT3yuk
- *Keep Your Powder Dry* – Personal DVD copy.
- WAAC promotional films on youtube:
  - 1943 WAAC Recruiting Film "We're in the Army Now" https://www.youtube.com/watch?v=kxNnG7aPAfg
  - WAACs https://www.youtube.com/watch?v=_BpxzMdvIA8
  - Women's Army Corps Part 1 "Women at War" https://www.youtube.com/watch?v=ALow_k85n2s
  - Women's Army Corps Part 2 https://www.youtube.com/watch?v=efCMW1qOiks

ONLINE

- Army.mil: https://www.army.mil/article/157175/man_in_the_motor_pool_lee_employee_passionately_shares_history_of_wwii_vehicles
- Arthur Benline obituary https://www.moaa.org/content/

about-moaa/scholarship-fund/faces-of-donorsFolder/CAPT-Arthur-J--Benline,-USNR-and-Mrs--Peggy-Cornell-Benline/

- Details about Palm Beach: newyorksocialdiary.com/palm-beach-social-diary-addison-mizner-the-afterlife/

- Grauman's Chinese graumanschinese.org/1927-1928.html (for information on the *Noah's Ark* premiere)

- Hollywood Gastronomical Haunts (for information on Café Lafayette): http://laheyday.blogspot.com/2015/07/what-went-before-2312-w-7th-street_29.html

- How World War II Changed Thanksgiving 75 Years Ago https://blog.newspapers.com/how-world-war-ii-changed-thanksgiving-75-years-ago/

- IMDB.com: Various

- Media History Digital Library: http://mediahistoryproject.org/fanmagazines/

- "Mythic Landscapes of the Boom and Bust Weedon Island, Florida" Florida Historical Society (Sheila K. Stewart) (Volume 15, No. 4- Volume 96, No. 2) Florida Historical Quarterly https://www.jstor.org

- Newspapers.com: various

- Noah's Ark premiere latimes.com/entertainment/movies/la-et-mn-chinese-theatre-20170518-htmlstory.html

- Oliveborden.net

- Rationing - https://www.sarahsundin.com/make-it-do-meat-and-cheese-rationing-in-world-war-ii-2/

- Realtor.com – 627 N. Hillcrest listing: https://www.realtor.com/realestateandhomes-detail/627-N-Hillcrest-Rd_Beverly-Hills_CA_90210_M21547-70803

- SFGate (for information on Dante Sanitarium): https://www.sfgate.com/bayarea/article/San-Francisco-medical-options-in-1924-6836434.php#photo-9414824

- Tampa from Prohibition to Organized Crime: http://www.tampa-pix.com/tampa1940s7.htm

- Tea Association of the USA (for tea leaf reading) http://www.teausa.com/14531/reading-tea-leaves

- Vintage St. Peter: Making Movies on Weedon https://stpetecatalyst.com/vintage-st-pete-weedon-islands-brief-reign-as-a-center-for-movie-making/

- The Weedon Island Story: http://www.weedonislandpreserve.org/pdf/WIBookWeb.pdf

- Wikipedia (On the Spot) https://en.wikipedia.org/wiki/On_the_Spot_(play)

- World War II: Then and Now: Ilene Hall served as a driver in the WACS https://www.cantonrep.com/x1784773218/World-War-II-Then-and-now-Ilene-Hall-served-as-a-driver-in-the-WACS

RECORDS
- Olive Borden military file #A-201285 - National Military Personnel Records Center, St. Louis, MO

TOURS
- Museum of Women in the Army- Fort Lee, Virginia
- Museum of the Quartermaster – Fort Lee, Virginia
- U.S. Army Transportation Museum – Fort Eustis, Virginia
- Lee Holland's Motor Pool Garage – Enon, Virginia

Made in the USA
Middletown, DE
13 August 2023